THEORIES OF JUDGMENT

The exercise of judgment is an aspect of human endeavor from our most mundane acts to our most momentous decisions. In this book Wayne Martin develops a historical survey of theoretical approaches to judgment, focusing on treatments of judgment in psychology, logic, phenomenology, and painting. He traces attempts to develop theories of judgment in British Empiricism, the logical tradition stemming from Kant, nineteenth-century psychologism, recent experimental neuropsychology, and the phenomenological tradition associated with Brentano, Husserl, and Heidegger. His reconstruction of vibrant but largely forgotten nineteenth-century debates links Kantian approaches to judgment with twentieth-century phenomenological accounts. He also shows that the psychological, logical, and phenomenological dimensions of judgment are not only equally important, but fundamentally interlinked, in any complete understanding of judgment. His book will interest a wide range of readers in the history of philosophy, philosophy of mind, and psychology.

WAYNE MARTIN is Reader in Philosophy at the University of Essex. Since 2002 he has served as the General Editor of *Inquiry: An Interdisciplinary Journal of Philosophy* and he is author of *Idealism and Objectivity: Understanding Fichte's Jena Project* (1997).

MODERN EUROPEAN PHILOSOPHY

General Editor
ROBERT B. PIPPIN, *University of Chicago*

Advisory Board
GARY GUTTING, *University of Notre Dame*
ROLF-PETER HORSTMANN, *Humboldt University, Berlin*
MARK SACKS, *University of Essex*

THEORIES OF JUDGMENT

Psychology, Logic, Phenomenology

WAYNE M. MARTIN
University of Essex

DAMAGED

CAMBRIDGE
UNIVERSITY PRESS

CAMBRIDGE UNIVERSITY PRESS
Cambridge, New York, Melbourne, Madrid, Cape Town, Singapore, São Paulo

CAMBRIDGE UNIVERSITY PRESS
The Edinburgh Building, Cambridge CB2 2RU, UK

Published in the United States of America by Cambridge University Press, New York

www.cambridge.org
Information on this title: www.cambridge.org/9780521840439

First published 2006

Printed in the United Kingdom at the University Press, Cambridge

A catalogue record for this book is available from the British Library

ISBN-13 978-0-521-84043-9 hardback
ISBN-10 0-521-84043-0 hardback

for Karen Pilkington
1959–2000

CONTENTS

FIGURES

ACKNOWLEDGMENTS

I have benefited from opportunities to present versions of this material to a number of helpful and challenging audiences, first in a pair of graduate seminars at UC San Diego (1999) and UC Irvine (2000), and then in a pair of lectures at Stanford University (2002). Various portions and drafts have been submitted to the scrutiny of audiences in colloquia at UC Riverside (2003), the UCSD History of Philosophy Roundtable (2002, 2003), the UCSD Department of Cognitive Science (2001), and at the meetings of the Southern California Philosophy Conference (2002) and the International Society for Phenomenological Studies (2002, 2003). I am grateful to the many friends, students, and colleagues who lent me their attention and engagement. A version of Chapter 3 appeared in *The New Yearbook for Phenomenology and Phenomenological Studies*; I wish to thank the editors and publishers for permission to use that material here. Support for the project was provided in the form of sabbatical leave from UCSD, and by a grant from the UCSD Center for the Humanities.

The time has long since passed when I could identify all the people who have helped me think about the theory of judgment. I hope that I shall not be thought ungrateful if I thank them here only collectively so that I might single out just one. Karen Pilkington started graduate school with me at Berkeley in 1986, and it was in a series of our conversations on the bench outside Moses Hall that I first tried to think seriously about the nature of judgment, and about how one might succeed where Hume failed. Karen died in March 2000, after a long and painful series of illnesses. I have often thought about her as I have worked on these materials, and have sorely missed the opportunity to continue our conversations.

The material presented in this book is the product of work undertaken during my twelve-year affiliation with the Philosophy Department at the University of California, San Diego. In many ways it is a reflection of the vibrant and contentious intellectual environment that I was privileged to participate in there. Although I have since left San Diego, I would like to count this book as my modest contribution to the extraordinary output of that still-young department. I am grateful to those who provided me the opportunity to work and learn there.

PRINCIPLES OF CITATION

I have used the author-date style of citation throughout, with the following exceptions: in citing Kant's works, I refer to the pagination of the academy edition, except in the case of *Critique of Pure Reason*, where I have used the usual A and B pagination. Citations to Heidegger's doctoral dissertation, *The Doctrine of Judgment in Psychologism* (1913), are given with the abbreviation FS, citing the pagination of the 1972 edition of *Frühe Schriften*. Citations to works in the Loeb Classical Library are given with the abbreviation LL, followed by the author, volume, edition, and page reference, e.g., LL Lucian III 1921: 385.

INTRODUCTION: THE FACES
OF JUDGMENT

This is a book about judgment, and about the long history of attempts to understand it. It is said that one can learn something about a community by considering how it adjudicates disputes. Is judgment reached by majority vote? by contests of strength or the casting of runes? by deferral to elders or experts? In each case the procedure of judgment is revealing: revealing about the world of the judges and revealing about the sources of authority within the community. The same is true of individuals: we can hope to understand something important about ourselves (perhaps ultimately about the kind of *beings* we are) if we can understand what it is to judge. The task of judgment is everywhere in human life, whether in sorting the mail, casting a vote, or salting the soup. But what do we do when we judge? What process do we undergo? What stance do we adopt toward ourselves and others? What authority do we invoke and submit ourselves to?

To embark on an investigation of these matters we require some initial characterization of judgment. What range of phenomena is to be investigated under this rubric? I have no definition to offer, but rather begin with some tautologies and examples.

Judgment is what judges do. Obviously this is not a definition (it is blatantly circular and obviously incomplete), but it has the virtue of directing our attention from the outset to the idea that judgment is in some sense an activity of cognitive agents. To judge is to do something. Judges solicit evidence, which they weigh, interpret, and assess. In

1

passing judgment a judge reaches a conclusion on the basis of such assessment. In wood-paneled courtrooms these activities are carried out with solemnity and ceremony, but they are at work in all manner of mundane judgment as well. When we judge we somehow reach a conclusion in response to evidence.

A judge is a figure of authority and responsibility. This is obvious when one thinks about black-robed judges: they are formally invested with the authority to decide certain questions. They incur various responsibilities in doing so: the responsibility to weigh evidence fairly, to support their judgments rationally, to reply to objections as they are raised. But it is no less true of mundane judgment. To pass a judgment is in some sense to occupy a position of responsibility – laying claim to the authority to reach a decision about some particular matter and thereby incurring the responsibility for having done so. Such claims to authority can, of course, be challenged, just as any particular judgment can be challenged; but the claim to authority is a central part of what is involved in passing judgment. To judge is thus to situate oneself (or to find oneself situated) in a framework of norms and ideals.

Some judgments are snap judgments. Emphasis on the responsibility and authority involved in judgment might suggest that judgment must be undertaken slowly and deliberately. But I follow ordinary language in resisting this view. Consider some examples: cycling at dusk I exercise judgment in adjusting my course as various obstacles appear in the light of my headlamp. I walk down the aisles of the library stacks looking for a call number, eyes flitting from book to book, deciding in each case whether to stop, to continue, or to back up. Playing speed chess I make my move without allowing myself time to think through its consequences. In each of these cases I make judgments – I reach a conclusion that is in some sense responsive to evidence – even though I don't undertake any conscious deliberation and I experience my judgment as issuing more-or-less instantaneously. This is not to say, of course, that my act of judgment takes up no time. As we shall see, issues about the timing of judgment are an important area of empirical research. The point here is simply that judging need not involve any *experienced* duration, nor does it require that I explicitly or deliberately review evidence in order to be responsive to it.

Judgment occupies a place in both theory and practice. The formation of judgments is involved both in deciding what to believe, and in deciding what to do. The baseball fan exercises theoretical judgment in reckoning the Yankees' chances against the Sox in the postseason. Here the outcome of deliberation is a belief, formed in response to evidence. The baseball manager employs practical judgment in deciding whether to send the runner or risk a double play; here the outcome of deliberation is an intentional action. As we shall see, these varieties of judgment have often been studied separately. But there is a level at which one can recognize a common phenomenon here. Indeed, according to one venerable tradition an intention simply is a judgment to act.

In attempting to develop a theoretical understanding of judgment, or even in trying to articulate a more-or-less reflective account of what judgment is, one encounters a persistent difficulty. It is this difficulty which structures the investigations which follow. Judgment, as I would like to put the point, shows three different faces (is there a tertiary form of *Janus-faced*?) and because of this, the theory of judgment must navigate three sets of theoretical commitments. Much of the history of the theory of judgment is the history of the entanglement of these various competing commitments.

A first face of judgment is psychological. Judgments figure in the explanation of the behavior of intelligent organisms, and accordingly the notion of judgment figures in psychological theory. The sense of psychology can here be taken quite broadly. Whether one is investigating ordinary or extraordinary voluntary actions, patterns of consumer or voting or mating behavior, capacities for perceptual discrimination, or the framing of alternatives in deliberative calculations, appeals to judgment frequently play a role in psychological explanation. Accordingly, judgment has been a topic of psychological investigation from Plato and Aristotle to neuroscience and market research.

A second face of judgment is logical. In judgment a responsible cognitive agent reaches a conclusion in response to reasons and evidence. In this sense at least, judgment is an activity of rational beings, guided by inferential structure somehow manifest in a body of evidence. Taken very broadly, logic is the study of inferential structure. Accordingly, judgment has been investigated in logic, and the activity of judgment must in some sense be governed by logical principles. The theory of judgment has in fact played a prominent role in the history of logic, and logicians from Aristotle to Frege made important contributions in this area. Indeed, until recent times the so-called "Doctrine of Judgment" formed one of the major subdivisions in logic textbooks. The reason for this is not far to seek. It is of the essence of judgments that they are party to logical relations: some pairs of judgment contradict one another; some, taken together, entail others. Logic investigates these inferential features of judgments. The centrality of the theory of judgment has been somewhat submerged in modern mathematical logic, but we shall see that debates in the logical theory of judgment were at the heart of the revolution that gave rise to the modern logical tradition.

The studies which follow take up aspects of both the psychological and logical theory of judgment, and selectively investigate the history of these two bodies of theory. But I am also concerned here with a third face of judgment: its phenomenological face. Judgments figure in the course of human experience – sometimes seamlessly and in the background, on other occasions in ways that utterly grip our attention. Any adequate phenomenology of experience must accordingly come to terms with the phenomenology of judgment. What is it like to judge? How do judgments manifest themselves as such in our experience?

Everything associated with the idea of phenomenology is a matter of controversy – from the meaning of the term to the coherence of the theoretical enterprise to particular purported phenomenological methods and results. In steering a course through these controversies, let me begin with a dogmatic definition. As I shall use the term, phenomenology is the study of the structure of experience, particularly of the ways in which things (entities, objects) manifest themselves in experience. The word "things" is here to be understood in the broadest possible sense: objects, actions, events, relations, persons, numbers, ideals, mistakes, character defects, desires, and fears all manifest themselves in my experience, and phenomenology as I understand it has a legitimate concern with all these things and many more beside. What is characteristic of the phenomenologist's investigation, however, is a concern not so much with the objective nature as with the subjective appearance of such things. In this sense, phenomenology seeks to investigate and articulate the ways in which things manifest themselves *for subjects*; it investigates the seeming of things in contrast to their being.

Already with such a characterization I will have stepped on toes. On one side, there will be those who object to the idea of building the notion of the subjective into the basic characterization of phenomenology. Particularly since Heidegger, one branch of phenomenology has set itself in opposition to the very notion of the subject, and accordingly finds objectionable any characterization of phenomenology which definitionally assures a place for subjects. At another extreme, there are those who pursue phenomenology as a distinctive strategy of investigation into the objective biological workings of conscious organisms, proposing a conception of phenomenology according to which its ultimate object of investigation is the functioning of brains. On my characterization, by contrast, brains are just one of the many things which manifest themselves in experience (and in this case only in rather specialized experience). Phenomenology's concern with them is strictly with their subjective manifestation; it takes no particular interest in their objective nature. It is beyond my purposes here to enter into debates with these other conceptions of phenomenology. (For an illuminating discussion of the alternatives see Cerbone 2003; we shall return in due course both to the neuroscience of judgment and to Heidegger's phenomenological investigations.) At this point I simply want to be clear about how I shall be using the term. Accordingly, it is perhaps worthwhile to emphasize some negative corollaries of my dogmatic definition.

Phenomenology is not the proper name of a particular philosophical tradition. Starting in the late nineteenth century, a series of philosophers and psychologists embraced the term "phenomenology" as the name for a distinctive philosophical approach and at times for a specific theoretical agenda. Brentano, Husserl, Heidegger, Merleau-Ponty, and Levinas were the most prominent representatives of this tradition, although many others (Twardowski, Ingarden, Chisholm, Føllesdal, Dreyfus, etc.) have played a role in its development. Some of the work of these self-described phenomenologists will concern us in this study, but phenomenology as I understand it extends far beyond the members of this particular philosophical tradition, and it includes these figures only insofar as their work falls within the definition just proposed. Much of the history of phenomenology with which I shall be concerned lies outside this tradition – whether prior to it (e.g., phenomenological claims found in British Empiricism and German Idealism), or otherwise independent of it (e.g., in phenomenological lessons from Northern Renaissance painting or neuroanatomical research).

Phenomenology does not necessarily privilege the first person point of view. Phenomenology as I define it is characterized by a particular theoretical ambition – to understand and articulate the ways in which things manifest themselves in subjective experience. This definition leaves entirely open the question of how to achieve that goal. In particular, phenomenology has no defining commitment to a method of introspection or self-reflective intuition. Phenomenology is certainly concerned with the first person perspective – that is, after all, a perspective that we characteristically occupy as subjects – but it makes no particular claims about the authority of such a perspective or the epistemic status of results obtained from it.

Phenomenology is not committed to a foundationalist agenda. At various times in its development, the pursuit of phenomenological theory has coincided with a strong foundationalist conception of philosophy, and in particular with the idea that a theory of subjective experience is needed to provide proper foundations for other scientific endeavors. The argument, roughly, was that since all scientific investigation ultimately *relies* on subjective experience, no science can be properly grounded unless one *begins* with a theory of subjective experience. My own view is that this bit of reasoning is fallacious; certainly the definition of phenomenology I propose here is not in any way committed to it. Phenomenology, as I understand it, is one investigation among many – albeit a rather unusual one in a number of respects that will concern us.

Phenomenology is not to be understood as the investigation of qualia or "subjective feels." In recent work in the philosophy of mind, much of the discussion of subjective experience has been focused around (indeed, one might well say: obsessed by) the problem of understanding qualia. Qualia are typically defined as the so-called "raw feels" of conscious life – the itches and tickles, the "blueness of the blue": the sensory qualities which manifest themselves in consciousness and are arguably exhausted by their being so manifest. The obsession with qualia is in large part an accident of the particular history of the mind-body problem in twentieth-century philosophy of mind. I shall not try to recount that history here, but content myself to say that phenomenology as I define it has no particular commitment to or indeed interest in qualia. In part this is because the very idea of qualia is part of a particular theory of experience – a theory according to which non-intentional sensory atoms occupy a fundamental place in our conscious lives. I do not myself subscribe to that theory, but more importantly, I see the characteristic concern of phenomenology as lying with the *structure* of experience, rather than with its particular content. Qualia, if indeed there are any, are not themselves part of the structure of experience; they are (or would be if they existed) part of its filling. In interrogating the structural features of experience, the appeal to or study of qualia simply doesn't get us anywhere. As I wait at the bus stop, it is part of the structure of my experience that I expect the bus to come. But neither the waiting nor the expectation is in any way captured by an attempt to somehow describe the ineffable "subjective qualitative feel" of my experience.

So far, this preliminary discussion of phenomenology has sought to avoid controversies more-or-less by fiat. But a further area of controversy concerning phenomenology is of direct relevance to the project as a whole. The question here: is any such thing as phenomenology possible at all? Can subjective experience ever be objectively investigated? I am cognizant of this problem, and I am deeply concerned with it. Indeed one of the purposes of the book is to find out whether there can be a body of phenomenological results. But while I am interested in this question, I am not going to tackle it directly. Phenomenology has often been beset by what we might call a problem of infinite deferral. Phenomenological writings seem forever to be at work on establishing the proper methodology of their undertaking or specifying its exact significance. Actual phenomenological results can seem always to lie over the horizon of some anticipated but never published second volume. This is perhaps more a problem of reputation than reality, but it is, at any rate, a vice to be avoided. Accordingly my approach here is to look at cases where phenomenology has already been at work – in particular at the work of developing a phenomenological account of judgment. My hope is that by assessing some actual phenomenological undertakings and concrete phenomenological successes and failures we shall find ourselves in a better position to assess the question of its possibility.

In what follows I approach the problem of judgment by focusing on these three faces of judgment and the theoretical entanglements they have spawned. My method is historical. The four central chapters of the book present a series of case studies, each undertaking detailed examinations of episodes in the history of the theoretical treatment of judgment. In choosing the cases to study I have adopted the prospector's strategy of mining where plates collide – focusing on moments in the history of the judgment problem where these three bodies of theory come into contact and conflict with one another. The argument is thus at once historical and philosophical. I show that the problem of judgment runs as a continuous thread through much of the history of modern philosophy, often uniting traditions and specializations that are otherwise seen as sharing little in common. In large part, however, the history I recount is a history of philosophical failure. In each study I show how seemingly promising approaches to the problem of judgment led more-or-less directly to theoretical impasse. The problem of judgment, it turns out, proves remarkably resistant to solution – even across a diverse range of disciplines and methodologies. But the philosophical lessons are not entirely negative, and in each case I argue that the failed approaches exhibit substantive leads and constraints for an adequate theory of judgment.

In marking out this terrain I have been speaking of judgment as a problem, and this locution requires some explanation. In philosophy as in many other domains, research gets going when large-scale issues can be tackled in the form of more-or-less well-defined puzzles. In orienting ourselves it will be useful to have at hand some of these smaller-scale problems that have provided theoretical leverage in this history of the investigation of judgment. By way of anticipation, I should perhaps add that research sometimes progresses by solving such puzzles, but in other cases gains ground by exposing problematic assumptions at work in the posing of the puzzles themselves.

Perhaps the most ancient and notorious problem concerning judgment is the so-called *problem of the copula*. The copula is that little grammatical device which makes all the difference between saying "Socrates, wisdom," and saying that Socrates *is* wise. In the latter case I have expressed a judgment, while in the former I have simply named a person and a property. Moreover the latter constitutes a truth-evaluable unity, while the former is nothing but a list. How should we understand the work of the judgment-making copula? Whence the peculiar unity that it marks? The problem of the copula is one of the venerable problems in the history of logic, and an adequate account of judgment requires that it be either solved or dissolved.

Closely related to the problem of the copula is the *problem of affirmation*. To make a judgment is to affirm the truth of some claim or content. Hence in order to understand judgment it is necessary to explain the difference between the mere occurrence of some psychological or semantic content and the affirmation of that content as true. As we shall see, the problem of affirmation has figured in all three domains of theory that will concern us in this study. A correlate of the problem of affirmation is the *problem of negation*. In thinking about the function of the copula it is natural to think of judging as an act of combination or synthesis. In judging that Socrates is wise I seem to forge a judgmental unity by combining the idea of "Socrates" and the idea of "wisdom" in a way that somehow reflects the unity of the person and the property. But if we go this route then what are we to say about negative judgment? Is negation to be understood as an act of separation? But what kind of unity can be effected through separation?

A fourth problem might be dubbed the *problem of agreement and disagreement*. If you feel pain from your gallstones and I don't, this difference between our psychological states does not amount to any kind of agreement or disagreement between us. But when the difference between our psychological states is one of judgment we have the makings of disagreement. What is it about identity and difference of judgment that amounts to (and allows for) agreement and disagreement? We will find that all these problems open up on to a broader set of *problems about truth and intentionality*. A judgment, after all, is always a judgment about something, and is evaluable as true or false.

But the ultimate stakes in this domain cannot be fully captured in the form of well-defined theoretical puzzles, for they concern our implicit and explicit self-understanding. How do we implicitly understand ourselves when we engage in judgment? How do we situate ourselves in the world? And what forms of recognition do we owe to the many other judges among whom we find ourselves judging? We will find, I hope, that pursuit of the various problems of judgment will allow us to gain some insight into these broader philosophical issues.

The book that follows is divided into five chapters. The first chapter deals with three attempts to tackle the problem of judgment experimentally. The three cases can all be classed very broadly as psychology, but the psychological approaches vary widely. Two of the experimental approaches are relatively recent cases from the field of neurophysiology: Benjamin Libet's much-discussed work on cerebral initiative and conscious intention and Michael Shadlen's work on the neural computations that implement decision in Macaque monkeys. I approach these experimental strategies by considering how they navigate a theoretical problem bequeathed by a much earlier set of psychological experiments concerning judgment – experiments reported by David Hume in his *Treatise of Human Nature* (1739). Hume famously approaches the problem of judgment by focusing on the problem of affirmation: what is the difference, Hume asks, betwixt merely entertaining an idea and actually believing it? Hume devises an experiment which is meant to settle the question, and proposes his theory of belief on the basis of his results. Hume's experiment is clearly a failure, but I argue that it exhibits a substantive constraint on any theory of judgment, a condition that I call *the content identity condition*: whatever the difference between merely entertaining some claim and judging it to be true, it must be possible for judgment to vary while the content of judgment remains the same. More broadly, Hume's investigation exhibits a form of dependence of psychological on logical questions about judgment, and I consider how the two bodies of modern experimental work have managed this dependency.

The chapters that follow turn to the history of logic, particularly in the period stretching roughly from the French Revolution to the outbreak of the First World War. This period (the nineteenth century, expansively construed) was one of intense unrest and experimentation in logic, and it was a period in which the proper characterization of judgment was fiercely debated among logicians. It is perhaps the most concrete contribution of this study to recover this largely forgotten history of the logical theory of judgment, and to show how some of its forgotten figures – Herbart, Drobisch, Lotze, Maier, Lipps – contributed to a new understanding of the logic, psychology, and ultimately the phenomenology of judgment. My survey of this tradition begins in the second chapter with a reconstruction of the main episodes in a century-long dispute about existential judgment, a debate spawned by Immanuel Kant. Kant very explicitly draws on the logical theory of judgment in developing his account of the role of judgment in human experience – what Kant calls "transcendental logic." My discussion focuses on Kant's characterization of judgment as a form of combination or synthesis, and on the problems created for that approach by Kant's own famous claim that "being" or "existence" (the "*ist*" in "*Gott ist*") is not a predicate. I show how this claim creates an anomaly for Kant's general logic, and I track four generations of nineteenth-century logicians as they resort to increasingly radical strategies for resolving it. This crisis created for the synthetic construal of judgment begins with Fichte, who complains that Kant had not applied his critical spirit to logic itself, and culminates in Brentano's revolutionary claim that synthesis or combination forms no part of the essence of judgment.

The third chapter considers the role of the theory of judgment in the revolution that gave rise to modern symbolic logic, particularly in the work of the seminal logician, Gottlob Frege. The focus of my analysis in this case is Frege's introduction of the so-called "judgment stroke" in his innovative logical calculus, *Begriffsschrift*. I argue that Frege's attempts to explicate the judgment stroke drive him to acknowledge a limit of the expressive capacity of logic. Frege's logical standard in the theory of judgment both requires and precludes a symbolic mark of judgment, and his attempts to define the judgment stroke accordingly end in paradox. I propose an interpretation of these limits drawing on two claims from Heidegger's philosophical logic – the claim that the copula is necessarily ambiguous between its truth-claiming and unity-marking functions; and the claim that logic presupposes an understanding of truth that it must borrow and cannot articulate. In the course of making this argument, I consider the sense in which Frege should be considered a logical revolutionary, and criticize Frege's explanation of the redundancy of the truth predicate.

The fourth chapter turns to Martin Heidegger's contributions to the theory of judgment. Although they are now rarely discussed, Heidegger's earliest writings focused of the theory of judgment, particularly in logic. My discussion focuses on Heidegger's doctoral dissertation of 1913, *The Doctrine of Judgment in Psychologism*. I review his critical engagement with four theorists who sought to ground the logic of judgment in empirical psychology, and I show how, in the course of these exchanges, Heidegger articulates two methods that can be used in investigating the distinctive phenomenology of judgment. The first of these methods is the explicit position of the dissertation itself – what Heidegger himself calls "logicism." The second borrows important elements from the psychologistic theories Heidegger criticizes, and can best be described as a phenomenology of judgmental comportment. On this latter approach, one articulates the character of judgment in experience not by some introspective procedure (a strategy that fails miserably in Hume and those who have failed to learn from Hume's failure) but rather by articulating the comportment or orientation that a judge adopts in passing judgment.

In the final chapter I take some tentative steps toward unraveling this judgmental comportment. As a source and resource I use a series of paintings of a famous instance of judgment – the Judgment of Paris as portrayed by the German Renaissance painter, Lucas Cranach the Elder.

These studies of the history of the judgment problem are anything but exhaustive. Indeed it is hard to imagine a single book that could encompass a topic so large. I have nothing to say here, for instance, about the renaissance reform in logic, and its consequences for the theory of judgment, nor do I make any more than a passing reference to the debate in early modern philosophy over the voluntarist conception of judgment. Among ongoing research programs, my survey is again highly selective, leaving out, for instance, the rich research tradition on the psychology of judgment stemming from the ground-breaking work of Tversky and Kahneman. On the logical side, I have focused my attention on the tumultuous history of logic in the nineteenth century, a period in which the theory of judgment was central to the most important disputes and developments in logic. In doing so, however, I entirely neglect one of the most important logical research traditions pertinent to my topic: the decision-theoretic treatment of judgment under conditions of uncertainty. Even among those theorists whose work I do discuss, I have neglected large and pertinent tracts of theory. This is most evident (and perhaps egregious) in the case of Kant, where I have focused almost exclusively on what Kant calls the general logic of judgment, and have entirely omitted Kant's more famous claims about judgment, including his critique devoted to this topic. I excuse these omissions not because these cases are any less interesting or less important than those I have chosen to discuss, but rather with the pleas that any excursion in this arena must be selective if it is to be manageable, and that the forays undertaken here together provide the makings for a single arc of argument which I hope can advance our understanding of the topic.

Before getting down to the work of the specific case studies, it is perhaps worthwhile to conclude these introductory remarks by acknowledging a possible objection to the framing of the issues I have here proposed. In particular, it will not have escaped the attention of readers that I have been using the notion of judgment ambiguously. When a judge issues a ruling we distinguish between the act of judging and the judgment issued. We call both by the name "judgment," just as the term "assertion" applies both to my act of asserting and to what I assert, and "combination" can refer either to an episode of combining or to the product thereof. If we are not to be misled by this ambiguity, we must take care to distinguish between the *act* of judgment and the *content* of that act. The former is a dated episode in the life of some particular individual; the latter is typically a proposition. Yet on just this point some may suspect an elementary error in my framing of the questions to be pursued here. I have proposed that we might hope to learn something about ourselves as judges by focusing in part on the treatment of judgment in logic. But it is only judgments as contents (propositions) that would seem to fall within the theoretical purview of logic, since it is only the *content* of a judgment that can serve as a premise or conclusion of an inference. It would thus be a mistake in principle, it seems, to turn to the logic of judgment in the hopes of learning something interesting about ourselves as judging agents. To suppose otherwise is to set off down the slope toward the fallacy of psychologism: the confusion of the logic of inferential relations with the psychology or phenomenology of inferring.

I shall not try to reply in detail to this objection here, since relations between these different senses of judgment form the object of this study as a whole. Certainly we must exercise care in navigating the act–content distinction as it applies to the case of judgment. We must also allow room, I believe, for a species of logical truth that obtains quite independently of the contingent psychological facts about judgment. At the same time, however, we must find a way of construing the act of judgment as a strict correlate of the content expressed thereby. For it is only in virtue of some such a correlation (what Husserl called "noetic-noematic correlation") that we can secure our conception of our subjective experience as disciplined by rational constraints.

THE PSYCHOLOGY OF JUDGING: THREE EXPERIMENTAL APPROACHES

> One is always faced, then, with the unacceptable alternative of not
> attempting to study a primary phenomenological aspect of our human
> existence in relation to brain function because of the logical impossibility
> of direct verification by an external observer.
>
> Libet 1985: 534

Judgment is, among other things, a characteristic capacity of certain
intelligent organisms, and it is thus natural to turn to empirical psychology to investigate it. Our initial set of case studies are accordingly drawn
from psychology and its history. In particular, I consider in this chapter
three attempts to tackle the problem of judgment experimentally. Two
cases come from modern neuropsychological research; the third is by now
ancient history: the eighteenth-century psychological experiments due to
David Hume. The three experimental approaches diverge dramatically
in their methodologies and in their conception of psychology, yet each
exhibits the pattern which is the subject of this book: the entanglement of
logical, psychological, and phenomenological constraints in the theory of
judgment. My discussion aims both to document these entanglements
and to show how, in at least two cases, they lead to experimental failure.
But I also seek to extract positive results, exhibiting a substantive logical

I am grateful to David Owen, Dallas Willard, and Jeff Yoshimi for comments on an earlier
draft of this chapter.

constraint on the theory of judgment (Hume's content identity condition) and a variety of patterns whereby experimentalists have sought to integrate the various faces of judgment.

My discussion is divided into six parts. The first section reviews two recent experimental protocols used in investigating the neurophysiology of judgment. The middle sections (the bulk of the chapter) are then devoted to a detailed assessment of Hume's experimental protocol: section 2 reviews Hume's experimental approach in psychology; section 3 presents his failed experiments pertaining to judgment. In section 4 I consider a common diagnosis of Hume's failure and argue for its inadequacy. Section 5 offers an alternative diagnosis, beginning from the logical considerations which structured Hume's experimental approach and shaped his impasse. The final section then returns to the modern experiments to consider how they navigate the pattern of entanglement which thwarted Hume's account.

1 The neurophysiology of judging: two experimental protocols

I begin with some widely discussed and controversial experiments carried out in Benjamin Libet's laboratory at UC San Francisco. The results were originally reported in a series of articles in the early 1980s[1] and were reviewed by a distinguished group of philosophers and scientists in a much-cited article in *Behavioral and Brain Sciences*.[2] Libet's experiments continue to attract a lot of attention, most recently in a volume of essays extending and assessing his experimental results.[3] Libet works in the experimental tradition which seeks to advance our understanding of neural processes and architecture on the basis of very precise time measurements of neural and conscious events. The study of the timing of cognitive events goes back to the beginnings of empirical psychology, being one of the research tools pioneered by Wundt and others in the late nineteenth century. In the modern development of this technique the units of time at stake are very small (down to tens of milliseconds) – small enough to afford glimpses of the transmission of electrical impulses through the nervous system.

Libet himself was a major player in this research tradition long before his work bearing on the theory of judgment. His experiments from the

---

[1] Libet 1982, 1983.
[2] Libet 1985.
[3] Libet, Freeman, and Sunderland 1999.

early 1960s are widely cited for the demonstration of what has come to be called "Libet's half-second" – the 500 millisecond duration required for a direct neural stimulus to rise to the level of conscious experience.[4] The early methodology involved the direct electrical stimulation of the brains of conscious human subjects. Using this technique Libet argued that it takes a stimulus of at least a half-second duration for a person to evolve a state of consciousness for a new experience – in short: to feel a shock. The procedure may now seem rudimentary but the result was significant, particularly in the context of a tradition which tended to treat consciousness as a kind of instantaneous presence of a perceptual environment. As one recent commentator puts it: "The time it takes to settle a fully-tuned spread of neural representation means that we must constantly run half a second behind reality – although for some reason we never notice the fact."[5]

The experiments that concern us here come nearly twenty years later, but as we shall see, Libet is still very much concerned with that 500 millisecond margin. The basic experimental protocol was as follows. Human subjects were asked to perform simple, voluntary, self-paced, repetitive exercises. Volunteer research subjects sat in a laboratory and performed very simple voluntary movements – flexing either a wrist or finger. Their instruction was to do this at their own initiative, without prior planning or further prompting cues from laboratory personnel. Libet then used electro-physiological monitoring of the research sub-jects at two separate sites: nerve activity in the arm was monitored by electromyogram (EMG) while opposite hemisphere cerebral monitors recorded brain activity.

Using this protocol, Libet's laboratory generated the results shown in Figure 1.

Notice some of the key features of this data. The wiggly lines are generated by the opposite hemisphere neural monitors, and they show us the dynamic electrical environment of the brain. Notice the scale here: 1,000 milliseconds against 10 microvolts (1 millisecond = 0.001 seconds; 1 microvolt = 10^{-6} volts); the brain, it turns out, is not only extremely fast, it is also remarkably energy efficient. In the first two columns of graphs (RP I and RP II) we see a steadily rising level of electrical activity, followed by a sharp drop off. The difference between RP I and RP II is the length and slope of the initial rise. Libet – following a number of

---

[4] Libet 1965, 1966.
[5] McCrone 1999: 119 and ch. vi.

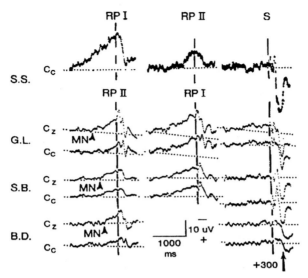

Figure 1: Libet's Readiness Potentials
Source: Libet 1985: 531

others[6] – calls this pattern of activity the Readiness Potential – hence RP. Libet characterizes an RP as "a scalp-recorded slow negative shift in electrical potential generated by the brain."[7] Its systematic correlation with voluntary movements suggests that it is a neural event involved in initiating such activity. The vertical lines on these graphs then map the muscular activity onto this neural activity. That is, the vertical lines mark the points where muscular activity is initiated. Summing up so far: what we have is voluntary movement preceded by a characteristic pattern of neural activity.

These basic characteristics of Readiness Potentials had already been demonstrated by a number of other researchers. Libet's key contribution was to map this activity onto the subject's phenomenology. That is, he sought to incorporate the subject's own experience into the timeline of neural and motor activity. Indeed Libet's unswerving determination to accommodate phenomenological data within neuroscientific research is one of the distinctive marks of his experimental approach: "The

---

[6] Gilden, Vaughan, and Costa 1966; Kornhuber and Deecke, 1965.
[7] Libet 1985: 529.

objective was in fact to compare the time of onset of the *conscious intention* to act and the time of onset of associated *cerebral processes*."[8]

But Libet also recognizes the difficulty that faces the experimentalist who concerns himself with phenomenology:

> Because subjective experiences are not directly accessible to an external observer, it may be logically impossible for the external observer to determine directly any feature of the experience. ... One is always faced, then, with the unacceptable alternative of not attempting to study a primary phenomenological aspect of our human existence in relation to brain function because of the logical impossibility of direct verification by an external observer. Or one can attempt to evaluate the accuracy of the introspective report and gain confidence in its validity by applying indirect controls, tests, and converging operations.[9]

So what is Libet's solution? How are we to undertake phenomenological as well as electro-physiological monitoring of the subject's decision to act? Libet's strategy was to begin from the ability of the research subjects to monitor their own experience:

> In the present experimental paradigm subjects agree to comply with a variety of instructions from the experimenter. One of these is an expectation that the subject is to perform the prescribed motor act at some time after the start of each trial; another is that he should pay close introspective attention to the instant of the onset of the urge, desire or decision to perform each such act.[10]

While reflecting on their own conscious activity, the research subjects were then instructed to attend to an oscilloscope, on which was displayed a clock face with a revolving marker (see Figure 2).

The marker moved rapidly around the clock face, making a revolution every 2.5 seconds. Each unit on the face thus represented 43 milliseconds. After each trial the subjects were asked to recall the "clock time" of the onset of their experienced intention to act.

The results of Libet's experiments are plotted on the timeline shown in Figure 3. The timeline gives us three main points to compare. EMG marks the initiation of muscular activity as recorded by the electromyogram, and is here used as the zero point for the timeline. RP marks the initiation of the Cerebral Readiness Potential. Finally, W marks the

---

[8] Libet 1985: 530.
[9] Libet 1985: 534.
[10] Libet 1985: 534.

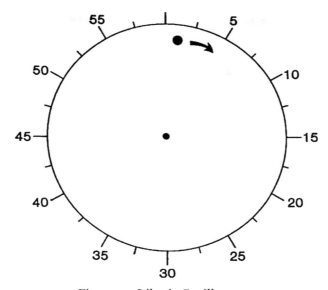

Figure 2: Libet's Oscilloscope
Source: Libet, Freeman, and Sunderland 1999: 50

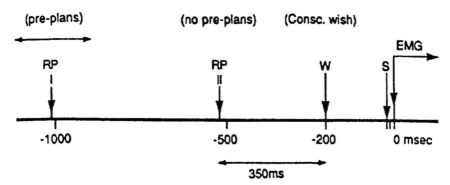

Figure 3: Libet's Timeline
Source: Libet, Freeman, and Sunderland 1999: 51

subject's own reported awareness of the "urge, desire or decision" to act.
I shall return below to some of the other features on the timeline – most
importantly S, and the distinction between RP I and RP II. These details
turn out to be important, but the main result to notice is this: the onset of the

RP systematically *precedes* the reported conscious decision to act. In other words: the brain seems to get started on action about half a second before consciousness knows about it. This was the result that attracted attention and revived the worry that consciousness might after all be wholly epiphenomenal. Libet did not himself subscribe to the epiphenomenalist conclusion, but he found the need to invoke quite imaginative hypotheses in order to preserve a causal role for consciousness on the timeline of action.[11]

A second set of experimental results comes from primate research. The results in this case are due to Michael Shadlen's work on neural computation and decision in Macaque and Rhesus monkeys – an ongoing research project undertaken first at Stanford and later at the Primate Research Facility at the University of Washington.[12] Shadlen's monkeys are trained to carry out a variety of tasks involving perception in a complex visual field. I shall not here reconstruct all the details of Shadlen's remarkable experiments, but confine myself at this stage to a brief description of the experimental set-up and a statement of one of Shadlen's conclusions.

Under Shadlen's protocol, monkeys are shown a video monitor displaying a pattern of blinking and moving light-points. Against the background of the randomized flashing on the screen, a small portion of the light-points exhibit movement either to the right or to the left. The monkeys are trained to recognize the direction of this movement, hold their forward gaze for a short delay period and then redirect their gaze to a target either to the right or to the left, depending upon the direction of the detected movement (see Figure 4). In effect, the monkeys are called to perceive, make a decision about what they see, and then act upon what they decide. Shadlen's experiments focus on the neural basis of that middle step – the decision that mediates between perception and motor response. His conclusion concerns the neural implementation of that decision. In particular, he attributes it to a cluster of neurons in the lateral intraparietal (LIP) region. I postpone for now consideration of the basis for Shadlen's anatomical conclusion.

Neither of the two cases I have presented here are explicitly conceived or designed as research into judgment. Shadlen casts his project as an investigation of decision, while Libet's work has mainly been discussed as a

---

[11] Epiphenomenalism is the thesis that the mind and body do stand in causal relations, but that the causal traffic runs only in one direction: bodily changes have consequences for consciousness, but mental events do not cause physical changes. For Libet's positive account of conscious agency, see Libet 1985: 538ff, and Libet, Freeman, and Sunderland 1999: 51–53.

[12] Shadlen *et al.* 2001.

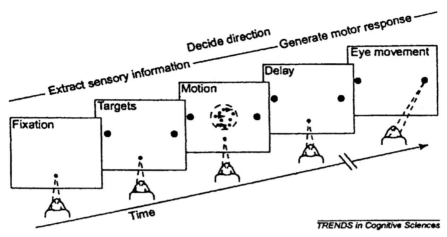

Figure 4: Shadlen's Direction-Discrimination Task
Source: Shadlen *et al.* 2001: 11

contribution to the understanding of voluntary action and the problem of free will. But both sets of experiments are in an important sense empirical investigations of judgment. In both cases the research subjects are tasked with making a decision – a decision about when to act in Libet's case; a decision about what is seen and what to do in the case of Shadlen's monkeys. The experiments are designed to shed light on the biological implementation of such decisions. Perhaps to some these decisions will seem too rudimentary or trivial to merit the name judgment. But we need not entangle ourselves in the demarcational issue at this point. What matters is that these cases exhibit important features of judgment, and that they can teach us something about the difficulties of psychological research in this domain. I return below (section 6) to consider the significance of these contemporary experimental approaches for the theory of judgment. But I turn first to consider in some detail a much older set of experiments – those reported by David Hume in his 1739 *Treatise of Human Nature*.

2 Hume's experimental approach

Hume's *Treatise* bore an important but often forgotten subtitle: "Being an Attempt to Introduce the *Experimental Method* of Reasoning into Moral Subjects."[13] In calling for an experimental method in philosophy,

[13] Emphasis added.

Hume is hoping to follow what he takes to be the Newtonian lead. Newton had reduced the complex motions of physical nature to a few simple laws, and Hume hoped to do the same for the motions of the mind. The data in this enterprise are to be gathered mainly (though not exclusively) through careful experimental observation of what Hume calls perceptions (mental content) in the stream of human consciousness. The experiments are to be designed so as to exhibit the primitives of our conscious lives – what Hume calls impressions and ideas – in their simplest behavior. In the normal course of human experience, the simple elements of consciousness manifest themselves only as parts of more complex aggregates, and their simple behaviors are often lost in the context of more complex forces. We need an experimental approach in order to exhibit the simple behaviors vividly, for it is at that level that we can hope to find the most basic principles of human psychology.[14]

The experiment with which we shall be concerned comes fairly deep in the first book of the *Treatise*, in the context of Hume's extended investigation of our idea of a causal connection. By this point in the *Treatise*, Hume already has a fair number of results in hand, so I begin with a brief review of a few salient points of terminology and psychological doctrine. The most important piece of background for our purpose is Hume's general account of psychological content and its primitives. This is, of course, the classical empiricist account of the stream of consciousness, understood as the successive presence in my experience of complexes of simple perceptions. The specific content of my experience, on this account, simply is the specific character of those conscious primitives (their qualitative feel) and the spatio-temporal order of their appearance. These psychological simples come in two basic varieties, according to Hume. *Impressions* are (roughly) the contents of direct sensory experience, together with the quasi-sensory content characteristic of the various emotions. *Ideas* are copies of these impressions, such as those that occur in memory or imagination. Impressions and ideas are both species of a broader class – *perceptions*, in Hume's vocabulary.

---

[14] For Hume's account of the application of the experimental method to "moral subjects" see the Introduction to Hume 1739; for a discussion see Stroud 1977: 1–16. Some of Hume's experiments are thought experiments, as in the famous case where Hume asks us to imagine a visual spectrum with a missing shade of blue. But others are actual experiments, as when he argues for the idea of a visual minimum (a smallest visible extension) by instructing the reader to make a mark on a surface, then slowly to back away until it is no longer visible, thence returning to the point where it first appears.

"Perception" for Hume simply names the broadest class of mental content. What differentiates perceptions is both their specific quality (whether the sound of the word "Paris," the taste of green tea, or the palpable felt quality of visceral fear) as well as what Hume calls their "force and vivacity" – the intensity with which they occur. Hence, for instance, when I look at my tea cup I have an impression of it; when I turn away and recall it to mind, I have a corresponding idea – essentially a paler, less forceful copy of the impression.

The particular issue that concerns us pertains to the psychological phenomenon of belief. Hume's discussion of belief is quite short in the *Treatise* – only a few pages in a book of several hundred – but it is clear that Hume attaches considerable importance to it. He repeatedly claims that this is one of his most original contributions to psychology, and it is the topic to which he immediately returns in the Appendix that he attached to the final installment of the book. It is also fair to say that this is an area where he was never fully satisfied with the account he provided.[15]

Before considering Hume's experimental protocol, we must be clear about two terminological issues. First it is important to appreciate that Hume is not investigating belief in the sense of "faith" or "trust" – as when we talk about believing in a friend or having faith in God. Hume has in mind the more commonplace variety of belief: *assent to an idea*. To believe an idea is to hold it as true. A second problem of terminology pertains to the term "incredulity." Hume's most concise formulation of his experimental question turns on the contrast between belief and incredulity: "I ... ask: Wherein consists the difference betwixt incredulity and belief?"[16] But there is an ambiguity here. Sometimes Hume focuses his investigation on the difference between belief and *disbelief* – the difference between believing an idea to be true and believing it to be false. Indeed one of Hume's formulations casts the question in exactly these terms: "Wherein consists the difference betwixt believing and disbelieving any proposition?"[17] But much of his attention is devoted to incredulity in the sense of *lack of belief* – what Hume calls "the mere conception of an idea." When I "merely conceive" an idea, I entertain it without forming *any judgment* concerning its veracity. Accordingly, Hume sometimes formulates his question in terms of the "difference

---

[15] For a discussion of Hume's claim to originality in the theory of belief, see Owen 2003.

[16] Hume 1739: 95.

[17] Hume 1739: 95.

betwixt the simple conception of ... an object and the belief of it,"[18] or (most tellingly for our purposes) between "the ideas of judgment [and] the fictions of the imagination."[19]

What is of particular significance for our purposes is that Hume sets out to answer his psychological question at least in part through pheno- menological investigation. He does not attempt to distinguish incredu- lity from belief by finding some relevant difference of neural activity or overt behavior. He attempts rather to articulate the difference by distin- guishing the ways in which our ideas manifest themselves in experience. To follow out Hume's lead is thus to be called to interrogate our own experience of judgment and to articulate its specific character. In this sense, it is to be called to phenomenological enquiry.

By formulating the problem of judgment in these terms, Hume would seem to have posed a question which every sane person ought to be able to answer. This is, after all, a matter on which we are all already experts. We are constantly besieged by ideas, and yet we rarely encounter any difficulty in sorting the ones we believe from the ones we merely enter- tain or disbelieve. Indeed we treat the chronic inability to mark this distinction as a pretty sure sign of delusional disorder.[20] In some way, then, we all already know the difference between these two sets of ideas and we typically mark the distinction with little more than a moment's reflection. All we need do, it seems, is to make explicit the knowledge we so readily deploy implicitly all the time. This is a characteristic promise of phenomenological investigation.

But if there is something promising about Hume's phenomenological posing of the judgment problem, there is also something troubling about it. For as we shall see presently, Hume's attempt to answer his

---

[18] Hume 1739: 94.

[19] Hume 1739: 629.

[20] There are, of course, many cases where I find myself unsure *what* to believe about some particular matter. ("Who do you think will win the Pennant ten years from now?" "I don't know what to believe about that; I just don't have enough relevant information.") In such cases I encounter an ordinary cognitive limit, but there is no failure of self-knowledge. I know perfectly well that I have no opinion about the matter. It is something quite of a different order and altogether more extraordinary to find myself unable to decide *whether* I am believing or not. This sort of confusion does on occasion occur, but when it does it is usually under conditions of considerable cognitive distress, where I find myself sufficiently torn as to find myself epistemically quite disoriented. Think, for example, of a person in the throes of a religious crisis, who at a certain point finds himself unable to say whether or not he any longer believes in the existence of God. Such a person is not simply unsure whether God exists; he is unsure *whether he believes* that God exists. The limit in this case is a limit of self-knowledge.

phenomenological question turns out to be a rather spectacular failure. Moreover, when we examine that failure we find ourselves faced with the question as to whether *any* phenomenological answer is forthcoming. In this way, Hume marks an important precedent for those of us who are tempted by phenomenology.

3 Hume's experimental failure

Here as elsewhere, Hume's approach is experimental in the sense specified above. We are to isolate pairs of ideas such that one is merely conceived or disbelieved while the other actually believed. In order to exhibit the relevant difference in as pure a form as possible (one of the aims of the experimental approach) we seek to minimize extraneous or independent variables. The optimal procedure would be to undertake a "side-by-side" comparison by finding two ideas which vary only in belief status, excluding all independent variables. Unfortunately this optimal set-up turns out to be experimentally impossible, since one and the same person cannot both believe and disbelieve the same idea at the same time. Accordingly we must satisfy ourselves with the closest possible departures from the optimal case. In the case of disagreement we find the same idea believed and disbelieved at the same time, but occurring in two discrete individuals. When a single person changes her mind, we find the relevant difference in the same individual with the same idea, but with difference of temporal position. Yet a third case takes two similar but not identical ideas occurring at the same time within the same individual, with one believed and one merely conceived or disbelieved. At different points Hume has something to say about all of these second-best cases, and in each case the question we are to pose is the same: how does the difference manifest itself in conscious experience?

So much for Hume's protocol; let us turn now to his reported experimental results. Famously, his claim is that the difference in each case is a difference in the force and vivacity of the two ideas. In particular, he reports that believed ideas occur more forcefully and vivaciously than those which are merely entertained. Hume: "Belief does nothing but vary the manner, in which we conceive any object, it can only bestow on our ideas an additional force and vivacity."[21]

---

[21] Hume 1739: 96.

Now this answer is, it must be said, deeply implausible on its face. Indeed Hume's purported confirmation of the result reads like a pretty effective refutation. Here's Hume's phenomenological report:

> [This will] be found to be entirely conformable to every one's feeling and experience. Nothing is more evident, than that those ideas, to which we assent, are more strong, firm and vivid, than the loose reveries of a castle-builder. If one person sits down to read a book as a romance, and another as a true history, they plainly receive the same ideas, and in the same order; nor does the incredulity of the one, and the belief of the other hinder them from putting the same sense upon their author. His words produce the same ideas in both; tho' his testimony has not the same influence on them. The latter has a more lively conception of all the incidents. He enters deeper into the concerns of the persons: represents to himself their actions, and characters, and friendships, and enmities: He even goes so far as to form a notion of their features, and air, and person. While the former, who gives no credit to the testimony of the author, has a more faint and languid conception of all these particulars; and except on account of the style and ingenuity of the composition, can receive little entertainment from it.[22]

This is one of those wonderful moments in a phenomenological enterprise where one gets a revealing glimpse into the life of the experimenter. Certainly it tells us something about Hume's novel-reading (or perhaps about the novels he was unlucky to have chosen). And it tells us something about why he was such a successful writer of history. But it just gets the wrong result for the theory of belief.

The most obvious problem is that there are many ideas which carry considerable force and vivacity, but which nonetheless are not believed to be true. For my part, at least, the scene of Anna Karenina hurling herself in despair before a moving train is among the most forceful and vivacious of my ideas. Tolstoy's rendering of the account produces not only "entertainment," but just the sort of vivid presence that Hume reports from reading histories. Yet I don't for a moment confuse the forcefulness of this idea with veracity. And to take the opposite case: if I ask myself whether, in fact, somewhere in nineteenth-century Russia, a distraught woman hurled herself before a train, my answer would be yes. No doubt the engineers had to cope with many such suicides – particularly after the appearance of Tolstoy's novel. But in this case my idea of the suicide is not at all forceful and vivacious, despite being believed. On the face of it, then, Hume's distinction fails to capture the phenomenological facts.

---

[22] Hume 1739: 97–98.

Now perhaps a defender of Hume will cry foul at these purported counter-examples. After all, Hume explicitly allows for the influence of "the style and ingenuity of the composition," and it is clearly this variable which is at work in my idea of Anna Karenina. Hume's own experiment, by contrast, holds this variable constant by considering the same book read in two different ways. This is a fair objection, but not enough to save Hume's account. Suppose that Herzog's *Fitzcaraldo* had been one of those films that concludes with the old radio-drama line: "The story you have just heard is true ... " Sitting in the theater after seeing the film for the first time, I find myself called upon to believe a set of ideas that, a moment before, I had merely entertained. Here we have the time-variant version of Hume's experiment: same person, same idea, change of belief-state. As the closing credits begin to roll, I have the idea of an opera-lover in Quito who dragged a ship over a mountain. When I get to the final line, with its claim to veracity, I have the same idea occurring now as a belief. How do the two ideas differ? Not, I submit, in their vivacity. After the veracity-claim I find myself with one more reason to mutter: "That's remarkable." I may find myself wondering about various issues that had not occurred to me before. (Which native group was it that assisted him? Were they also involved with the film-project?) But the idea itself retains the same considerable vivacity it had a moment before; believing it adds no appreciable force. Indeed, speaking for my own case, I doubt that it could possibly have further vivacity than it already had.

There are further complications here, which are important and interesting for the interpretation of Hume's work. The crucial problem lies in interpreting the term "force and vivacity." We have already seen that this is a central term in Hume's psychology – marking not only the difference between merely conceiving and believing an idea, but also between sense impressions and ideas. The gradient of force and vivacity is thus of considerable importance to Hume's psychological theory. But it also harbors an ambiguity. It might be read as a generalization of the phenomenon of visual brightness – as if the lamp is somehow turned up on the slide projector of consciousness, the sights and sounds made more vividly present. Call that the phenomenological reading: my sensory experience of the tea cup is simply more vividly present to consciousness than my memory of it after the perceptual fact. But Hume's notion can also be read psycho-mechanically. In this sense an idea is more forceful and vivacious if it carries, so to speak, more psychological momentum – if it has more impact on my beliefs and actions. Remember that Hume is trying to follow the Newtonian lead here, so talk of "force" needs to be read in light of the mechanical paradigm.

I won't here try to resolve this ambiguity in Hume's terminology. At any rate, I am sure that there is no simple resolution of it.[23] For our purposes, however, it doesn't matter which way we go, since in either case Hume's result is false to the phenomenological facts. Certainly the phenomenological reading cannot capture the difference between merely entertaining and actually believing an idea, since one can have extremely vivid ideas that one does not believe, and contrariwise believed ideas that are almost entirely lacking in vividness. My idea of Anna Karenina at the station is an example of the first (vivid without being believed). My idea of my tenth birthday party is an example of the second (believed but not at all vivid).

The mechanical reading may seem to have a better claim here, since it does seem that believed ideas generally have more impact on my actions and further beliefs than merely entertained ideas. But there are at least two problems here as well. First, to go this route would seem to require that I know what I believe only indirectly – by knowing something about the impact of the ideas on my actions and belief. But this is certainly not normally the case. Somehow I seem able to know which ideas I believe non-inferentially. I don't have to wait and see; I don't have to undertake comparative statistical studies of my subsequent behavior. More seriously, the psycho-mechanical answer is also false to the phenomenological facts. Some of the most momentous ideas in our experience are ideals: Infinite Justice, the City of God, the Kingdom of Ends. Such ideas can be enormously influential in shaping actions and beliefs, and so score high on the psycho-mechanical scale of force and vivacity. But those who adopt these ideals and act accordingly do not thereby commit themselves to the belief that Infinite Justice or the Kingdom of Ends actually exist. Forcefulness in the psycho-mechanical sense does not require belief.

[23] See, e.g., Hume 1739: 624, where Hume describes forceful and vivacious ideas as "more present to us," and as having "a greater firmness and solidity," but immediately goes on to add that the mind is "more actuated and mov'd by them." A few pages later "force and vivacity" becomes "force and influence" (Hume 1739: 627). In the footnote on logic, forceful and vivacious ideas are described as being "strong and steady." There is, in short, no way fully to extricate the phenomenological from the mechanical commitments in Hume's position.

4 A psychological straightjacket?

I won't go on further in arguing against Hume's position, since in fact it has no defenders. Even Hume himself, writing only a year later in the Appendix to the *Treatise*, feels the need to modify his position substantially. What I am more interested in here is the diagnostic question. Where did Hume go wrong? How did he find himself saddled with these plainly inadequate experimental results? The answer turns out to be both complex and revealing.

Certainly a major part of Hume's failure can be put down to the principle that observation is theory-laden. Phenomenologists have sometimes wanted to claim a distinctive authority for the investigation of subjective experience. Because of the peculiar immediacy of our own self-knowledge, it is argued, phenomenological investigation should be able to get out in front of all theorizing, taking its lead strictly *from the things themselves*. But this is at best an impossible ideal and at worst simply wrong-headed. In phenomenological observation, as in all observation, we tend to find what we know to look for, and theoretical precommitments are accordingly everywhere at work shaping our experimental observations.

In this case, Hume approaches his phenomenological experiment already committed to a psychological theory that leaves him looking for complexes of sensory contents ("perceptions") varying in force and vivacity. Upon phenomenological reflection he finds just that. The psychological commitments predelineate the phenomenological possibilities, but they are ultimately too constraining, too sparse to handle the phenomenological facts. As Stroud describes Hume's failure: "he tries to answer his question about belief within the confines of an impossibly narrow theory."[24]

This first diagnosis of Hume's failure is in many ways borne out by what we find in his later thoughts on this topic, particularly in the Appendix to the *Treatise*, but also in the treatment of incredulity and belief in the later *Inquiry* (1748). Already in the Appendix, Hume is ready to acknowledge the failure of the account he had given in the body of the *Treatise* itself. Indeed, reflecting on a book which spans more than 600 pages and an astonishing variety of topics, belief is the first of the two "articles" which Hume feels the need to revisit in the Appendix.[25] In this subsequent treatment, we see Hume valiantly but vainly trying to find some room to maneuver in the "impossibly narrow" space dictated by his

---

[24] Stroud 1977: 74.
[25] Hume 1739: 622ff.

psychological theory. That theory allows only for ideas and impressions, each characterized by a distinctive sensory or qualitative character, and by a degree of force and vivacity. Recognizing the position of the *Treatise* as inadequate, Hume makes the only move open to him. If belief is not a degree of force and vivacity then it must be distinctive qualitative character. Accordingly he now reports a "certain feeling or sentiment" which accompanies those of our ideas which we believe:

> When we are convinc'd of any matter of fact, we do nothing but conceive it, along with a certain feeling different from what attends the mere reveries of the imagination. And when we express our incredulity concerning any fact, we mean, that the arguments for the fact produce not that feeling.[26]

This position predictably leads to phenomenological surrender. Hume confesses to finding himself "at a loss for terms to express his meaning,"[27] and suggests that the definition of belief is "a very difficult, if not an impossible, task ... as if one should endeavor to define the feeling of cold, or passion of anger."[28] But he also insists that we should expect such limits when a psychologically primitive content is at issue. "In philosophy we can go no further, than assert, that [belief] is something felt by the mind, which distinguishes the ideas of the judgment from the fictions of the imagination."[29] Indeed, Hume now sees the main mistake of the *Treatise* as overstepping that limit – attempting a definition where only analogical description is possible.[30]

But none of this marks a phenomenological advance, and the position of the Appendix turns out to be just as phenomenologically inadequate as was its predecessor within the *Treatise* itself. The problem, of course, is that there is no ineffable sentiment of belief, no matter how badly Hume's psychology may require it. There is no little light, no characteristic surge of feeling any more than there is a distinctive crispness or vividness that marks out some ideas as believed. Hume's claims to the

---

[26] Hume 1739: 624. Hume insists that this move in fact retains something of his original position. An impression is, on Hume's account, characterized by its greater force and vivacity, and he is sure that they convey some of that energy to the ideas they accompany. According to the position of the Appendix, however, belief itself is strictly speaking an impression – a distinctive sentiment or feeling – that accompanies ideas, rather than being a degree of the force and vivacity of the believed ideas.

[27] Hume 1739: 629.

[28] Hume 1748: 61–68.

[29] Hume 1739: 629.

[30] For the clearest statement of this diagnosis, see Hume 1748: § V, Pt ii.

contrary are based in theoretical need rather than in the phenomenological facts. Hence, the first diagnosis of Hume's failure: his straightjacket psychology falsifies his phenomenological observations.

While there is considerable truth to this first diagnosis, it cannot
suffice as a diagnosis of Hume's experimental dead-end. For Hume's
phenomenological pinch continues to make itself felt even when his
psychological constraints are loosened. Suppose, for instance, that one
enriches Hume's psychological resources as many twentieth-century
analytic philosophers wanted to: by adding the resources of propositions
and propositional attitudes. Once again Stroud's take is representative:
"We have an idea of, e.g., the book's being on the table, but when that
idea figures in a belief it is a belief *that* the book is on the table. ...
Hume's theory does not account for this fact."[31] Belief, on this view,
is neither a primitive quasi-perceptual content nor a feature of such
primitives but a stance or attitude one takes toward a propositional
complex.

It is hard to deny that the appeal to propositional content marks an
advance in characterizing belief, but does it in fact leave us any better off
when faced with Hume's experiment? Once we admit the enriched
psychology, Hume's question immediately recurs: how do we manage
to distinguish "betwixt" different propositional attitudes? What identifies some of my attitudes as "believings," others as "merely entertain-
ings," and still others as hopings, desirings, bemoanings, etc.? When this
question has been addressed at all it has typically been in dispositionalist
or broadly functionalist terms: a belief differs from a case of incredulity
by playing a different role in disposing me to actions of one sort or
another. This is all well and good but it famously says nothing about
the manifestation of this functional difference *in my experience*. If we try to
fill the phenomenological lacuna, we quickly find ourselves once again in
Hume's pinch, unable to say what we so readily know. So Hume's failure
is not sufficiently explained by his psychological constraints.

A more radical diagnosis blames phenomenology itself. Perhaps
Hume's experiment fails precisely because he poses his experimental
question in phenomenological terms. Perhaps he ought to give up his
armchair for a lab-bench, or perhaps he ought to give up on the very
category of conscious experience altogether. Whatever the preferred
alternative, one might well find in Hume's failure a striking example of

---

[31] Stroud 1977: 257–58.

the impotence of phenomenological investigations. When challenged to articulate the difference between two fundamentally different psychological states that figure centrally in our experience, phenomenology seems to be left with nothing to say. Perhaps there is simply nothing to tell. I shall not attempt at this stage to rebut this diagnosis, although ultimately we shall see that it is indeed too despairing. For now it will be enough to forestall phenomenological surrender by considering a third diagnosis of Hume's failure – one that is rooted, as it happens, much more closely in the details of Hume's own experimental report.

5 Hume's logical constraints

When we look to Hume's text, we find that his experimental observations do indeed betray the influence of theory. Significantly, however, the influence comes as much from Hume's logic as from his psychology. This is the first of several surprises. Hume is celebrated as a key figure in the history of many branches of philosophy – metaphysics, epistemology, ethics, and so on, but we do not usually count him in the history of logic, save of course for his skepticism about induction.[32] But Hume himself described Book I of the *Treatise* as presenting his logic,[33] and his concern with logical themes is nowhere more explicit than in this short section on belief. A long footnote to the section engages Hume's logical rivals, and Hume's arguments explicitly turn on considerations about inference and quantification. We find here a pattern that will concern us in much of what follows: the reliance on logical theory in shaping phenomenological and psychological research. The issues here are complex, and we shall return to many of them in later chapters. Here I confine my attention to two points.

The first is a point in *quantification theory*. Quantifiers are terms like *some, all, each and every*. Their proper treatment has been a major area of controversy in the history of logic, and indeed modern logic is often said to have begun with a new strategy for dealing with quantification. In his discussion here, Hume is particularly concerned with what has come to be called existential quantification – the logic of existence-claims. It seems odd at first that this logical point appears in the context of a psychological and phenomenological analysis of belief, but Hume finds

---

[32] There is, for instance, no bibliography entry for Hume in Kneale and Kneale's monumental study of *The Development of Logic*.

[33] "The sole end of logic is to explain the principles and operations of our reasoning faculty, and the nature of our ideas. ... The author has finished what regards logic." Hume 1739: 646.

a direct relevance. Believing an idea certainly seems to add *something* to my experience, and an obvious candidate for addition is the idea that the envisioned thing or state of affairs *exists*. Gazing out my office window I combine various perceptions and find myself entertaining the idea of a solar hang-glider – a hang-glider that rides the solar wind. Offhand I have no idea whether such a thing is possible, and in fact have very little sense of what the solar wind is anyway. But suppose that I subsequently come to believe that there is such a contraption. We might suppose that I have now effected a further combination – combining the complex idea of a solar hang-glider with the idea of existence. What rules this out, Hume argues, is the logic of the quantifier: "[I]n that proposition, *God is*, or indeed in any other, which regards existence, the idea of existence is no distinct idea, which we unite with that of the object, and which is capable of forming a compound idea by that union."[34]

Hume defends this position with several arguments. He claims, first, that we simply have no bare idea of existence and so cannot possibly add it to any other idea. And he claims, as Kant later would, that our idea of anything – whether of God or a solar hang-glider or a hundred thalers – is not in any way enriched in advancing the relevant existential claim.[35] He concludes that "exists" cannot express a distinct idea that is combined with or predicated of another idea. We can recognize here a logical position that would be reiterated famously by Kant in his refutation of the Ontological Argument, but which would take another 150 years to work its way into logical doctrine, and another 200 years before it would become the universally-received view about quantification: logically speaking, quantifiers are not predicates, but operators over contents.

In the long footnote, Hume goes on to use this logical analysis to argue against the traditional logical theory of judgment as synthesis – a topic to which we shall return in detail in the next chapter. But in the text itself Hume seeks to establish a broader result. He claims that in moving from an idea of something to the belief that it exists, *the content of the idea remains unchanged*:

> But I go farther; and not content with asserting, that the conception of the existence of any object is no addition to the simple conception of it, I likewise maintain, that the belief of the existence adds no new ideas to

[34] Hume 1739: 96n.
[35] Hume 1739: 94: " 'Tis ... evident that the idea of existence is nothing different from the idea of any object."

> those, which compose the idea of the object. When I think of God, when
> I think of him as existent, and when I believe him to be existent, my idea
> of him neither encreases nor diminishes.[36]

This is another surprising result. One would have thought that the same
process whereby I come to believe in the existence of a solar hang-glider
(reading about it in the newspaper, for instance) would also add considerably to the content of my idea. But Hume insists that the difference
between mere conception and belief must be independent of any such
enrichment.

Hume's defense of this claim comes from an unexpected quarter: his
analysis of the form of disagreement, dispute, and adjudication. The
initial point here concerns the structure of bare difference of opinion:

> Suppose a person present with me who advances propositions, to which
> I do not assent, that Caesar dy'd in his bed, that silver is more fusible than
> lead, or mercury heavier than gold; 'tis evident that not withstanding my
> incredulity, I clearly understanding his meaning, and form all *the same*
> *ideas which he forms.*[37]

In its bare logical form, we have disagreement only when there is some
content, some set of ideas, that someone asserts and another denies.
Where this condition is absent, we may think we disagree; we may even
go on at some length quarreling – talking at cross purposes, as we say. But
logically speaking the disagreement is apparent rather than real. *Genuine*
disagreement requires a common disputed content. This requirement of a common content is often formalized in venues of public adjudication: the
criminal trial begins with a reading of the indictment, a debate begins
with a resolution. Notice that a participant in such practices must be
capable of first entertaining and subsequently forming a judgment concerning the same set of ideas. In the course of the trial or debate many
further ideas are associated with the indictment or resolution. But at the
end of the day the juror must form a judgment about *the very ideas* that
were first expressed in the original indictment. It is only when those same
ideas occur in a verdict that the adjudication finally comes to an end:

> 'Tis confest, that in all cases, wherein we dissent from any person; we
> conceive both sides of the question; but ... we believe only one. [Until
> we form our belief,] we may mingle, and unite, and separate, and

---

[36] Hume 1739: 94.
[37] Hume 1739: 95, emphasis added.

confound, and vary our ideas in a hundred different ways [but] we have in reality no opinion.[38]

The logical structure of disagreement and dispute thus exhibits what I shall call *Hume's content identity condition*. Whatever the difference between believing, disbelieving, and merely conceiving an idea, it must be such as to allow the content in question to remain the same.

This requirement of sameness of content is rooted in the logical function of judgment. It is a requirement that we find in some form wherever we engage in logical practices: practices such as proof, refutation, inference, etc., as well as collective adjudication or reasoned dissent. A logical practice puts inferential principles to work, and in doing so it requires identity of content through variation of logical status. Examples: Euclid's proofs begin with a statement of a thesis, followed by a proof which establishes *the same thesis* as a theorem. To follow out a reductio proof I first suppose and subsequently reject *one and the same* thesis. Most broadly, formal validity requires univocality: a symbol must retain its sense throughout the course of a proof. If our beliefs and judgments are to play a role in these logical practices and be party to logical relations, then they must be capable of retaining their content while their logical status varies.

From this conclusion, Hume establishes a result that substantially shapes his subsequent experiment. The difference he seeks to discover experimentally cannot consist in the addition or subtraction of an idea; it must consist rather in a variation of what Hume calls "its manner of conception": "But as 'tis certain there is a *great difference* betwixt the simple conception of the existence of an object, and the belief of it, and as this difference lies not in the parts or composition of the idea, which we conceive; it follows, that it *must lie in the manner, in which we conceive it*".[39]

This by itself may seem a rather modest or even trivial result. Significantly it is when Hume tries to *specify* that manner of conception that his account gains substance and also goes substantially wrong. But the result here is not trivial, insofar as it is rooted in the content identity condition. In concluding that belief is a distinctive manner of conception, Hume is insisting that the content of a belief must retain its identity when credulity varies. This is a substantive constraint, and one that leaves Hume with limited options within the framework of his psychological theory. As we have seen, Hume's psychology dictates

[38] Hume 1739: 96.
[39] Hume 1739: 94–95, emphasis added.

that the content of experience at a particular moment simply is the specific set of "perceptions" (impressions and ideas) occurring at that moment. The only variation which can leave that content unchanged is a change in force and vivacity with which those contents occur:

> When you wou'd any way vary the idea of a particular object, you can only encrease or diminish its force and vivacity. If you make any other change on it, it represents a different object or impression. ... So that as belief does nothing but vary the manner, in which we conceive any object, it can only bestow on our ideas an additional force and vivacity.[40]

Hume's own experimental record thus suggests a third diagnosis of his failure. His experimental results are driven not simply by an overly narrow psychological theory, but by his attempt to satisfy an entangled set of logical, psychological, and phenomenological constraints – the three faces of judgment. His logic dictates that an idea must retain its identity through change of credulity status. His psychology dictates that the content of a psychological state simply is the particular set of perceptions occurring at a particular time. For Hume, phenomenology comes last, and must answer to these prior constraints. But Hume can find no way to satisfy the constraints without falsifying the phenomenological facts.

6 Libet and Shadlen on the faces of judgment

Let me return to the two modern experimental approaches described at the outset of this chapter. In particular, we can now consider how these experimental protocols navigate the trio of commitments in which Hume's experiments became entangled. How are the logical and pheno-menological faces of judgment managed in the design of these neuro-psychological experiments?

We have already seen that Libet explicitly seeks to integrate the psychological and phenomenological faces of judgment by situating the conscious experience of a decision or intention on the timeline of an unfolding neuromuscular episode. In considering how Libet effects this integration, it is particularly instructive to consider how he manages two concrete experimental obstacles. A first problem arises in accounting for the time-lag involved in phenomenological reporting. As we have seen, Libet's research methodology relies on the subject's ability to report the time of onset of the conscious intention or decision to act.

---

[40] Hume 1739: 96.

But such reporting itself takes time. Since the time increments under the protocol are so small, even a slight phenomenological reporting delay could significantly skew the resulting timeline. A delay of even half a second would mean that the conscious intention itself came *before* the Readiness Potential, even though the *report* of the intention comes afterwards. Libet recognizes this problem and so builds into his experimental protocol a procedure designed to yield a value for this reporting delay. With the subject's hand shielded by a screen, a slight, near-threshold skin stimulus is applied – essentially a light pinprick. The subject uses the oscilloscope timer to report the conscious awareness of the sensation. Using this standard, Libet finds a 50 ms phenomenological reporting delay.[41] Using this reporting margin to correct the values of the subject's report of a conscious intention to act, he concludes that the conscious intention occurs approximately 50 ms before the subject's report, but still about 300 ms after the onset of the Readiness Potential.

Libet's second experimental problem is noise – those background signals that every experimenter must manage in order to isolate the values to be determined. In Libet's experiment there are two main sources of noise in the data. Background electro-physiological noise from ongoing neural activity makes it difficult to discriminate the onset of Readiness Potentials from other electrical events in the brain. But there is also noise in the phenomenological data: the many ongoing conscious events – some associated in some way with the action, others entirely unrelated – which make it difficult to specify the exact time of onset of the conscious intention or decision to act. Part of Libet's management of noise involves simply keeping the subject calm, stationary, and undistracted, thereby minimizing extraneous signals in both the neural and phenomenological data stream. Remaining neural noise is managed by attuning cerebral monitors to neural areas known to be involved in generating the relevant motor signals, and by employing techniques of mathematical smoothing. But how does one cope with phenomenological noise? In particular, how is the subject to pinpoint the experienced intention in the context of all the other conscious experience associated with voluntary action? Here instructions to subjects become crucial:

> The subject is ... instructed to allow each ... act to arise "spontaneously," without deliberately preplanning or paying attention to the

---

[41] This is the significance of S in Figure 3.

"prospect" of acting in advance. The subjects did indeed report that the inclination for each act appeared spontaneously ("out of nowhere"), that they were consciously aware of their urge or decision to act before each act, that they felt in conscious control of whether or not to act, and that they felt no external or psychological pressure that affected the time when they decided to act. Thus, in spite of the experimental requirements, the basic conditions set out above for a voluntary act were met. .... [O]ne could study the cerebral processes involved in such an act without confusing them with deliberative or preparatory features that do not necessarily result in action.[42]

In effect, Libet's strategy is to contrive a setting for action in which the intention to act is maximally isolated from any process of reasoning, deliberation, anticipation, or preplanning, and then to urge subjects to refrain from any such extraneous conscious activities.[43]

These details of Libet's experimental technique are significant. The strategy for correcting reporting-error brings out an important tendency of the experiment as a whole: the assimilation of intentions to something like discrete sensations in a conscious stream. For subjects in Libet's set-up, reporting on a conscious intention is directly akin to reporting on the sensation of a light pinprick. Notice how this quite directly reproduces Hume's assumptions about consciousness as a stream of discrete "perceptions." If I am one of Libet's subjects I can only successfully carry out my assigned task if I can discover my "intention, decision or urge to act" as a passing item to be fished out from the stream of consciousness. This in turn points to a deeper presupposition of Libet's protocol: the assumption that the experienced temporality of conscious awareness can be projected without distortion onto the temporal schemata dictated by clock faces and timelines. This may or may not be a fair assumption,[44] but it is crucial to see that Libet's instructions to his research subjects impose the requirement without questioning it.

For our purposes, however, the most important point to notice here is that both these experimental details tend to efface the logical dimension of intention and judgment. We have already seen from Hume's case how

---

[42] Libet 1985: 530.

[43] In debriefing sessions research subjects did sometimes "confess" to having engaged in preplanning (Libet 1985: 532). Libet proposes that the difference between cases of preplanning and cases of "fully spontaneous" action correlates to the difference between RP I (preplanning involved) and RP II (no preplanning). See Libet, Freeman, and Sunderland 1999: 51.

[44] The canonical challenge to it is, of course, Division Two of *Being and Time* (Heidegger 1927a). For a more accessible treatment of the same themes see Heidegger 1927b: § 19.

difficult it is to satisfy the logical constraints on judgment within the framework of the empiricist stream of consciousness. The empiricist stream simply lacks the logical structure needed to satisfy even such a basic logical requirement as the content identity condition. But Libet makes matters considerably worse with the systematic isolation of decision and intention from the deliberative processes and logical practices in which they find their logical significance. A Libetian intention is to be thoroughly isolated from any such logical context. The instruction to "act spontaneously" here in effect requires (impossibly) that one act without any reason at all. In short: Libet's strategy for integrating the psychology and phenomenology of judgment requires him to drain judgment of its logical significance.

Such a strategy may indeed have its experimental rationale, but it is ultimately self-defeating and unsurprisingly generates pressure to falsify the phenomenological facts. The most dramatic example of this pressure comes with Libet's now-notorious appeal to the so-called "trigger-or-veto hypothesis." Anxious to preserve some role for consciousness in voluntary action, Libet hypothesizes that conscious intention comes into play not in initiating action, but in either triggering or vetoing a plan of action that has already been put in motion by the brain. On this view, we are in fact deceived if we think consciousness *initiates* action, but it nonetheless plays a role in those final 300 ms preceding action – a final conscious valve (near the pineal gland, perhaps?) which allows cerebral initiatives to be put into action. This is a desperate and ultimately misguided metaphysical move,[45] but what matters to us is that it is another striking example of theory-driven phenomenology. The trigger or veto hypothesis is, after all (and among other things) a phenomenological hypothesis: a hypothesis about a structural feature of subjective experience in intentional action. But it is not suggested by or faithful to anything in our experience of consciousness in action.

We find a very different interplay of the faces of judgment in Shadlen's experiments, which exhibit quite a different model for meeting the demands of the logical, psychological, and phenomenological masters. Since Shadlen's conclusion is physiological, and since his research subjects are monkeys, one might well suppose that he manages to steer clear of any entanglement with the logical or phenomenological dimensions of judgment. But this is not at all the case. When we look to Shadlen's

---

[45] For a point-by-point compatiblist reply see Freeman 1999.

evidence for his anatomical conclusion, we find that it draws quite directly on the phenomenological and logical setting of the decisions he investigates. Significantly, Shadlen's argument begins from *a logical description of a phenomenological field*. The monkey's field of perception is a bounded dynamic field characterized by a high level of visual noise, a task, and an emerging pattern. The monkeys sort out a significant trend in this perceptual environment. Shadlen's strategy is to analyze this field of experience for its logico-mathematical structure. What, in particular, are the logical and mathematical resources suited to recognizing the requisite significance in the perceptual field with which the monkey is presented? The logical task here is in effect to accumulate conditional probabilities, up to a threshold issuing in a binary outcome. This is, of course, just the sort of calculation for which neural computers are suited. Shadlen argues that the accumulating probabilistic evidence can be effectively managed by a mathematical function which calculates the logarithmic value of a conditional probability – the log of the likelihood ratio. The anatomical task is then to find the neural array that effectively implements that function, given the probabilistic values of the perceptual field. The details of this analysis are rich and subtle, but the point I want to emphasize here is this: Shadlen's analysis takes its orientation from what we can aptly describe as *a phenomeno-logical analysis of a judgment or decision*.[46] His investigation *begins* with a description of a phenomenological field, identifies the logico-mathematical structure of that field, and then looks for the neurophysiological mechanism that effectively works the inference. In this case the psychology does not drive the phenomenological analysis; it is much rather warranted by it.

For the experimentalist, the faces of judgment provide a challenge for experimental design. In this chapter we have seen three models for approaching that challenge. Hume uses logical and psychological considerations to constrain his phenomenological options, and finds himself forced to falsify the phenomenological facts. Libet integrates psychological and phenomenological results only by systematically suppressing the logical dimension of judgment and imposing the structure of clock time on his subjects' phenomenological reporting. In Shadlen's case the starting point for a psychological investigation of decision is the logico-mathematical structure of a field of experience. The perceptual

---

[46] I borrow the term "phenomeno-logical" from Castañeda 1969.

"decisions" carried out by Shadlen's Macaques are of course a far cry from the judgments which prominently consume human attention. Our judgments commonly have a much richer setting – both logically and phenomenologically. In the remainder of this study I take a lead from Shadlen's example, not in looking for the physiological implementation of judgment, but in investigating its underlying phenomeno-logical structure.

2

JUDGMENT AS SYNTHESIS, JUDGMENT AS THESIS: EXISTENTIAL JUDGMENT IN KANTIAN LOGICS

He [Kant] was not so disinclined as he ought to have been toward common logic, and did not destroy it from the ground up as his philosophy truly required, and as we here undertake to do in his name.

Fichte 1812: 111–12

Not only does the combination of representations not suffice to bring about a judgment, it is often not even necessary. This can be seen from the so-called existential propositions: *es regnet, es donnert, es gibt ein Gott* (it is raining, it is thundering, there is a God).

Brentano 1870–77: 99

I turn now from the history of psychology to the history of logic, a theme that will occupy us through most of the remainder of this study. The history of formal logic may well be as abstruse a topic as one can hope to find; nonetheless, it proves to be a rich source in the history of the judgment problem. In this chapter and the two that follow I take up themes and disputes from the long history of attempts to provide a systematic logical representation of judgment; I focus on cases where logical doctrines have shaped and influenced phenomenological investigation. In this chapter my strategy is to track a logical dispute that

I am grateful to Bill Blattner, Bill Bristow, Dave Cerbone, Ryan Hickerson, Pierre Keller, Hans Sluga, and Eric Watkins for comments on earlier versions of this chapter.

spanned nearly a century in the supposedly quiet history of logic before
Frege and Russell. The disputed question can be very simply stated: how
should logic analyze or construct singular existential judgments? What,
in short, is the logical form of "Pierre exists" or "There is a table in our
seminar room"? I examine the struggle over this question as it stemmed
from Kant, and spanned a century of Kantian logic in the nineteenth
century. I use that history to argue that there is a fundamental instability
in Kant's philosophical position, predicated as it is upon the model of
judgment (and indeed thinking and intelligence generally) as a form of
combination or synthesis. I show how Kant's own treatment of singular
existential judgment as positing (*setzen*, θέσις) led to the overthrow of the
model of judgment upon which he had relied.

The work of the chapter is divided into two main parts. The first three
sections review Kant's logical treatment of judgment, mainly as it figures
in his account of inference (general logic), but touching also on elements
of his theory of judgment in experience (transcendental logic). I formu-
late the problem of singular existential judgment and consider the
resources for handling it within the formal framework of Kantian
logic. The second part of the chapter turns to the ensuing debate, as
logicians working in the Kantian tradition tried to accommodate the
non-synthetic forms of judgment Kant had himself identified. Once
again the clearest result here is negative. As Brentano would starkly
put it: Combination forms no part of the essence of judgment.
Brentano's attempt to provide an alternative leads to innovative logical
results but also to a phenomenological impasse.

1   Kant's loan from logic

The Critique of Pure Reason is a book with few figures amid its 800 pages of
text. There are two lists organizing Principles and Analogies, and a graphic
arrangement of Antinomies; but the only prominent figures are two isomorphic tables presenting the forms of judgment and the pure a priori
categories of experience. If books are buildings then these can be the flags
atop Kant's citadel. The first table is a result in the general logical theory of
judgment – a product of the logician's characteristic focus on the *form* of
reasoning, in abstraction from any concern with its subject matter or
content. It specifies the possible forms of judgment and provides a tool
which can be used both to construct judgments and to exhibit their
differential contributions to inference. The second table is a result in
what Kant calls transcendental philosophy – the attempt to investigate

and articulate the a priori conditions and necessary limits of knowledge (*Erkenntnis*) and experience (*Erfahrung*). Kant uses these results in assembling the bases for the celebrated doctrine of the transcendental deduction: the claim that any experience or knowledge of an object must rely on the categories of substance and accident, cause and effect, plurality and totality, possibility and necessity, etc. The two figures provide emblems for a strategy that pervades the *Critique*. Kant himself famously describes his loan from logic as the *Leitfaden* – the clue or guiding thread – of his argument, and it is visible again and again in the *Critique*. Other examples: the ideas of reason are derived from the forms of syllogism (categorical, hypothetical, disjunctive); the very idea of a dialectic is taken from the logical enterprise of exposing the illusions of logical fallacies. Among Kant's many loans from logic, however, one is fundamental: the conception of judgment as a kind of combination or synthesis.

The understanding of judgment as synthesis is ancient, dating at least to Aristotle, who characterizes judgment as "a putting together and a taking apart" – *synthesis and diairesis*. And it follows a natural lead from language: as I combine words to form an utterance, so I combine concepts to form a judgment. Moreover, the synthetic construal of judgment provides a research strategy for investigating the phenomenological character of judgment, a research strategy that Kant systematically exploits. Rather than looking for some distinctive qualitative "feel" of judgment, the phenomenologist looks rather for the characteristic ways in which we *combine* our representations in forming a judgment.

Kant's own commitment to the synthetic construal of judgment is most explicit in the various versions of the lectures on logic, each of which formulates a definition of judgment in terms of combination or synthesis. Kant's formulation in the Vienna Logic is representative:

> A judgment is *generaliter* the representation of the unity in a relation of many cognitions. A judgment is the representation of the way that concepts belong to one consciousness universally, objectively. If one thinks two representations as they are combined together and together constitute one cognition, this is a judgment.[1]

At the core of this definition is the idea of judgment as a distinctive form of combination. In judgment, two (or more)[2] representations are "combined

---

[1] Ak. 24: 928. Young 1992: 369.

[2] In Kant's logic, categorical judgments (which according to Kant constitute "the basis of all the remaining judgments") require at least two concepts, a subject and a predicate. Hypothetical and disjunctive judgments require either trios of concepts or higher-order

together [*zusammen verbunden*] and together constitute one cognition." What is characteristic of this combination is its distinctive form: a judgment forges a subjective unity which in turn represents an objective unity – a "unity in one consciousness" which is nonetheless "universal, objective." Judgment, on this characterization, exhibits a kind of bipolar unity. Subjectively, a judgment is the combination of representations – e.g., the concepts "human" and "mortal." This subjective unity represents an objective unity: the belonging together, objectively and universally, of human beings and liability to death. The objective unity is in turn the truth-maker for the subjective unity which represents it. And it is in virtue of the whole structure that judgments are truth-evaluable at all.

An important but also potentially confusing example of Kant's synthetic construal of judgment can be seen in his treatment of the analytic–synthetic distinction. The potential confusion stems from one of the annoying ambiguities in Kant's terminology. In one sense, Kant uses "*Synthesis*" to mean combination (*Verbindung*) in general.[3] To say, in this sense, that a judgment is synthetic simply means that it is formed by synthesis, by the combination of concepts so as to represent an objective unity. But Kant also very prominently uses "synthetic judgment" as the opposite of "analytic judgment." In this case a synthetic judgment is simply one that is not an analytic tautology: its predicate concept is not already contained in its subject concept:

> In all judgments in which the relation of a subject to the predicate is thought, this relation is possible in two different ways. Either the predicate B belongs to the predicate A as something which is (covertly) contained in the concept A; or B lies outside the concept A, although it does indeed stand in connection with it. In the one case I entitle the judgment analytic, in the other synthetic.[4]

Kant's definition here has been much discussed and contested, particularly since Quine's famous attack. But for our purposes the key thing to note is the explicit restriction of the scope of these logical categories. The analytic–synthetic distinction is defined only for judgments which

---

combinations of categorical judgments. Since all judgments, according to Kant, are either categorical, hypothetical, or disjunctive, it follows that all well-formed judgments of Kantian logic require at least two concepts comprising their matter. These construction rules are explicit in the Vienna Logic (Ak. 24: 933–34), the Dohna-Wundlacken Logic (Ak. 24: 763–65), and are implied by the definitions in § 21ff in the Jäsche Logic. Young 1992: 372–73, 497–98, 601.

[3] The passage at A77–78/B103 (quoted below) is a famous example.

[4] A6/B10

involve the combination of concepts. Hence both analytic and synthetic judgments must be synthetic in the broader sense, comprising a synthesis of subject and predicate.

In what follows I shall mainly be concerned with the deployment of the synthetic construal of judgment in Kant's general logic, that is in his account of the basic forms and rules of inference. But it is worth taking note of the fundamental place the synthetic construal of judgment occupies within Kant's broader argument. In the *Critique*, Kant's commitment to the synthetic construal of judgment is explicitly introduced at the outset of the transcendental logic, and informs the strategy and results of the rest of the work. In justifying his reliance on logic, Kant relies on a claim of isomorphic identity. In particular, he claims that the same function which produces judgments out of concepts also produces objective experience out of a sensory manifold: "The *same function* which gives unity to the various representations in a judgment also gives unity to the mere synthesis of various representations in an intuition; and this unity, in its most general expression, we entitle the pure concept of the understanding."[5] Within the architecture of the *Critique*, this claim occupies the position between Kant's two flags, between logic and transcendental philosophy.

The "same function" is, of course, a form of synthesis, which becomes the main focus and basic notion in Kant's account of experience and knowledge. In a memorable passage which sets the agenda for the whole of the transcendental logic, Kant writes: "Synthesis of a manifold is what first gives rise to knowledge. . . . [S]ynthesis is that which gathers together the elements of knowledge, and unites them to form a certain content. It is to synthesis, therefore, that we must first direct our attention, if we would determine the first origin of our knowledge."[6]

But, of course, not just any synthesis will do. The most general capacity for synthesis of representational content is, according to Kant, the imagination. But imaginative combination alone does not make a claim to truth or present us with an object. It is, in Kant's phrase, "a blind but indispensable faculty." In order to produce knowledge or experience, synthesis must introduce what Kant (notoriously and somewhat misleadingly) dubs *a transcendental content*: "The same understanding [which] produced the logical form of a judgment, also introduces a transcendental content into its representations."

[5] A79/B104–5, emphasis added.
[6] A77/B103.

The term is confusing because, on Kant's view, this "transcendental content" is not so much an additional *content* of representation as it is a characteristic *form*. Our experience presents us with a world in virtue of its being *combined* so as to make a claim to truth; accordingly, representational content must be so combined as to forge a unity – a unity in a single consciousness that itself represents an objective unity to which it answers. Since this is precisely the form of unity forged in the judgmental synthesis of concepts, Kant claims title to bring the synthetic construal of judgment across the divide from general to transcendental logic.[7]

The same function thesis is pivotal in Kant's overall argument in the *Critique* and it exhibits the deep and fundamental reliance of Kant's transcendental philosophy on the logical theory of judgment as synthesis. But what concerns us here is what lies within the confines of Kant's general logic of judgment – setting aside its purported transcendental application in a study of the structures of experience. On the side of general logic the basic elements of Kant's approach can be stated quite simply. As in all of Kant's logic, the analysis is hylomorphic: a judgment is analyzed as a distinctive combination of form and matter. The matter of a basic judgment is a pair of concepts; higher-order judgments take simpler judgments as their matter. But the logician's concern is with a judgment's form – the mode in which these pairs are combined. All judgments have the synthetic form of judgment defined above; more fine-grained specifications of form are then provided by using Kant's table, choosing one form from each of the four triads of Quantity, Quality, Relation, and Modality.

2 An exercise in Kantian logic

With this background in place we can now tackle an exercise in Kantian logic. What is the logical form of singular existential judgment? Figure 5 provides a worksheet for those who want to play along.

Some of the answers are easy. In quality "Pierre exists" is clearly affirmative. In modality it is surely assertoric. Modern readers may pause a moment at the old logical term "categorical." But since the alternatives are hypothetical and disjunctive, it seems clear that this must be the right form of relation. (Let me assert, affirmatively and categorically: *Pierre exists*.)

---

[7] For a nuanced study of Kant's strategy see Longuenesse 1993, which also provides a detailed study of the definitions of judgment in Kant's *Nachlaß*. Longuenesse builds on a tradition of attention to Kant's general logic, notably Reich 1932 and Brandt 1989.

Pierre exists.

1. Analytic or synthetic?[a]

2. Form: (choose one from each trio):

I

Quantity

Universal

Particular

Singular

II	III
Quality	*Relation*
Affirmative	Categorical
Negative	Hypothetical
Infinite	Disjunctive

IV

Modality

Problematic

Assertoric

Apodeictic

Figure 5: Kant's Table of Judgment Forms
Source: Kant A70/B95

[a] I here wish to thank the referee who beat my quiz by pointing out that the analytic–synthetic distinction is not, for Kant, a distinction of general logic, since its application turns on the specific matter of a judgment rather than its form.

With the category of quantity we encounter the first complication. The answer here might seem to be straightforward: "Pierre exists" would certainly seem to be singular in quantity – concerning, as it does, a unique individual. But strictly speaking there are only two forms of quantity in Kant's general logic of judgment, although three appear on his table of forms. For the logician's purposes, Kant claims, judgments are either universal or particular. In a universal judgment I say of all Ss that they are P; in a particular judgment I say that some are. Although the table lists "singular" as a third form, singular judgments are, for logical purposes, treated equivalently to universal judgments. In short, "Socrates is wise" is treated as "All Socrates are wise." On this basis we ought strictly to say that "Pierre exists" is, on Kant's account, universal in quantity.

On the question of analyticity, Kant's answer is about as clear as Kant gets. Certainly it is hard to see how Pierre's existence could be reported in an analytic tautology. Invoking the authority of "all reasonable men,"

Kant insists that no judgment of existence is analytic.[8] Since nothing, as it were, exists by definition, a singular existential claim must be synthetic.

But now we meet the first hint of trouble. On the solution just given, "Pierre exists" and "Pierre is wise" have the same logical form. "Pierre is wise" is certainly affirmative, assertoric, categorical. And its quantity – however we decide to resolve that issue – would presumably be the same as that of "Pierre exists." "Pierre is wise" is also – with all due deference to Pierre – synthetic. So *Pierre is wise* and *Pierre exists* do not vary in logical form. This result will seem odd to anyone raised in the logic of the twentieth century, where existential judgments make fundamentally different contributions to inference than do predications. But it should also seem odd for Kant, since it seems to contradict his own celebrated thesis that "exists" is not a real predicate. In what follows I explore this oddity and its consequences.

3   Four Kantian approaches to singular existential judgment

In this section I consider four ways of responding to this difficulty, each drawing from Kant's own discussions. The first three can be found in Kant's discussion of the ontological argument in the *Critique*;[9] the fourth comes from the essay "On the Only Possible Proof for the Existence of God" (in particular the "First Reflection" in that essay).[10] Let me begin by listing them; I'll then add a few remarks about each.

A. "Existence is not a real but a logical predicate."
B. "Logically, existence is the copula."
C. "Being is obviously not a real predicate ...; it is the positing of a thing."
D. "Something existent is God."

A   Existence is not a real but a logical predicate

In the context of his discussion of the ontological proof for the existence of God, Kant famously takes up the question of the logical form of "God exists." He claims that in this and all existential judgment, "existence" or "being" (the *ist* in *Gott ist*) is not to be treated as a real predicate. A real

---

[8] A598/B626.
[9] A592–603/B620–631.
[10] Ak. 2: 70–77.

predicate, in Kant's terms, is a predicate capable of adding to or "amplifying" a subject concept. If I say that my hundred thaler coin is copper then I add content to my representation of the coin. If I say that it is money then I unpack content already contained within my subject concept. In the first case my judgment is synthetic; in the second it is analytic. But Kant argues that "exists" does not function in either of these ways. I neither add to nor unpack my concept of God in saying that God exists.

Notice that so far this is strictly a negative claim, and hence not a solution to our exercise. Let us concede: "God exists" does not use existence as a real predicate. So what is its logical form? Here there is a modern answer that lies all-too-readily at hand: existence is not a real predicate; it is a quantifier. Since Frege and Russell, logicians have sharply distinguished predicates and quantifiers as types of logical terms. In the now-familiar calculi, predicates together with names constitute atomic propositions, while quantifiers figure only in complex contexts which take such atomic sentences as bound contents. This model is now so fundamental to our logical analysis that we readily see it as the natural positive correlate to Kant's negative thesis. "Exists" is not a real predicate, so the thought goes; it is a quantifier governing a complex content.

It is crucial to recognize that this is *not* Kant's proposal here. Notice his formulation: *"Exists" is not a real predicate; it is a logical predicate.* Kant's proposal is that "exists" *really is a predicate*; it is just not a real one. But what does this mean? What exactly is a logical predicate? For Kant, the claim that "exists" is a logical predicate is closely connected to his oft-repeated principle that the logician abstracts entirely from the content of reasoning and concerns himself only with its form. The content of a categorical judgment is a pair of concepts (a subject and a predicate), but for the logician they can be any concepts. In this sense, any concept can be a predicate, including existence. To be a logical predicate, then, is to be a predicate *for the purposes of logic* – in particular for the logician's project of exhibiting the differential contributions of judgments in inference. And for these purposes, existence can indeed serve as a predicate. Consider these examples:

> Pierre exists.
> Therefore nothing non-existent is Pierre.
>
> Pierre exists.
> All existent things have a beginning.
> Therefore Pierre has a beginning.

The first is an immediate inference by the rule of contraposition; the second a mediate inference – a syllogism of the first figure. Both are valid in virtue of their form; and the logician takes no interest in their matter. "Pierre exists" effectively becomes "Pierre is an existent thing" – or better (in light of the point about the forms of quantity): "All Pierres are existents." And "existent" then functions perfectly properly as a predicate. It had better. The inference rules in Kant's logic all require premises with subjects and predicates. So unless he can treat existence as a predicate, the Kantian logician is left unable to model inferences with existential premises or conclusions.

Once we are clear about Kant's notion of a logical predicate – and about the difference between Kant's move and Frege's – we immediately find ourselves back with the result that troubled us earlier: if existence is a logical predicate then "Pierre exists" and "Pierre is wise" have the same logical form.

B "Logically, 'exists' is the copula"

A second strand in Kant's analysis of singular existential judgment suggests a different solution: that "exists" functions not as a predicate but as a copula. In the *Critique* this suggestion follows the negative claim and is explicitly identified as a matter of general logic. "Existence is obviously not a real predicate; .... Logically, it is merely the copula of a judgment."

This suggestion is certainly puzzling, and it is not clear just in what sense Kant advances it.[11] Nonetheless we can make sense of it given the treatment of the copula in Kant's logic. The copula is typically the third term in a subject-predicate judgment (the *is* in "Socrates is wise") and its treatment has been much contested in the history of logic. For Kant, the copula serves as a marker of logical form – both of the form of judgment in general, and (by its inflection) of a specific form for a particular judgment:

> In every judgment there occurs (1) the matter of the judgment, that is, subject and predicate. ... The 2nd thing in each judgment is its form. The copula *est* always expresses this. This copula is posited *simpliciter*, now, if it indicates the relation of two concepts in their connection[;] but

[11] Since there is very little elaboration of this point in the text, the force of the remark is somewhat unclear. It may be that Kant's point here is that "being" functions as a copula in categorical judgments, not that it functions as a copula in existential judgments.

if it expresses the relation in the opposition of these concepts, then it is accompanied with the word *non*.[12]

The crucial point here is that the copula expresses the form of a judgment. It is not, on Kant's treatment, part of the matter or content of a judgment – like some kind of glue that holds subject and predicate in one piece. It is rather a symbol of the form of unification: much as a wedding ring serves as a symbol of union in a marriage. Like a ring it need not always be worn, since the marriage of subject and predicate is not effected by the copula, only symbolized by it. Inflections of the copula (is, is not, may not be, etc.) serve as a rough indicator of form; a precise specification is given with Kant's table.

Here we can see what is puzzling about the suggestion. If a copula is a mark of synthesis then it ought to mark the combination of one concept with another. But if "exists" is a copula rather than a predicate-concept then there does not seem to be anything for the subject-concept to be combined with. There are no marriages of one party, and there is no obvious role for a mark of synthesis in a judgment of one concept. The most we can say is that "exists" serves as a marker of some distinctive judgmental form; we have not yet said what that form is.

C *"Being is obviously not a real predicate . . .; it is the positing of a thing"*

Kant seems to take the decisive step in characterizing the form of existential judgment when he describes it as "positing": "If now, we take the subject (God) with all its predicates (among which is omnipotence) and say 'God is,' or 'There is a God,' we *attach no new predicate* to the concept of God but *only posit* it as being an object that stands in relation to my concept."[13]

Some philological context is helpful here. "Posit" translates Kant's *setzen* – to put or to place. These are themselves the Latin and German equivalents of the Greek 'thesis' ($\theta\acute{\epsilon}\sigma\iota\varsigma$), whose primary meaning is also to place or set. "Thesis" is, of course, itself an etymon of syn-thesis: to put or place together. In thinking about its application here, it is useful to have in mind the mathematical sense of positing – as when I posit a number in the course of a proof ("Posit an integer greater than n . . . "). Kant's claim, then, is that in judging Pierre to be wise I combine my concepts, but in judging that he exists I posit him.

[12] *Blomberg Logic*: § 292; see also *Jäsche Logic*: § 24.
[13] A599/B627, emphasis added.

Kant's move here has the great advantage of recognizing a fundamentally different form of judgment in singular existential judgment – a thesis rather than a synthesis. We shall return below to consider the fate of this proposal, but for the purposes of our exercise it presents an immediate problem. If existential judgment is not a combination of concepts – if, as Kant here insists, an existential judgment "attaches no new concept" – then judgment is not in general what Kant's logic defines it to be: a subjective synthesis that represents an objective unity. For in the case of singular existential judgment, judgment is not synthesis at all.

D "Something existent is God"

So far, the solutions we have considered fall into one of two camps: either they fail to recognize any logical difference between existential judgment and predicative synthesis, or else they overflow the limits of Kant's general logic of judgment. But in at least one place Kant proposes a solution that remains faithful to the principles of his logic, while at the same time recognizing a difference of form. The proposal is made in the early essay on the only possible proof for the existence of God. Already there (in 1763, at a time when Kant still thought that there could be a theoretical proof for the existence of God) Kant claims that being is not a predicate. But his position in the 1763 essay is in effect that existence is a subject. "Strictly speaking, the matter ought to be formulated something like this: 'Something existent is God.'"[14]

Within the confines of the logic of synthesis this is a striking proposal. The idea is that in making an existential judgment I do not start out by representing Pierre, whom I then characterize as existent. On the contrary: I start out by representing all the existing things and then say that something in that motley collection is Pierre. In its logical form, "Pierre exists" is thus neither singular nor universal but particular: some *part* of the collection is Pierre. "Pierre exists" thus turns out to like "some barns are red": affirmative, assertoric, categorical, particular. Pierre may not find this very flattering, but at least here we have a difference to point to. At the same time, the analysis respects the principles of the logic of synthesis, effectively treating "existent" as a concept – a subject term to which "Pierre" is predicatively combined.

But this treatment of the form of existential judgment has important ramifications for its matter. For on this treatment, all existential

[14] Kant Ak. 2: 75.

judgments effectively have the same subject term – a Spinozist idea that would have a significant afterlife in Hegelian monism. Significantly, Kant drops this solution in the later discussions (to the best of my knowledge, anyway), although the idea resurfaces in the claim of transcendental logic that judgment is the synthesis of a representation with the unity of apperception.

These various suggestions for the treatment of singular existential judgment bring into view an important tension in Kant's thought, and a problem for his strategy of leaning on logic in developing a theory of the structure of experience. We can see the tension operating at several different levels. In its narrowest form it manifests itself in the divergence between these different strategies for handling singular existential judgment. Here the problem is not that Kant *lacks* a treatment of singular existential judgment but that he suffers from an overabundance of them. On the one hand, we have treatments that accommodate singular existential judgment to the synthetic construal of judgment and to the logic which presupposes it. Singular judgments are treated as universal; existence becomes a concept available for use as predicate (as in Solution A) or as a subject (as in Solution D). But these solutions would seem to be inconsistent with the treatment of singular judgment as a form of thesis or positing in which we "attach no new predicate" but rather posit an object in relation to my concept.

The significance of this tension becomes clearer when we see it in light of a deeper tension in Kant's notion of logical form – a tension that is nowhere more explicitly on view than in his explanatory notes concerning the table of judgment forms.[15] The first of these notes explains Kant's inclusion of the form of "singularity" on the table of judgment forms, despite the fact that, as we have seen, Kantian inferences treat singular judgments as universal in quantity. Kant justifies the inclusion by distinguishing two standards that can be employed in enumerating the forms of judgment. The logician concerns himself strictly with "the employment of judgment in syllogisms," in which case the form of singularity is omitted. But if one concerns oneself rather with what Kant here calls "the moments of thought in general" then singularity deserves its own place:

> If, therefore, we estimate a singular judgment (*iudicium singulare*) ... as knowledge in general, according to its quantity in comparison to other

[15] A71–76/B96–101. I am grateful to Jeff Yoshimi for his account of these notes.

knowledge, it is certainly different from general judgments (*iudica communia*), and in the complete table of the moments of thought in general deserves a separate place – though not, indeed, in a logic limited to the use of judgments under one another [*untereinander*].[16]

For the construction of inferences, a judgment about Pierre is effectively modeled as a judgment about all the Pierres, provided that Pierre's concept can be suitably specified so as to represent only one individual. For the analysis of judgments "under one another" – i.e., in a proof – such a treatment suffices. But such a treatment fails to capture what is distinctive about *singular* judgment as a discrete cognitive form – as a "moment of thought in general" or "in comparison to other cognition."

This bifurcation in the notion of logical form illuminates the divergence in Kant's treatments of *existential* judgment, and can be used to render them at least consistent. For the purposes of inference, existence can be treated as a concept (either subject or predicate) and existential judgment can be modeled in the logic of synthesis. But while this treatment suffices for syllogistic proof, it fails to capture the form of existential judgment as a distinctive mode of thought in its own right – as a form of positing or thesis rather than of synthesis or combination.

But if Kant's various proposals can in this way be rendered consistent, there are consequences for his broader strategy. As we have seen, Kant's central loan from logic is the synthetic construal of judgment, with the attendant model of human understanding as a computational combination of representations. As we have seen, Kant's model of judgments as the combination of concepts is directly appropriated in transcendental logic as the model of judgmental synthesis of sensory content under a concept. But if singular existential judgment is not combination, if judgment is not in general synthesis, then the loan needs to be renegotiated. In particular, if singular existential judgment has one form in logic but quite a different one in knowledge in general, then Kant is not entitled to claim that the same function is at work in both arenas.

4 The logical accommodation of thetic judgment

I turn now to gather the logical aftermath. The first three sections of this chapter provided an introduction to Kantian logic and tackled a problem that arises within Kant's logic of judgment. I suggested a Kantian

---

[16] A71/B96.

solution to that problem but also identified three manifestations of a tension in Kant's position. In what follows I trace the history of this problem in the nineteenth-century tradition that explicitly tackled it. Such a treatment will require that we become familiar with some unfamiliar characters, working logicians of mid-nineteenth-century German logic. We will see how they attempted to incorporate Kant's treatment of singular existential judgment within the framework established by Kant's own synthetic logic. This led to more and more extreme revisions of logic, reaching one culmination in Brentano's logic, which explicitly rejects the synthetic construal of judgment and proposes that all judgments should be treated as existential.[17]

The first decades of nineteenth-century German logic are now mainly remembered as a period of Hegelian dominance and radical logical proposals: dialectical logic, material logic, the purported rejection of the principle of non-contradiction. But alongside the Hegelian movement there persisted a logic that can best be described as *normal* by comparison. I use "normal" here in a sense borrowed from Thomas Kuhn.[18] In mid-nineteenth-century Germany there was, in Kuhn's sense, a "normal science" of logic, explicitly relying on a paradigm provided by Kant. Kant's logic provided a canonical accomplishment, a standard textbook for training practitioners, and a working apparatus for the logical analysis of judgments and inferences. At the same time, it generated problems of normal science requiring solutions, with standards of success and failure established by the logical practice itself. In Kant's own treatment of singular existential judgment it encountered an anomaly to be resolved.

So here is our question: how did the normal working logicians of the nineteenth century manage the apparent anomaly of singular existential judgment? How did a logic designed to handle judgments of the form "S is P" handle judgments whose grammatical form is "S is" or "there is a P"? There are many voices in the history of this logical unrest; in what follows I focus my attention on two logicians in particular: Moritz Wm. Drobisch and Franz Brentano – a heroic logical normal and a logical subversive.

Moritz Drobisch (1802–1896) was, in effect, Fichte's logical grandson, by way of Johann Friedrich Herbart (1776–1841) – the founder and

---

[17] I am indebted to Ryan Hickerson for helping me to appreciate the significance of Brentano's contributions to the logical theory of judgment.
[18] Kuhn 1962.

namesake of the "Herbartian School" of logic. It will be worthwhile to begin with a brief review of this lineage, which turns out to be of considerable significance to our topic.

Herbart had studied with Fichte at Jena, and although he very prominently broke with Fichtean idealism, he nonetheless took up Fichte's call for a "destruction of logic in Kant's name." For Fichte, the two most fundamental judgments are the judgments "I am" and "it is," the judgments expressing our self-consciousness and our consciousness of an object respectively. Fichte had argued that neither of these judgments expressed the combination or synthesis of representations; they are much rather to be treated as positings – the positing of I and not-I. Fichte's *Wissenschaftslehre* treated these two acts of positing as the basic constitutive functions of human subjectivity, and he famously wrote as if "*setzen*" were the only root verb in the German language. Fichte himself recognized that such an approach had important ramifications for logic, but these were never his own main concerns. He insisted on several occasions that an adequate logic would have to be based on the *Wissenschaftslehre* and not presupposed by it. But in his published works he never squarely faced this task, nor did he attempt to provide the promised (and deeply paradoxical) "deduction of logic." Among his students it was Herbart who made the most important first steps in this direction.

At the heart of Herbartian logic was the claim that categorical judgments lack existential import. To say that Cyclops are one-eyed, for instance, or that square circles are impossible, is certainly not to assert the existence of Cyclops or square circles.[19] An existence claim, Herbart proposes, must accordingly be recognized as an independent, non-categorical judgmental form. In these judgments, Herbart claims, there is only a predicate, introduced "without limit or condition": "Everything changes in the representation of these judgments, where there is no subject for the predicate. There arises in this way an *existential proposition*, which one misinterprets if one treats the concept of being as the original predicate."[20] Among traditional logicians, Herbart complains, these judgments have been neglected, even though they are well-represented in ordinary language and play a fundamental logical role. He goes on to introduce a set of examples which would receive considerable attention over the subsequent decades of German logic: *es friert, es regnet, es blitzt, es donnert* (it is freezing, it is raining, there

---

[19] Herbart 1813: §§ 53, 35–37.
[20] Herbart 1813: 111.

is lightning, it is thundering), and he introduces new terminology to cover these judgments. They are, he claims, "existential propositions" (*Existentialsätze*) or "thetic judgments" (*thetische Urtheile*). Their root form is not "S is P" but rather "it is P" or "there is P" (*Es ist P*), where "it" (*es*) functions not as a subject concept but only to mark the empty place of the subject position.

Among the logicians of the Herbartian school, it became standard to credit Herbart with having "discovered existential propositions."[21] In retrospect we can see that he was introducing logical terminology to acknowledge a form of judgment upon which Kant and Fichte had already insisted. But it is one thing to name a new judgment form; it is quite another to integrate it into logical theory and a working inferential system. In Herbart's logic, existential judgments were quite literally tacked on as a final section in the logic of judgment, following a faithful replication of Kant's synthetic treatment in accordance with the table of forms. The task of integrating this addition was taken up in detail by Herbart's student and disciple, Moritz Drobisch. The chief work here is Drobisch's *Neue Darstellung der Logik nach ihren einfachsten Verhältnissen*, which first appeared in 1836 and then in many subsequent editions over the course of half a century. The work falls squarely within the Kantian-Herbartian tradition, in its definitions and organization, in its many explicit references to Kant's logical apparatus, and in its frequent claims to be following Herbart's innovations.[22] It is historically significant in part for its attempt to apply logic in mathematics (a Mathematical Appendix constructs mathematical proofs using Drobisch's logical apparatus), but for us its significance lies in its attempt to provide a Kantian logic that can systematically incorporate the thetic judgments that Kant had identified and Herbart named. In the changes made to the successive editions of Drobisch's text one finds a record of a crisis underway in Kantian logic.

Drobisch's central logical innovation lies in his distinction between two distinct forms of judgment, which he dubs "*Beschaffenheitsurteile*" and "*Beziehungsurteile*." These are difficult terms to translate, but for reasons that will become clear I render them as "*attributive judgments*" and "*referential judgments*" respectively. The distinction is incipient in the first edition of Drobisch's *Logic* (1836) but emerges fully in the second edition (1851), which Drobisch himself describes as "a completely rewritten work, almost a new book." My discussion follows Drobisch's third edition

[21] See for instance Drobisch 1836: 49; see also Brentano 1874: 211.
[22] See Drobisch 1876 for Drobisch's retrospective reflections on Herbart's accomplishments.

(1863), by which time the distinction had quite thoroughly reshaped his logical treatment of judgment.

Drobisch's point of departure is the Herbartian analysis of categorical propositions, which he treats as non-existential and intrinsically hypothetical in form:

> The judgments, "God is just," or "the soul is not transitory," no more include the claims that a God exists, or that there are souls than "the Cyclops are one-eyed," "the Furies have snakes for hair," or "Ghosts appear at night" unconditionally posit the subjects: Cyclops, Furies, Ghosts. Rather, all these judgments say only that *if* one posits the subject then the predicate applies as a determination of its features [*Beschaffenheiten*]. ... This important point was first recognized by Herbart.[23]

For Drobisch, an attributive judgment (*Beschaffenheitsurteil*) expresses a relation among concepts, specifying either its genus or some among its species, or attributing some property to its instances. But an attributive judgment does not take a stand on whether or not those concepts are instantiated. Because attributive judgments express a relation, they require a minimum of two concepts to serve as the relata. Symbolically, they are represented as "S is P" or "SxP", where S and P are concepts and x is a form of relation. Such judgments cannot be used to express an existential claim, insofar as the existence of an S is always implicit as an undischarged antecedent in a conditional. "Cyclops are one-eyed" becomes "If there is a Cyclops then it is one-eyed." "The soul is not transitory" becomes "If there is a soul then it undergoes no change." Generally: "If S is, then S is P." Existence cannot be treated as a predicate in an attributive judgment, for to do so would yield a tautology: "If there is a Cyclops then it exists."

How then is a judgment of existence to be formulated? Drobisch provides his answer in his treatment of referential judgments (*Beziehungsurteile*):

> The simple answer is: through condition-less judgments, that is, those in which the conditioning subject term is ... absent altogether or in which there is only an empty place for one. ... [T]here results the form of judgment:
>
> There is P [*es ist P*],

---

[23] Drobisch 1863: 59–60.

where the small word "*es*" ["it" or "there"] indicates the empty subject position. We can call such judgments "thetic" or "absolute."[24]

For Drobisch, "S is P" and "There is P" become the root forms for two broad families of judgment. We use attributive judgments to express relations among our concepts; we use referential judgments when existence is expressed. In each case the root form can be inflected and modified to express a whole range of more complex judgments. Drobisch's treatment concludes with a memorable catalog of thetic forms:

> Examples: There is lightning; it is raining; there is fire; there are forebodings;[25] there is a God; there is no devil, there are no witches, and so on; there are religious, irreligious and agnostic men; there are neither fairies nor elves nor goblins; there is either providence or fate; it is true, that everything good is beautiful; it is not true that if virtue is not rewarded then all morality is an empty illusion.[26]

"These thetic judgments," Drobisch insists, "have an independent meaning, and should not be treated as categorical judgments."

Drobisch's distinction between attributive and referential judgments allows what Kant's own logic did not: the formal recognition of judgments involving only a single concept. Drobisch integrates such judgments into logic essentially following Kant's own approach. Thetic judgments vary in all the usual ways: in quantity, quality, modality, and relation. And they are subject to a range of principles of combination, both for producing complex thetic judgments from simple ones, and for combining thetic judgments in mediate and immediate inferences. In effect, Drobisch normalizes the anomalous phenomenon. He shows how the apparently anomalous case of singular existential judgment can be integrated into a Kantian formal representation of judgment and apparatus of inference. The generations of students who were taught logic from Drobisch's textbook learned a logical practice which recognized singular existential judgment as a distinct logical form of judgment governed by its own set of inference rules.

There is, however, an important sense in which Drobisch's accommodation of thetic judgment remained incomplete. For although his logical practice recognized and made use of existential judgments as judgments

---

[24] Drobisch 1863: 60.
[25] "*es gibt Ahnungen.*" This is a tricky phrase to translate. It seems to come from a proverb: "There are inklings and insights [*Es gibt Ahnungen und Einsichten*] that one cannot express, but only act upon."
[26] Drobisch 1863: 61.

of a single concept, his definitions and general characterizations of judgment tended systematically to leave such judgments out of account, or even to exclude them. This is because, despite his expansion of logical forms, Drobisch perpetuates the traditional definition of judgment in general as essentially involving the combination and division of conceptual representations; that is, he retains the synthetic construal of judgment. In his general introduction to the work, he defines judgments as the combination and separation of concepts (*Die Verknüpfung und Trennung der Begriffe*)[27] and at the opening of the division devoted to judgment, he requires of every judgment at minimum a subject, a predicate, and a copula:

> Every judgment consists therefore of three elements: 1) the subject, the concept concerning which the assertion is issued; 2) the predicate, which includes that which is asserted about the subject; 3) the copula, the form of the assertion, which is either affirming or denying, and either ascribes the predicate to the subject or refuses it [*das Prädikat dem Subjekt entweder beilegt oder abspricht*].[28]

The result is a curious imbalance in Drobisch's work. His logical practice recognizes and deploys a form of judgment which is excluded by his own definition of judgment and by his general requirements on a well-formed formula. The tension we found in the Kantian position has here been sharpened into a formal inconsistency in symbolic logic.

Drobisch himself recognized the problem, and the traces of his struggle with it can be found in the many additions (*Zusätze*) and changes made to the later editions. Some of the changes amount to a merely cosmetic qualification of the principles which generate the problems. For instance, all the editions include the requirement that a well-formed judgment include both a subject and a predicate, but between the second and third editions Drobisch drops the word "*immer*" (always) from the sentence: "*das Urteil wird nämlich immer aus drei Stücken bestehen.*"[29] In a *Zusatz* introduced in the second edition, he suggests that judgments of one term (for instance: "Cannonfire!" or "Fire Alarm!") can be treated as enthymatic (*enthymematisch*),[30] but he offers no suggestion about how the enthymeme is to be filled out in accordance with the form specified by his definition and formal requirements. In a note included from the third

[27] Drobisch 1863: 11.
[28] Drobisch 1863: 44–45, § 40.
[29] Comparing Drobisch 1851: § 39 to Drobisch 1863: § 40.
[30] Drobisch 1851: § 46z, 54.

edition on, he finally acknowledges the difficulty of providing a unified definition of judgment applying to the full range of forms he relies on: "It is not easy to provide a simpler explanation of judgment than the one given here. It always comes out dualistically, if it aims to be clear [*Es fällt immer dualistisch aus . . .*]."[31] In short: in Drobisch's logical system, judgment seems at root to be two different things. In some judgments I sort and combine my representations; in others I say that something beyond my representations exists. Drobisch himself ultimately despairs of uniting these two forms in a single non-disjunctive definition.

In one *Zusatz* Drobisch explicitly considers an alternative to the definition of judgment in terms of synthesis.[32] One might, he suggests (considering a suggestion from Herbart that is clearly traceable to Kant), define judgment as the cognition of an object under concepts (*Erkenntiss eines Gegenstandes durch Begriffe*) – a definition which says nothing of synthesis and which is readily applicable to judgments which involve only a single term. But Drobisch refuses this way out, and his reasons are instructive. Judgment is indeed necessary for cognition of an object, he holds, but its "original significance" (*ursprüngliche Bedeutung*) is determined "independently of real objects and within the domain of the merely represented." For Drobisch, judgment is narrowly an activity of the mind (*ein Denkform*), and accordingly its provenance is exclusively representations. Given this approach, judgment can involve various kinds of sorting and combination and calculation over representations, but in Drobisch's phase, "*es geht über die Vorgestellte nicht aus*" – it does not transcend the domain of what is represented.[33]

Drobisch sought to resolve an anomaly in Kantian logic, by showing how the paradigmatic logical characterization of judgment could accommodate singular existential judgment. But the strategy Drobisch used was insufficiently radical. The logical accommodation ultimately failed, because it attempted to graft a form of judgment onto a core theory that tends systematically to exclude it. If judgment is essentially the combination of representational content, if it is a form of thinking having conceptual representations as its domain of activity, then it cannot ultimately accommodate judgments that do not at root involve the combination of representations. It would fall to a more radical generation of logicians to make a more fundamental break.

---

[31] Drobisch 1863: § 40z, 45.
[32] Drobisch 1863: § 9z, 11.
[33] Drobisch 1863: 11.

5 Thetic logic

Franz Brentano is now best remembered as a founding figure of modern phenomenology, the one who vigorously introduced the problems of intentionality into the study of conscious experience, and appealed to "intentional inexistence" to analyze its structure. Solving the problems bequeathed by Brentano's work became one of the organizing strategies not only among his many influential students (Husserl, Meinong, Twardowski, Marty) but also among philosophers of mind a century later (Chisholm, Dennett, Quine, Dretske, Fodor, Searle, McGinn ...). We shall return below to consider the contribution of the phenomenological tradition to the problems of judgment, but our interest here is rather in Brentano's work as a logician. Brentano's logical doctrines have not been widely discussed, and the neglect is in retrospect explicable.[34] His most detailed logical writings were published only posthumously in 1956, and his influence and accomplishment in this area, though significant, were doubly eclipsed: first by his role in the emergence of a distinctively phenomenological school, and then by the broader logical revolution to which Brentano had contributed but which ultimately overswept him. (Brentano's main logical doctrines were first set out in 1874, and his calculus was elaborated in detail by 1877; Frege's *Begriffsschrift* was published in 1879.) Nonetheless, Brentano's logical accomplishments merit our attention. Why? Because in Brentano's logic the dispute over the logical representation of existential judgments turns subversive, directly challenging the longstanding characterization of judgment as synthesis. Brentano and his collaborators formulated the first modern system of inference that systematically eschewed any appeal to judgment as a synthesis of representational content.

---

[34] For some exceptions to the general neglect of Brentano's logic, see Chisholm 1982, and important discussions by Simons 1984 and 1987, and the Italian logician Roberto Poli 1993, 1998. By contrast, important studies of the reform of logic in this period leave Brentano entirely out of account (Dummett 1993, Willard 1984), and Barry Smith's account of Brentano's contributions to the tradition he calls "Austrian Philosophy" (1994) skims over Brentano's logical contributions. Two essays by Burnham Terrell (1976, 1978) deal with Brentano's treatment of quantification; for replies see Fischer and Miller 1976 and Chisholm 1976. Perhaps the most intriguing appropriation of Brentano's logical proposals is Kuroda 1972, which uses Brentanian logic in the analysis of Japanese syntax, and is still regularly cited in linguistics research. See, e.g., Sasse 1987, Ladusaw 1994, McNally 1997, 1998.

Brentano's most celebrated work is his *Psychology from an Empirical Standpoint*, first published in 1874. The seventh chapter touches directly on logical topics, and Brentano already there stated the main elements of his logical treatment of judgment: he rejects the synthetic construal of judgment; he insists that all judgments are essentially existential in form; and he provides (in overview) the formal argument required to establish these conclusions in detail. In order to see these logical positions fully elaborated, however, we must work from Brentano's posthumously published logic lectures from the 1870s (Brentano 1870–77), and from the work of Brentano's collaborators, particularly Franz Hillebrand and Anton Marty,[35] who worked closely with Brentano in the construction and elaboration of the new logical framework he had established.

In the logic lectures, the first glimpse of Brentano's revolution is symbolic. Where the tradition had identified "S is P" or "SxP" as the fundamental schema for judgment, Brentano proposes instead (A+) or (A−):

> The most universal schema for assertion accordingly reads: "A is" (A+) and "A is not" (A−). ... This form of expression contains everything that belongs to a simple judgment: a name, which names the object of judgment [*das Beurteilte*], and a sign which indicates whether the object of judgment is to be acknowledged or denied [*anzuerkennen oder zu verwerfen sei*].[36]

For Brentano, the fundamental elements of a judgment are not a subject and predicate in synthesis but rather a name (A), together with an indication of affirmation (+) or negation (−). It is hard to overestimate the significance of this rupture in a tradition which had long followed Kant and Aristotle in defining judgment in terms of synthesis.

Brentano acknowledges straightaway that his approach marks a break from that tradition, and that he owes us some principled grounds for rejecting the longstanding logical precedent: "This means a break with the traditional doctrine that every proposition consists of subject and predicate, and that the fundamental form [*Urform*] of judgment is 'A is (or is not) B.' One cannot repudiate so old a tradition unless one provides the grounds for one's divergence from it".[37]

This opens a forthright and explicit attack (prior to Frege's or Russell's) on the subject-predicate analysis of judgment – a logical

---

[35] Hillebrand 1891, Marty 1908. Franziska Mayer-Hillebrand also deserves mention here; it was she who assembled the source documents into a single treatise.

[36] Brentano 1870–77: 98.

[37] Brentano 1870–77: 98.

position that he rather dramatically describes as *"die Hauptfehler"* of traditional logic: "They [traditional logicians] remained of the false opinion that judgment is essentially a combination of representations."[38]

Brentano states his case against the synthetic construal of judgment in section 75 of his logic lectures, and his argument draws on several lines of argument we have excavated. He credits John Stuart Mill with the recognition that synthesis is not sufficient for judgment, although as we have seen the point can be traced at least to Hume. In simply entertaining a compound concept ("a golden mountain") or in posing a question ("Was Mohammed a prophet of God?") we find the combination of concepts without judgment; hence synthesis cannot by itself suffice for judgment:

> We have seen that a combination of representations can take place without a judgment being given. J. St. Mill ... already remarked that if I say "golden mountain," this is a combination of representations [*Verbindung von Vorstellungen*], but nonetheless not a judgment. ... Mill also showed that, whether I now believe or deny that Mohammed was a prophet of God, I must combine the two concepts "prophet of God" and "Mohammed" with one another.[39]

Recognizing this, one might then set out to discover what *in addition to synthesis* is required for judgment – whether by seeking out a particular form of synthesis (as in Kant) or by seeking some additional element present in judgmental synthesis (as in the appeal to the representation of "objective validity" – a position Brentano associates with Mill). Brentano cites Mill's memorable remark: "To determine what it is that happens in the case of assent or dissent *besides putting two ideas together*, is one of the most intricate of metaphysical problems."[40] But Brentano argues that such an approach is "wholly misguided" (*vollkommen mislungen*). This is because synthesis is not only insufficient for judgment; it is not necessary either. His argument on this point invokes the by-now celebrated examples: "Not only does the combination of representations not suffice to bring about a judgment, it is often not even necessary. This can be seen from the so-called existential propositions: *es regnet, es donnert, es gibt ein Gott* [it is raining, it is thundering, there is a God]."[41]

At least in the case of elementary judgments, Brentano argues, "the multiplicity of elements [*Mehrgliedrigkeit*] is in no way a necessary

---

[38] Brentano 1870–77: 125.

[39] Brentano 1870–77: 98–99.

[40] For Mill's argument see Mill 1843, Bk I, ch. 5, esp. § 1.

[41] Brentano 1870–77: 99.

property of judgment."[42] Brentano accordingly draws his revolutionary conclusion: since the combination of representations is neither necessary nor sufficient for judgment, we ought to abandon the tradition which defines judgment in terms of synthesis: "We have shown that the combination of subject and predicate and other similar connections are in no way part of the essence of judgment."[43]

In articulating and defending this argument, Brentano both draws on but also forthrightly criticizes the Kantian-Herbartian tradition we have been tracking. As with most German logicians of this period, his treatment of the forms of judgment is peppered with commentary on Kant's table, and he credits Kant with recognition of the crucial point that existence is not a predicate, and with the treatment of existential judgment as positing. But Brentano ultimately describes the Kantian position as "an unclear and contradictory halfway measure," complaining that Kant "allowed himself to be misled into classifying existential judgments as synthetic [as opposed to analytic] propositions."[44] The problem is that Kant recognizes a form of judgment that requires no conceptual multiplicity, and yet at the same time applies the analytic–synthetic distinction, thereby presupposing a pair of concepts in judgmental synthesis. Brentano's assessment of the Herbartian position is similarly mixed. He credits Herbart with the introduction of thetic judgment, thereby putting an end to the longstanding requirement of conceptual multiplicity in judgment, but he criticizes him for treating thetic judgment as a rudimentary form "alongside" (*nebenher*) the traditionally recognized categorical judgments.[45] For Brentano, such a position represents an insufficiently radical reform of the traditional approach: existential judgment is not to be treated simply as one form alongside others; it is much rather the basic form of all judgment.

This brings us to Brentano's second major innovation in the logical representation of judgment. For Brentano, the case of existential judgment is not simply a counter-example to the characterization of judgment as synthesis – an outlier against a general pattern of synthetic judgment. Its place is much more central than that. Ultimately, he argues, existential judgment is the root form of all judgment: "The fundamental form of judgment [*die Urform des Urteils*] is the thetic or

[42] Brentano 1870–77: 101.
[43] Brentano 1874: 222.
[44] Brentano 1874: 211.
[45] See Brentano 1874: 211; Brentano 1870–77: 124.

absolute."[46] The argument for this thesis is extensive and intricate. Where Herbart had argued that categorical judgment must be supplemented by thetic or existential judgment, Brentano argues that once thetic judgment is introduced, the categorical forms of judgment are strictly dispensable – reducible to complexes of thetic judgments. Establishing this result in detail takes up much of the text of the logic lectures. The first stage of the argument is to show that all the judgment forms recognized in Kantian logic can be "translated" (*übersetzt*) or "reduced" (*zurückgeführt*) to affirmative or negative existential judgments or conjunctions thereof.[47] He then sets out to construct axioms of proof and inferential figures sufficient to capture all the traditionally recognized valid inferences, now making use of only thetic premises and conclusions. In short, he undertakes to transpose Kantian logic into a strictly existential idiom.

The full details of this logical undertaking cannot be recounted here, but a few examples will provide a sense of the project. As we have seen, a basic judgment in Brentanian logic takes one of two forms: (A+) or (A−), either the affirmation or the denial of the existence of A. "Pierre exists" accordingly becomes (P+); "there are no goblins" becomes (G−). The traditional categorical forms are then treated as what Brentano calls "double judgments" (*Doppelurteile*).[48] Some care must be taken with this term. The "doubling" involved in a Brentanian double judgment is neither conjunction nor predication. It is not formed by combining two simple existential judgments (A+ & B+), nor by combining two concepts in a predicative unity, but rather by compounding the name or concept in a simple existential judgment. Hence, for instance, "Some S is P" becomes (SP+); "No S is P" becomes (SP−):

> The categorical proposition, "Some man is sick," means the same as the existential proposition, "A sick man exists," or "There is a sick man." The categorical proposition, "No stone is living" means the same as the existential proposition, "A living stone does not exist," or "There is no living stone."

Some of the principles of the Brentanian translations are at first surprising. Using lower case letters to designate the negation of a

---

[46] Brentano 1870–77: xviii.

[47] "It can be shown with utmost clarity that every categorical proposition can be translated [*übersetzt*] without any change of meaning into an existential proposition." Brentano 1874: 213.

[48] See Brentano 1870–77: 113.

Classical	Brentanian
Some S are P	SP+
All P are Q	Pq–
Some S are Q	SQ+

Figure 6: Classical and Brentanian Syllogisms
Source: adapted from Brentano 1870–77: 210–11

concept, he proposes that the universal affirmative form of categorical judgment be rendered as follows: (Sp–). In this way the canonical affirmative judgment comes out as a negative: "All S are P" becomes in effect: "There are no non-P Ss," or "A non-P S does not exist."

The results are sometimes cumbersome, and not always intuitive. Compare a classical inference with its Brentanian transposition (see Figure 6). The validity of the transposed inference is certainly not as readily recognizable as that of the traditional schema, and this is not simply because of the familiarity of the traditional form. And matters get considerably worse when hypothetical and disjunctive syllogisms are involved, since every disjunctive or hypothetical premise must ultimately be recast as a sequence of negated existential conjunctions – an anticipation of Wittgenstein's truth tables. Brentano grants that his formulations may at times be awkward (*schleppend und unbequem*),[49] and allows that we may choose to acknowledge the traditional forms for simplicity of expression. But he insists that his translations show those forms to be dispensable; thetic judgment suffices for all the recognized inferences of classical logic.

Brentano's logic was destined to be surpassed and overshadowed before it was even published in any detail, but it nonetheless marks a watershed in the history of logic. In appearance it is utterly unlike any logic that preceded it; it operated with judgmental and inferential forms that differed fundamentally from those of its predecessors; and it provided the first modern calculus of proof that entirely renounced the construal of judgment as synthesis. Though now largely forgotten, it was the culmination of a century of logical foment.

But was it successful? There are of course different measures for the success of an inferential system. Certainly the Brentanian proposals were

---

[49] Brentano 1870–77: 123.

not without their difficulties. One of the most heated debates concerned Brentano's treatment of universal affirmative categoricals as existential negatives – the transposition of "All men are mortal" into "There are no immortal men." This transposition raises particular difficulty in connection with the fictional contexts to which the Herbartian analysis had appealed. One of the basic inference rules in Brentanian logic is that a *simple* existential negative entails any corresponding *compound* existential negative: (C−) entails both (CA−) and (Ca−). (If there are no honest men then there are neither tall ones nor short ones.)[50] But now consider Brentano's treatment of a universal affirmative concerning a fictional object. In the Brentanian framework, a judgment about a Centaur or a Cyclops must be rendered as either an existential affirmative or an existential negative. This seems straightforward in the case of a simple denial that Cyclops exist, but what are we to say of the judgment that, e.g., Cyclops are monocular? Under the principles of Brentanian transposition, this comes out as "There are no non-monocular Cyclops" (Cm−). That may seem fine until we recognize that "Cyclops are binocular" must accordingly be rendered: "There are no non-binocular Cyclops" (Cb−). By the inference rule governing existential negatives, (C−) entails both (Cm−) and (Cb−). Accordingly "Cyclops are n-eyed" is true for any number n.

A more fundamental problem concerns the principled limits on Brentano's revolutionary ambitions. Brentano's stated aim was to bring about a thoroughgoing revolution in logic – "a complete overthrow, and at the same time, a reconstruction of elementary logic."[51] While there is a sense in which he accomplished this, his revolutionary impulse was in the end fundamentally limited by the basic strategy of proof and legitimation that he adopted. As we have seen, Brentano effectively produced his logic by systematically translating or transposing the classically recognized forms. Moreover, his standard of adequacy for his completed system was in large part driven by his aim of capturing all traditionally warranted valid inferences.[52] These strategies amount to a significant drag on his revolutionary impulse – as if the would-be

---

[50] "Jeder richtige negative Urteil bleibt richtig wenn man seine Materie um beliebig viele Determinationen bereichert." (Brentano 1870–77: 209).

[51] Brentano 1874: 230.

[52] There were limitations to this aim, however. In particular, Brentano rejected those classical inferences whose validity turned on an assumption of existential import in the universal affirmative form. Hence, for instance, he rejects the classical inference rule of subalternation. See Brentano 1870–77: 205ff; and for a discussion Simons 1987.

revolutionary council seeks to legitimate itself by appeal to the very government it denounces and overthrows.

Certainly if success is to be measured by influence then Brentano's logic can at best be deemed a limited success. There did briefly emerge in Vienna what we might well describe as a new "normal science" of logic, explicitly taking Brentano's logical proposals as its point of reference and repudiating essential elements of the Kantian paradigm. Brentano's own logic remained unpublished until long after his death, but Marty, Hillebrand, Kraus, Meinong and others elaborated his logical proposals and tackled some of the central problems that arose from them. Through the mediation of his student Twardowski, Brentano indirectly influenced developments in twentieth-century Polish logic. For the most part, however, Brentano's influence in logic was limited to his immediate circle, and indeed the details of his logic were known only to those who attended his lectures in Vienna. The textbooks and problems of the new century would much rather take their orientation from the mathematical logics of Peano, Frege, and Russell.

For our purposes, however, there is a further set of questions to be raised about the adequacy of Brentanian logic. The logical history we have here recounted began with a loan from logic to phenomenology: Kant appealed to the logical representation of judgment in order to guide and illuminate his investigation of judgment as it figures in experience. The model of judgment he borrowed was the construal of judgment as the synthesis of representational content, and it was this model that informed his account of human thought and intelligence. What we have seen in this chapter is that Kant also planted the seed (or fired the shot?) that would ultimately lead to the repudiation of that model of judgment. His account of singular existential judgment as positing became the central source for a century-long movement which ultimately turned its back on the synthetic construal of judgment. Accordingly, a central question to be posed about Brentanian logic concerns what it offers as an alternative to the traditional synthetic account, and accordingly what alternative "guiding thread" it might provide for the phenomenological investigation of judgment.

This question is particularly pressing when formulated from the viewpoint of the classical logician Brentano seeks to displace. Brentano insists that the tradition has fundamentally erred in characterizing judgment as synthesis; *so what is his purported alternative*? What is judgment if not the synthesis of representational content? As we have seen, Kant's treatment of existential judgment as positing prompted the revisionist trend in nineteenth-century logic, but it calls out for some explication of its central notion. What exactly does it mean to posit an object? The traditional logician can justly claim to have a pretty good sense of what synthesis or combination is, and how it is an act that can be undertaken in thought. But what is involved in positing something? Attempts to answer this question tend to be formulated negatively. Logicians from Herbart to Brentano insist that thetic judgment is not combination and requires no conceptual multiplicity. It also seems clear that to posit something is not simply to create it. (I do not bring Pierre into existence in judging that he exists.) But when we attempt to go beyond these negative characterizations it is easy to slip into vacuous circularity. To posit Pierre is not to bring him into existence, we want to say, but rather to assert *that he exists*. In positing Pierre, I claim that *there is something* which answers to my description of him. But such answers are obviously circular if they are meant to explain or define the positing involved in existential judgment. So where the synthetic construal of judgment left us with a research program (what form of synthesis of concepts amounts to a judgment?), the characterization of judgment as positing threatens to leave us with an empty tautology: existential judgment is positing; positing is an assertion of existence.

In Brentanian logic, this issue is managed by appeal to the notion of acknowledgment or recognition (*Anerkennung*). As we have seen, Brentano treats thetic judgment as the basic form of all judgment, and his symbolic representation of such judgments is meant to reflect its essential character: a name represents an object which is then acknowledged or denied. But here again the threat of circularity looms. Naturally we want to know what such acknowledgment consists in. Clearly it is not the kind of acknowledgment that figures in the prefaces of books (the acknowledgment of influence or assistance) nor the acknowledgment of receipt issued by clerks and postal officials. So what kind of acknowledgment is it? The natural but plainly inadequate answer is that a thetic judgment acknowledges the *existence* of what it names. The circularity in defining the basic notion seems to reappear.

Brentano's strategy with this problem is revealing: in effect he embraces it. Any attempt to produce a non-circular definition or analysis of acknowledgment and denial must fail, he argues, because these notions are logically primitive and irreducible:

> All the difficulties that thwart the old account of judgment as a combination of representations can best be resolved if we abandon that doctrine

and suppose instead that that judgment is an *irreducible* act which is directed upon an object and which cannot be further analyzed. In other words, judgment consists in a particular relation to an object that can only be made clear through examples, and that we can express as "acknowledgment" or "denial."[53]

For Brentano, however, the indefinability of these notions does not leave us with a vacuous notion. Rather, the meaning of these terms is to be fixed by a kind of inner ostension. We cite examples to illustrate them, and we appeal to "inner sense" or "inner experience" to determine them. In other words, the determinacy of these terms is fixed phenomenologically:

> Our conclusion therefore is this: ... we must assume that ... a fundamental difference exists between judgment and representation. ... The arguments in support of this truth are as follows: firstly, *inner experience directly reveals the difference in the references to their content which we assert of representation and judgment.* Secondly, if this were not the distinction between them, there would be no difference between them at all.[54]

For Brentano, then, the basic character of judgment cannot be clarified through definitions or analysis but must be known through direct, first-personal acquaintance. We cannot expect to produce a non-circular definition of judgment but must simply know it from our own experience. On this point Brentano compares judgment to the phenomenon of love or hate. In all these cases, he claims, we have a primitive form of relation to an object, one in which the object in question is presented *in a distinctive way* – but in a way that is so basic that it can be aroused but never definitionally specified.

There are a number of observations to be made about this outcome. Notice first that Brentano here fundamentally reconfigures the relationship between logical and phenomenological claims concerning the character of judgment. Where Kant's theory of experience depended on results borrowed from logic, Brentano in effect makes logic depend on phenomenology. The basic notion in the logical representation of judgment depends for its determinacy on an appeal to "inner sense" or "immediate experience." But with this loan comes a debt that must somehow be discharged. Brentano insists that we can and must rely on inner sense to reveal the distinctive character of acknowledgment, and

---

[53] Brentano 1870–77: 100–1.
[54] Brentano 1874: 225, emphasis added.

hence of judgment. But it is far from clear that this claim can be vindi-cated. Here Brentano's final position is strikingly similar to Hume's position in the Appendix to the *Treatise*. Both assume that there is some primitive mental state, evident to introspective attention, which marks out the distinctive character of affirmation. If there is such a primitive – which is to be doubted – then treating it as inarticulably primitive is tantamount to an admission of phenomenological defeat. We can say nothing, it seems, about the experiential character of judging something to be true. Worse, it seems that phenomenology can say nothing about how this phenomenological primitive differs from the other primitives on which Brentano relies. How does the experience of acknowledgment differ from that of denial? How do these in turn differ from love and hate? Brentano's treatment of all of these as primitives serves to enforce a principled phenomenological silence. If, on the other hand, there is no such primitive, then we require some other means for fixing the sense of the basic terms in the logical analysis of judgment. Finally by making the basic notions of logic rest in this way on a kind of introspection, Brentano would soon encounter fierce resistance from those who saw in such appeals a dangerous corruption of logic.

As in so many other areas, Brentano's contributions to the logical representation of judgment bequeath a range of problems for his phe-nomenological successors. If judgment is at root existential judgment, if its basic character is thesis or acknowledgment rather than synthesis or combination, then we want to know what in our experience supports and sustains the logically basic capacity to identify and acknowledge those entities we judge to exist. In the fourth chapter, below, we shall take up Heidegger's contribution to these Brentanian problems. But I turn first to a nearly contemporary episode in the history of the logic of judgment: Frege's introduction of a logical symbol meant to represent or enact it.

3

THE JUDGMENT STROKE AND THE TRUTH PREDICATE: FREGE AND THE LOGICAL REPRESENTATION OF JUDGMENT

Can we add something more original, something that goes beyond the definition of the essence of truth as a character of the assertion? Nothing less than the insight that this definition, however construed, is, though unavoidable, nonetheless derivative.

Heidegger, *The Essence of Reasons*

When Frege published his logical calculus in 1879, the first symbol he introduced was the turnstile:

In explaining the symbol, Frege distinguishes its two parts. The horizontal portion is the content stroke, indicating that the symbols within its scope constitute, in Frege's words, "a possible content of judgment." The vertical portion of the symbol is dubbed "the judgment stroke," indicating that the content marked by the horizontal is recognized as true.[1] In laying down the formation-rules for his *Begriffsschrift*, Frege stipulates that in a well-formed inference, every autonomous premise must begin with this symbol. Hence modus ponens, for example, is constructed in *Begriffsschrift* as shown in Figure 7.[2] Frege's judgment stroke has not been well received by subsequent logicians and

I wish to thank Lanier Anderson, Ermanno Bencivenga, Adrian Cussins, Steve Crowell, John Haugeland, Michael Hardimon, Ryan Hickerson, Stephan Käufer, and Sam Rickless for comments on earlier drafts of the material presented in this chapter.

[1] Frege 1879: § 2, 111.
[2] Frege 1879: § 6, 117.

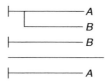

Figure 7: Modus Ponens in *Begriffsschrift*
Source: Frege 1879: § 6.

commentators. In the *Tractatus*, Wittgenstein dismisses it as "logically altogether meaningless."[3] Peano, in his review of the *Grundgesetze*, complains that the judgment stroke is otiose: "I fail to see the purpose of these conventions, which have nothing corresponding to them in [my] *Formulaire*."[4] Among recent commentators the assessment is, if anything, even more negative. Anthony Kenny describes it as "[an] unsatisfactory feature, too important to be glossed by benevolent paraphrase."[5] Baker and Hacker conclude that Frege's account of the judgment stroke is "flawed by misconceptions and confusions. ... The result is conceptual chaos."[6] The negative assessment may not be universal,[7] but it is reflective of a broad consensus that the judgment stroke is redundant at best and dangerously confused at worst. It is significant that the main contemporary logical calculi – the ones that undergraduates are now expected to master – seem to function perfectly well without a judgment stroke, despite leaning heavily on many of Frege's other logical innovations.

The unhappy fate of the judgment stroke stands in stark contrast to Frege's own assessment of its significance. In a particularly striking private note from the Summer of 1906, Frege asks himself: "What may I regard as the result of my work?" His answer consists of about ten lines of text. He starts by giving pride of place to his logical calculus: "It is almost all tied up with the *Begriffsschrift*," he writes, going on to recount several features of the system – its treatment of concepts and relations, generality, etc. But after five lines the fragment breaks off and Frege begins again: "Strictly I should have begun by mentioning the judgment stroke, the dissociation of assertoric force from the predicate."[8] We will have occasion to return to

[3] Wittgenstein 1921: 4.442.
[4] Peano 1895: 29.
[5] Kenny 1995: 34–35.
[6] Baker and Hacker 1984: 98.
[7] Peter Geach is one notable exception. See Geach 1965.
[8] Frege 1906: 184.

this remark below. For now note simply that Frege himself certainly does not think of the judgment stroke as meaningless or otiose. It lies, on his view, at the beginning of his logical contributions.

What is the judgment stroke and why did Frege think it so important? What role does it play in Frege's logical theory of judgment? Why has it been so roundly denounced by those who labored in the logical space Frege opened? What does its fate teach us about judgment, and about the limits of logical expression? In what follows I take up these questions in stages. In the first section I assess some standard accounting of Frege's contribution to modern logic, and consider the role played in Frege's revolution by his approach to the logic of judgment. In the second section I consider the role of the judgment stroke in that theory, surveying both apologist and critical positions. The third section takes up Frege's proposed paraphrase of the stroke, together with redundancy issues raised by the failure of that paraphrase. I argue that the failure of the paraphrase exhibits a limit in the expressive power of the judgment stroke itself, and in this sense a principled limit on Frege's logic of judgment. In the final section I draw on these results from Frege's project in order to illuminate two claims in Heidegger's philosophical logic.

1 The father of modern logic

Let me begin by suggesting that we need to rethink a few points that have become perhaps too familiar. Everyone knows that Frege is the father of modern logic – an unprecedented logical revolutionary. Every textbook seems to echo Russell's remark, crediting Frege with "the first serious advance in real logic [since ancient times]."[9] But what exactly was Frege's unprecedented, revolutionary contribution to logic? In virtue of what does he merit these oft-repeated honorifics? About this there is also a familiar textbook answer.[10] The core of the standard history has three elements. It is said, first of all, that Frege *invented mathematical logic*. He developed a calculus of proof which followed the mathematician's method of breaking down complex proofs into constituent steps; he introduced into logic mathematical concepts such as that of a function, and of course he sought to connect logic and mathematics by defining

---

[9] Russell 1914: 50. In fact Russell jointly credits Frege and Peano; this is less frequently echoed.

[10] For a concise statement of the textbook account see Beaney 1997: 47. For a canonical development of this line see Kneale and Kneale 1962: ch. 8, in particular 510–12.

basic mathematical notions in logical terms. Secondly, it is said that he *founded quantification theory*. He proposed rigorous definitions of quantificational terms like "all," "some," and "there is," and he invented formal calculating procedures and inference rules for deploying those quantifiers in proofs. In this sense we can say that he is the inventor of what we now call the predicate calculus. This in turn made possible a third celebrated contribution: *the first adequate treatment of the logic of multiple generality*. That is, the syntax of his quantificational calculus made it possible to capture in exact logical form such otherwise ambiguous sentences as "Every boy loves a girl," or "Every even number is the sum of two primes." These contributions were all in the service of Frege's most ambitious logical project: the logicist program of reducing mathematical to logical truth. But the accomplishments were also independent of that project – and they endured even after the collapse of the logicist program in the philosophy of mathematics.

We should not be surprised when the messy details of history do not conform to the neat sketches we find in textbooks. In fact, Frege was not the first to introduce mathematical techniques, concepts, and rigor in logic – a distinction which is much more due to the English mathematician and logician, George Boole, if not to Leibniz. (A few years ago only mathematicians and a few historians of logic knew Boole's name; in the age of Google searches everyone knows what a Boolean operator is and there are waitlists for community college courses in Boolean logic.) Boole's project of defining algebraic operators for logical functions was already well-established by the time Frege was writing. Indeed, one of the reasons that the *Begriffsschrift* failed to attract much attention on initial publication was that it was seen as a rather idiosyncratic version of work already being done by the Booleans. One of the very few reviews it received was by Ernst Schröder, who acknowledged it as clever but criticized Frege for reinventing the wheel:

> The present little book makes an advance which I should consider very creditable, if a large part of what it attempts had not already been accomplished by someone else. ... I consider it a shortcoming that the book is presented in too isolated a manner and not only seeks no serious connection with achievements that have been made in essentially similar directions (namely those of Boole), but disregards them entirely.[11]

The second part of the standard history claims that Frege was the first to offer a rigorous treatment of quantification. On this point the

---

[11] Schröder 1880: quoted in Sluga 1980: 68.

textbook account is often grossly unfair to the earlier logic. The traditional logic certainly did have a treatment of quantification, and the scholastic square of opposition amounted to a rigorous interdefinition of the various fundamental quantificational forms. (If all S are P then No S are not-P, etc.) This approach certainly differed from the Fregean one, and there are many reasons that one might prefer the modern treatment over the traditional. But it is simply inaccurate to say, as both Russell and Carnap did, that the traditional logic was forced to treat "All men" as the subject term in "All men are mortal."[12]

Within the parameters of the standard history, this leaves us with Frege's treatment of multiple generality. This is indeed a novel contribution on Frege's part, and it certainly serves to extend the scope and utility of logic. Moreover, it was a crucial innovation if logic was to be able to *express* – much less *prove* – the basic laws of arithmetic. But the logic student may well be left to wonder about the solemnity of his exercises on "Everybody loves somebody." Where in this should we locate Frege's logical *revolution*? A revolution is a turning around. Simply extending the scope and flexibility of logic does not of itself make Frege a logical revolutionary.[13]

If we turn from the textbooks to Frege's own self-assessment then we find a rather different frame for understanding his revolutionary contribution. In the Preface to the *Begriffsschrift* Frege offers the following characterization of what his book contributes to logic:

> The very invention of this *Begriffsschrift*, it seems to me, has advanced logic. I hope that logicians, if they are not put off by first impressions of unfamiliarity, will not repudiate the innovations to which I was driven by a necessity inherent in the subject matter itself. These deviations from

---

[12] "Metaphysical errors arose through supposing that 'all men' is the subject of 'all men are mortal' in the same sense as that in which 'Socrates' is the subject of 'Socrates is mortal.'" Russell 1945: 198; see also Russell 1914: 50 and Carnap 1930: 138. As we have seen, the logics Russell sought to overthrow treat the concept "man" as the subject of "All men are mortal." "All" is a marker of the form of the judgment (universal), and hence figures in neither subject nor predicate.

[13] Obviously these brief remarks do not settle the question of the adequacy of the standard history. Frege himself replied to Schröder's charge of reinventing the Boolean wheel. See Frege 1880–81. And certainly there are important differences of principle between the traditional treatment of quantification and that proposed by Frege. Furthermore, there are other areas in which the textbooks sometimes locate Frege's innovations: the interdefinition of sentential connectives; the sharp distinction between axioms and inference rules; the logic of relations, etc. I forego a fuller discussion of these various options in order to focus on Frege's own accounting of his logical contribution.

what is traditional find their justification in the fact that logic hitherto has always followed ordinary language too closely. In particular, I believe that the replacement of the concepts subject and predicate by argument and function will prove itself in the long run. ... What also deserves notice is the demonstration of the connection between the meanings of the words: if, and, not, or, there is, some, all, etc.[14]

The first point to note about this passage is the final line. The very accomplishments with which Frege is most frequently credited – the interdefinition of the connectives, the treatment of the quantifiers – are here billed as "also-ran." What Frege marks out as his more fundamental contribution is not an advance in quantification theory; it is an advance in our understanding of judgment. In particular, top billing is here given to the repudiation of the logical approach which treats a judgment as a synthesis of a subject and a predicate. Here we do indeed find a moment in the history of logic that is revolutionary in the literal sense of the word. In rejecting the subject-predicate logic of judgment, Frege is turning his back on the core analysis of judgment that had structured logical investigations since ancient times.

In order to appreciate the extent of Frege's revolution, it is instructive to compare his position on this issue with Russell's. In Russell we may seem to find the same revolutionary move. On Russell's account of the logical revolution, as on Carnap's, modern logic is "given wings" when it is "freed from the fetters" of subject-predicate analysis.[15] The traditional logic which took its departure from this analysis was, in Russell's phrase, little more than "solemn humbug"[16] that had become entrenched in the academic curriculum. But it is worth asking why – on Russell's account – logic must be liberated from subject-predicate analysis. Russell's main answer[17] concerns the logic of relations – particularly those relations such as "is the father of," or "is greater than," which are asymmetrical. Such relations, Russell claims, cannot be perspicuously analyzed in the

---

[14] Frege 1879: Preface, 106–7.
[15] Russell 1914: 68. For Carnap's discussion see Carnap 1930.
[16] Russell 1914: 42.
[17] Russell has other arguments as well. Most famously, he argues that subject-predicate logic is ontologically dangerous, since it is associated with "the belief or unconscious conviction that ... every fact consists in some thing having some quality." Russell 1914: 54–55. Russell elaborates this theme in his book on Leibniz, and at much greater length in his history of philosophy. I shall not attempt here to show that this argument is spurious – though it is still solemnly repeated.

traditional subject-predicate form. Accordingly, he argues, we ought to recognize relational form as a logical primitive.

The issues here are complex, but let me make a few observations about this claim. Consider one of Russell's own examples: the judgment that John is taller than Mary. How might we express this judgment as some set of subject-predicate judgments? Suppose we say that John is six feet tall and that Mary is five feet tall. Here we have two subject-predicate judgments, but together they say both more and less than the judgment they are meant to translate. They say more insofar as they specify heights in a way that is absent from the original judgment. But crucially they also say less. For from these two judgments we can only infer the original judgment if we add that six feet is longer than five feet. But, of course, here we have reintroduced a relational judgment. Accordingly, Russell proposes that this judgment – and indeed all judgments involving serial ordering – should be treated as ineliminably relational in form. In this case we introduce the two-place relation, "is taller than," taking John and Mary as its relata. In doing so, however, we overstep the limits of the subject-predicate logics.[18]

Russell knows, of course, that relational judgments can in one straightforward sense be accommodated within the traditional logical forms. We could, after all, simply treat "is taller than Mary" as a primitive predicate that is ascribed to John. It is worth emphasizing this point because it helps us to see where the real force of Russell's argument lies. If we treat "is taller than Mary" as a primitive predicate then we leave ourselves blind to some of the logical structure of the original judgment. In particular, our logical treatment will recognize no similarity between this predicate and "is taller than James"; nor shall we recognize that the original judgment entails both that someone is taller than Mary and that John is taller than someone. The crux of Russell's argument, then, is that the relational analysis is logically more perspicuous and thereby *extends the inferential power of logic*. In short: we should recognize relational judgments because doing so will yield a more powerful logic – in particular one that we might hope to be adequate to the logicist dream.[19]

---

[18] Russell 1914: 58–59.

[19] Arguably, the Russellian argument is undercut once set-theoretical resources are introduced in logic. If we help ourselves to such resources we can perfectly well analyze relational judgments in subject-predicate form: we need only take the ordered pair (John, Mary) as our subject term, and attribute to it the predicate: "member of the set of ordered pairs such that the former is taller than the latter." I am grateful to Gila Sher for helping me to appreciate this point.

For our purposes, however, the key point to notice here is the contrast between Russell and Frege. Russell is happy to allow that *some* judgments are of subject-predicate form, ascribing a quality to an object. His claim is that *not every judgment should be so treated.* When we look to Frege we find something different. For Frege, subject-predicate analysis does not need to be *supplemented* in logic; it needs to be *banished.* This is a point we see him emphasize over and over. Here are a few examples:

> From all this we can see that the grammatical categories of subject and predicate can have no significance for logic.[20]

> We shall completely avoid the expressions "subject" and "predicate," of which logicians are so fond.[21]

> Therefore it would be best to banish the words, "subject" and "predicate" from logic entirely.[22]

What we see here is a much more radical position than the one proposed by Russell. Frege and Russell are certainly agreed in seeing the old logic as "fettered" by its exclusive reliance on the subject-predicate analysis of judgment. And they are agreed that the logicist project can only be carried out if logic can free itself from those fetters. But Frege is Jacobin to Russell's Indulgent, demanding that the old forms be banished rather than supplemented. So the question we must now take up is: WHY? Why should the subject-predicate theory of judgment be banished?

Once again we find one answer developed in the *Begriffsschrift* itself. Section 3 opens by announcing the revolutionary banishment: "A distinction between subject and predicate finds no place in my representation of judgment."[23] It then goes on to justify the banishment with a famous argument. I quote the relevant passage in full:

> To justify this, I note that the contents of two judgments can differ in two ways: either the conclusions that can be drawn from one when combined with certain others also always follow from the second when combined with the same judgments, or else this is not the case. The two propositions "At Plataea the Greeks defeated the Persians" and "At Plataea the Persians were defeated by the Greeks" differ in the first way. Even if a slight difference in sense can be discerned, the agreement predominates. Now I call that part of the content which is the same in both the conceptual

---

[20] Frege 1897a: 141.
[21] Frege 1897a: 143.
[22] Frege 1891: 120.
[23] Frege 1879: § 3, 112.

content. Since only this has significance for the *Begriffsschrift*, no distinction is needed between propositions that have the same conceptual content.[24]

Frege's argument here turns on his notion of the "inferential significance" or "conceptual content" of a judgment. The inferential significance of a judgment is the bearing it has in proofs: two premises have the same inferential significance if and only if they have all the same consequences. His argument can be rendered in four steps. The first step introduces the distinction between two kinds of variation in the content of judgments: two judgments can vary either in ways that alter their inferential significance or in ways that leave their inferential significance untouched. The second step stipulates that logic is concerned only with such variations that alter inferential significance. The third step claims that there are transformations of judgments which exchange subject and predicate positions without altering inferential significance. (It is this premise that is supported by the example of the Persians and the Greeks.) The argument then concludes that the categories of subject and predicate are logically irrelevant. As in the Russellian argument, we find here an appeal to asymmetric relational judgments. But there the similarity ends. Russell sought to show that relational judgments cannot be perspicuously reduced to subject-predicate form; Frege claims that the very distinction between subject and predicate is logically irrelevant, since inferentially equivalent judgments can reverse subject and predicate position.

But the argument meant to establish this result is hardly decisive. A natural first line of defense for the traditional logician is to treat the two judgments as merely grammatical variants of one and the same subject-predicate judgment. There is nothing in the traditional framework which dictates that the grammatical subject of a sentence is to be identified with its logical subject. Kant's warning about this is explicit: "In logic, one holds to sense, not to words."[25] Since variations of expression can be merely grammatical or linguistic, the logical equivalence of Frege's two expressions does not directly bear on the viability of subject-predicate analysis.

But there are deeper issues here as well, and they suggest a second line of defense. Frege is, of course, right to point out that subject and predicate can – *given appropriate context and attendant transformations* – be exchanged for one another without change of inferential significance. But the qualification is important here. Subject and predicate certainly cannot be

---

[24] Frege 1879: § 3, 112–13.

[25] "In der Logik aber hält man sich am Sinn, nicht an die Wörte." See Pinder 1998: 2:441; Young 1992: 89.

reversed willy nilly; there is all the inferential difference in the world
between "all men are mortal" and "all mortals are men." The crucial
point is that such subject-predicate reversals are governed by purely
formal principles of inference. This was, in fact, a perennial topic of
concern in the traditional logics.[26] In particular, the principles of conversion and contraposition were meant to provide the inference rules for
what the traditional logics call "*metathesis terminorum*" – the reversal of
subject and predicate terms in immediate inferences.[27] The fact that
such transformations of subject and predicate are governed by purely
formal inference rules would seem to attest to the logical significance of
the distinction, rather than somehow ruling it out of logical order. Here
we might draw an analogy to sentential connectives in the familiar modern
calculi. With appropriate attendant variations, a disjunction can be trans-
formed into a conjunction: "p v q" is logically equivalent to "~(~p & ~q)."
Both have the same truth table; hence both have the same inferential
significance. But this hardly suffices to show that the distinction between
conjunction and disjunction is out of place in logic.

Let me be clear: I do not mean to suggest that Frege lacks resources
for criticizing subject-predicate analysis; and I am certainly not arguing
for a revival of scholastic logic. My point so far is, first, that Frege's logical
revolution turns in considerable measure on his contribution to the
theory of judgment; and second, that if we are to understand the significance of that revolution, then we must look beyond the standard
sketches and arguments. Certainly there is no shortage of places where
one might profitably look. In the *Nachlass*, for instance, there are a range
of arguments against subject-predicate logic that are independent of the
argument we found in the published writing. Alternatively, we might
focus on Frege's proposed alternative to subject-predicate analysis – in
particular his account of judgments in terms of the notion of a function.[28] In what follows I take a third strategy, following the lead from

---

[26] This dimension of the traditional logical project tended to get overlooked by the logical
revolutionaries of this period, who wrongly assumed that the traditional logics treated all
inference as syllogistic. See, e.g., Russell 1903: § 11: "The syllogism in all its figures belongs
to symbolic logic, and would be the whole subject if all deduction were syllogistic, as the
scholastic tradition supposed." Subject-predicate reversals were traditionally handled as
non-syllogistic or "immediate" inferences – what Kant treats as "inferences of the understanding." See, e.g., Kant, Ak. IX: 610.

[27] By the principle of contraposition, "All S is P" entails "No non-P is S." By conversion, "All S
is P" entails "Some P is S."

[28] The revisionist literature on Frege's revolution is by now unsurveyably large. For two
influential contributions see Sluga 1980 and Baker and Hacker 1984.

Frege's ten-line fragment. Accordingly, I turn now to consider the place of the judgment stroke in Frege's logical revolution.

2 The judgment stroke: critics and apologists

So what exactly is the judgment stroke? Any answer must begin from the relevant passage from the *Begriffsschrift*:

> A judgment will always be expressed by means of the symbol
>
> $$\vdash$$
>
> which stands to the left of the symbol or complex of symbols which gives the content of the judgment. If the small vertical stroke at the left of the horizontal one is *omitted*, then the judgment will be transformed into a *mere complex of ideas*, of which the writer does not state whether he recognizes its truth or not. For example, let
>
> $$\vdash A$$
>
> mean the judgment: "Opposite magnetic poles attract one another"; then
>
> $$- A$$
>
> will not express this judgment, but should merely arouse in the reader the idea of the mutual attraction of opposite magnetic poles, in order, say, to draw conclusions from it and by means of these to test the correctness of the thought. In this case we *paraphrase* using the words "*the circumstance that*" or "*the thought that.*"[29]

The first point to observe here is the reemergence of issues we encountered in Hume's discussion of belief. When Hume posed his problem about belief he did so by asking about "the difference betwixt merely entertaining an idea and actually believing it."[30] Frege's example of the magnetic poles seems to be drawing effectively the same distinction, a difference which Frege then marks graphically by the two strokes of the turnstile. The horizontal stroke thus indicates a complex of ideas "merely aroused in the reader"; the addition of the vertical stroke marks an affirmation of those ideas. What is striking about this parallel is the difference of domain between these two occurrences of the same distinction. For Hume, the difference between merely entertaining and believing an idea is a *psychological or*

---

[29] Frege 1879: s. 2, 111–12.
[30] Hume 1739: 94ff; see Chapter 1, sections 2–5.

phenomenological difference – a difference between two states of mind. Hume struggles to say what that difference is, but for him it is obvious that it is a psychological difference in the person who is having the ideas in question. For Frege, by contrast, the difference between merely entertaining and affirming is a distinction in *logic* – a distinction to be marked in a logical calculus. The distinction has somehow shifted from psychology to logic.

This shift itself provides the basis for one of the standard objections. Frege is, of course, an ardent opponent of psychologism in logic; he denies again and again that psychological facts are relevant to logic. But if we follow this anti-psychologism then it looks quite mysterious that Frege's logical symbolism should include this mark of judging a content to be true. After all, judging would seem to be a psychological act of some individual, and hence on Frege's own principles to be utterly irrelevant to logic. In the words of one critic:

> The very first new symbol which Frege introduces is what he calls "the judgment stroke." ... In his later work, Frege constantly emphasized the need to distinguish between logic and psychology. In this early passage, the distinction seems blurred. Frege is introducing a logical symbol, yet he does so in psychological terms: for he defines the symbol in terms of a contrast between judgment and combination of ideas. Now judgment is surely a mental act, and ideas are surely something in the mind.[31]

The worry here does not simply concern the consistency of Frege's views; it goes to the heart of his conception of inference. If we construct an argument according to the rules of the *Begriffsschrift*, each premise and the conclusion must begin with a judgment stroke. It thus begins to look – bizarrely – as if the inference holds *among various acts of judgment*. It is as if *my* act of judging B, together with *my* act of judging "if B then A" entails *my* act of judging A. But this is surely a mistake. We want to say that the inferential relation holds not among the acts of judging but among the contents themselves. This is one of Wittgenstein's objections: "Frege's assertion sign ... is logically altogether meaningless: in Frege (and in Russell) it only shows that *these authors* hold as true the sentences marked in this way. '⊢' belongs as little to the sentences as their number."[32]

Ironically, the very force of the objection is testimony to Frege's own influence. In the wake of Frege's otherwise uncompromising rejection of psychologism, we have become accustomed to the idea that

---

[31] Kenny 1995: 35.
[32] Wittgenstein 1921: para. 4.442, parenthetical; emphasis added.

psychological facts are irrelevant to logic. Accordingly, we take it as obvious that acts of assertion or judgment are quite irrelevant to the validity of the inference, which turns strictly on the relation that holds among the premises. So why should there be a mark of judgment in logic?

Already, then, we can see two related objections on which critics of the judgment stroke have relied. First, the stroke seems to violate Frege's anti-psychologistic principles, and second, it seems to be unnecessary for modeling inference. Whether or not I judge the premises to be true or false or simply suspend judgment as to their truth altogether, "p" and "if p then q" entail "q."

How might the stroke be defended from these criticisms? There is a small but elegant literature on this topic. The most widely cited defense of the stroke is due to Peter Geach, who in his 1963 Howison lecture at Berkeley confesses to "a missionary zeal" for Frege's innovation. The core of Geach's apology is the observation that proofs typically include propositions that are not themselves advanced as premises. Modus ponens, of course, contains the conditional premise, "if p then q." But while both "p" and "q" *occur* in the statement of the conditional, they are not themselves advanced or asserted as premises. Notice that if they were advanced or asserted, then modus ponens would amount to bla-tantly circular reasoning, insofar as its conclusion would already have been advanced among its premises. According to Geach, then, the judg-ment stroke marks a logical rather than a psychological difference – the difference between these two fundamentally different kinds of occur-rence of propositional contents within proofs.[33]

There is some important textual evidence which supports Geach's interpretation. In a paper comparing the *Begriffsschrift* to Peano's *Formulaire*, for instance, Frege writes as follows:

> In the formula
>
> $$(2 > 3) \supset 7^2 = 0$$
>
> ... a sense of strangeness is felt at first[.] ... [I]t appears as if something false,

---

[33] Thinking about the stroke in Geach's way, we can see a sense in which logicians continue to rely – albeit implicitly – on something like the judgment stroke. Modern systems of natural deduction, for instance, typically rely on some kind of distinction between premises and assumptions, or between discharged and undischarged assumptions. In a natural deduc-tion proof of a logical theorem, for instance, one typically makes assumptions which are then discharged. Accordingly, such a proof implicitly relies on a distinction between those propositions which are still bearing logical weight and those which are not. Read in Geach's way, we can see the judgment stroke as a device for explicitly marking this difference.

$(2 > 3, 7^2 = 0)$ is being asserted in that formula – which is not the case at all.[34]

He goes on to introduce the judgment stroke as a device for dispelling this "sense of strangeness":

> [F]or this reason I have introduced a special sign with assertoric force, the judgment stroke. This is a manifestation of my endeavor to have every objective distinction reflected in symbolism. With this judgment stroke I close off a sentence, so that each condition necessary for its holding is also effectively to be found within it; and by means of this selfsame sign I assert the content of the sentence thus closed off as true. Mr. Peano has no such sign . . . . From this it follows that for Mr. Peano it is impossible to write down a sentence which does not occur as part of another sentence without putting it forward as true.

In comparing his symbolism with one of its main rivals, then, Frege explicitly relies on just the point that Geach emphasizes.

Geach's solution has the merit of providing answers to the two main objections we have considered. In particular, it shows how the judgment stroke can be seen as marking a logical, rather than a psychological distinction. What is less clear on Geach's account is why the judgment stroke would be so important to Frege. (Recall again the ten-line fragment: an account of Frege's contribution to logic should *begin* with the judgment stroke.) After all, it is not as if prior logicians had systematically confused autonomous premises and embedded contents. As Peano observed, the difference is always clear from the context. Here, of course, Frege will reply that in logic, "nothing should be left to guesswork" – that every inferentially significant difference of form should be marked in a logical calculus. But we are left to wonder why the judgment stroke marks the *basis* of Frege's logical contributions rather than merely a modest step toward the ideal of a fully perspicuous logical symbolism.

After a long hiatus there seems to have been a recent revival of interest in the judgment stroke, and two recent articles advance alternative rationales. In a recent number of *Erkenntnis*, Dirk Greimann argues that Frege's description of the judgment stroke as a mark of assertion is misleading, and that the stroke functions rather as what Greimann calls a "truth operator."[35] Another recent analysis proposes an

---

[34] Frege 1897b: 247.
[35] Greimann 2000.

independent rationale for this reading. Nicholas Smith's interpretation
relies on Frege's odd insistence that inferences can only hold among
premises that are both true and acknowledged as true.[36] This is, to say
the least, a surprising claim from a contemporary perspective. We have
come to think of inference in terms of validity, and to think of validity as
quite independent of soundness. Indeed, we are so accustomed to this
way of thinking that we can hardly recognize alternatives. But if indeed
inference requires true premises, as Frege seems to hold, then one can
see that the logician's formal representation of an inference must
include some marker of the truth of its premises.

These recent contributions to the literature on the judgment stroke
certainly advance the discussion, but they leave behind residual problems.
In particular, both Greimann and Smith intend their interpretations to
save Frege from the charge of psychologism by associating the judgment
stroke with truth rather than with the psychological act of asserting.
Greimann's account of the stroke as truth-operator is meant to remove
it from the domain of psychology, and Smith argues that the charge of
psychologism no longer holds once we appreciate the idiosyncrasies of
Frege's conception of inference. But it is far from clear that these claims
are sustainable. It would seem, after all, that to mark a content with a truth
operator simply is to assert it – or at least to purport to assert it. Hence,
Greimann's interpretation seems to leave a psychological residuum in the
Begriffsschrift. And while Frege's criterion for inference may indeed warrant the inclusion of the judgment stroke, it nonetheless seems to require
the inclusion of a marker of a psychological act – particularly given Smith's
strong reading which requires that premises be both true and acknowledged as true. One way or another, the psychologism issue persists.

If we take our bearing from Frege's ten-line fragment, then a third
line of defense suggests itself. The starting point in this case is Frege's
well-known insistence that a logical symbolism must avoid the many
logical defects of natural language. The most basic requirement of a
logically perfect language is that it be free of ambiguity. This means not
only that each symbol must have a single well-defined meaning, it also
requires that every logically significant difference of form be marked
symbolically. Now if we think about the subject-predicate construction in
ordinary language, there is an important sense in which this latter
criterion is not met. In both English and German, for instance,

---

[36] Smith 2000.

predicative unity is often marked by what traditional logicians and grammarians call the copula. The most common form of the copula is of course a form of the verb, "to be." Hence in English, the addition of the word "is" between the words "Socrates" and "wise" stands as a mark of predicative unity. Whereas "Socrates, wisdom" is a mere list, "Socrates is wise" is a proposition (in the language of the *Begriffsschrift*: a judgeable content). Where the copula itself is absent, we typically have other grammatical resources – in particular the inflection of the verb – to serve the same function. Significantly, however, this is not the only function served by the copula and other markers of predicative unity. When I utter "is" between "Socrates" and "wise," I not only mark my utterance as an act of predication; I also assert the truth of what is thereby marked. In this sense, the copula and other marks of predicative unity serve a double function. Now this sort of ambiguity is, by Frege's standard, just the sort of defect in natural language that the logician must avoid, and we can see the introduction of the judgment stroke as an attempt to remedy it. The judgment stroke is introduced to distinguish the two functions which are conflated in natural language.

This line of justification illuminates a number of the outstanding interpretative issues. First, it provides one answer to our earlier question about Frege's grounds for rejecting the subject-predicate analysis of judgments. *One* reason for finding the traditional analysis defective is that it relies on a form – predication – which is fundamentally ambiguous between a mark of propositional unity and a mark of assertion. Notice further that this interpretation conforms well with the remark from the ten-line fragment. Recall Frege's exact formulation: "Strictly I should have begun by mentioning the judgment stroke, *the dissociation of assertoric force from the predicate*" (emphasis added). We can also begin to understand the point Frege is making in the fragment – just what we couldn't make out on Geach's analysis. As we saw, Geach avoids the psychologism objection but fails to explain how the judgment stroke could be fundamental to Frege's logical contributions. But we can here see a sense in which the introduction of the judgment stroke marks Frege's basic departure from traditional logical analysis. The stroke marks his rejection of the basic category (predicative synthesis) upon which the traditional logic of judgment had been based. In this sense it is indeed a mark of revolution.

But if all this may help bring some clarity to the interpretative issues, it also serves to bring a new set of philosophical difficulties into view.

3 An abortive paraphrase and a redundant predicate

The third section of the *Begriffsschrift* concludes with an intriguing and widely criticized remark about the judgment stroke. Having just dismissed the notions of subject and predicate as irrelevant to logic, Frege now goes on to offer what seems to be a substantial qualification of this dismissal. He invites us to imagine a language which has but one predicate. Instead of saying that Archimedes was killed at the capture of Syracuse, one says in this language: "The violent death of Archimedes at the capture of Syracuse *is a fact*." In such a language, Frege writes, there would be no question of subject and predicate "in the usual sense," since there would be only this single predicate: *is a fact*. Remarkably, Frege then adds: "Our *Begriffsschrift* is such a language and the symbol ⊢ is its common predicate for all judgments."[37]

It is natural to read these remarks as an attempt to provide an idiomatic subject-predicate paraphrase of the judgment stroke – a way of appropriating it back into a natural language like German or English. The general strategy of the paraphrase is, in effect, to nominalize the whole judgeable content and then to treat it as the subject of a sentence whose predicate is simply "is a fact."[38] It is not clear whether Frege intends the paraphrase as a qualification of his criticism of subject-predicate analysis, or whether it is meant rather as a pedagogical device – an attempt to meet natural language halfway and thereby facilitate comprehension of the novel formulations he was about to introduce. Whatever Frege's intention, what is ultimately most important about the proposed paraphrase is its failure. Even Geach, who is otherwise sympathetic to Frege's innovation, counts these remarks as a misstep, and Frege himself would later characterize this kind of move as a miscarriage.[39]

The most salient problem is that the paraphrase makes the judgment stroke self-defeating. As we have seen, one intended function of the judgment stroke is to mark the difference between contents which are asserted as true and those which occur in a proof but are not asserted. Now, it might seem natural that such a distinction should be marked by the predicate "is a fact." It would seem, after all, that to mark a particular proposition as factual (i.e., as true) simply *is* to assert it. (Imagine

---

[37] Frege 1879: § 3, 113.
[38] See Baker and Hacker 1984: 91–95 for a treatment along these lines.
[39] Frege 1915: 252.

someone going down a list of the dead at Syracuse, somberly announcing in each case: "It is a fact.") Significantly, however, as soon as the mark of assertion is brought inside the scope of the asserted content, it fails to fulfill its assigned function. Consider the modification that Frege here proposes. We start with a subject-predicate judgment:

(1) Archimedes died a violent death at Syracuse.

Such a judgeable content can occur either as the content of an assertion or without being asserted as true. We therefore introduce the judgment stroke to resolve the ambiguity, explicitly marking the content as asserted:

(2) ⊢— Archimedes died a violent death at Syracuse.

Under Frege's proposed paraphrase we modify (2) as follows:

(2') The violent death of Archimedes at Syracuse is a fact.

But now we are back with the ambiguity that was to be avoided. I can, after all, merely entertain the idea that the death of Archimedes is a fact. The lesson applies quite generally: *if we build the mark of judgment into the content of what is judged, then the mark no longer serves its purpose*; for the new content can itself be either judged as true or merely introduced ("aroused in the reader," as Frege puts it) without itself being asserted or judged as true. The reason for the failure can be seen by applying Hume's content identity condition. A variation in belief state (between "ideas aroused in the reader" and asserted contents, for instance) must allow the content to remain identical; the variation thus cannot be marked by adding or subtracting some idea or representational content.[40] Frege's paraphrase fails to observe this constraint, and thus inevitably miscarries.

Now one might conclude, as Geach does, that the proposed paraphrase was a mistake, and that Frege simply ought to retract it. But the problem can not be so easily put to rest. For the paraphrase brings into view a problem that applies equally to the unparaphrased stroke. We can approach the issue here with a dilemma. We have already seen that Frege's conception of logic is shaped by his notion of inferential

---

[40] Hume 1739: 94 "But I go farther; and not content with asserting, that the conception of the existence of any object is no addition to the simple conception of it, I likewise maintain, that the belief of the existence joins no new ideas to those, which compose the idea of the object."

significance, which played a key role in his most prominent argument against subject-predicate logic. We have also seen that Frege identifies the inferential significance of a premise with what he calls its "conceptual content."[41] But now consider Frege's dilemma concerning the judgment stroke. In particular, pose the following question: Is the judgment stroke intended as part of the conceptual content of what is judged? If the answer is yes then the judgment stroke falls to the same fate as its paraphrase – it is built into the content of what is judged and so fails at its intended function. But if the answer is no, then by Frege's own standard the stroke ought to be excluded from a logical symbolism, since it lies outside the conceptual content, which alone is of logical significance.

One might suppose that this dilemma can be disarmed. Since the first horn is so clearly contrary to Frege's stated intentions, the solution might be thought to lie in some more careful articulation of the standard of inferential significance – a topic which famously concerned Frege in his later writings. But we should recognize that the dilemma arises out of a deeper tension – one that presses Frege toward the first horn, despite his express intentions. The *Begriffsschrift*, after all, is itself a language – albeit a highly "un-natural" one. Its explicit function is to inscribe (which is to say: express) all and only that which is of relevance to inference. This in itself may turn out to be a vain ambition. We can at least now see that it leaves the judgment stroke in an intrinsically unstable position: the stroke must somehow express something without itself being part of the content that is expressed. If it fails to express anything of logical significance then, of course, it is logically redundant. If it does express something, then the very fact of its inscription draws it into the expressed content, with the result that it fails to perform its intended function.

Both the failure of the paraphrase and the limit exhibited by that failure continued to occupy Frege's attention, largely in connection with his mature reflections on the logic of the truth predicate. This is, of course, a large topic, but one or two observations are here in order. Even if it cannot capture the sense of the judgment stroke, Frege's

---

[41] See, e.g., Frege 1879: Preface, 104: "[The *Begriffsschrift* is] intended to serve primarily to test in the most reliable way the validity of a chain of inference and to reveal every presupposition that tends to slip in unnoticed, so that its origin can be investigated. The expression of anything that is without significance for logical inference has therefore been eschewed. I have called ... that which solely mattered to me *conceptual content*." The identification of inferential significance with conceptual content is also explicit in the Plataea passage in *Begriffsschrift* § 3, cited above.

proposed paraphrase nonetheless suggests an important connection between the judgment stroke and the truth predicate. Indeed, it is useful to imagine the judgment stroke and the truth predicate as a pair of bookends at either end of the judgeable content. Like bookends, the two devices work in tandem: to prefix the judgment stroke is ipso facto to append the truth predicate; to judge is to judge as true. But unlike bookends, the work is not symmetrical. In particular, as Frege famously observes, the second bookend is strictly redundant, once the first is in place: "I judge that p is true" is equivalent to "I judge that p." But as we learn from the failed paraphrase, the second bookend cannot substitute for the first: simply using the truth predicate (or the "is a fact" predicate) does not amount to making a judgment. Frege's first explicit discussions of the redundancy of the truth predicate came later, but in retrospect we can see in the failed paraphrase Frege's first struggle with this celebrated logical problem.

But why exactly is the truth predicate redundant? What need have we for a predicate that can be universally – and hence it would seem vacuously – applied? And how could the truth predicate of all things be vacuous, given the enormous significance of a content's being true rather than false? Deflationists and ordinary language philosophers have sometimes suggested that the truth predicate is simply a mark of emphasis. To say that p is true, on this account, is simply a way of saying p louder, or a way of conveying that one intends to controvert someone who denies p. Others have emphasized that the truth predicate is useful despite its redundancy, since it allows for useful contractions such as "Everything Apollo says is true." Both of these accounts at least explain why our language would include a predicate that turns out to be strictly redundant.

Frege himself, however, doesn't approach the issue in this way at all. In those places where he does seek to explain the redundancy of the truth predicate, his explanation seems to turn on the significance of assertion or assertoric force. The most famous example of this explanation is found in a well-known passage in "The Thought":

> An advance in science usually takes place in this way: first a thought is grasped, and thus may perhaps be expressed in a propositional question; after appropriate investigations, this thought is finally recognized to be true. We express acknowledgement of truth in the form of an assertoric sentence. We do not need the word "true" for this. And even when we do use it the properly assertoric force does not lie in it, but in the assertoric sentence-form; and where this form loses its assertoric force the word "true" cannot put it back again. ... *This explains why* it is

that nothing seems to be added to a thought by attributing to it the property of truth.[42]

In these remarks and others like them, Frege seems to claim that the redundancy of the truth predicate is to be explained by the fact that it is already implicitly contained within the act of assertion or judgment. Call this the bookends explanation of redundancy: to make an assertion simply is to advance a particular propositional content as true; hence we add nothing but emphasis if we append the truth predicate to our assertion.

But if this is indeed Frege's explanation of redundancy we must insist that his explanation fails. It cannot be right because the truth predicate is redundant even where there is no assertion. To assert that p is indeed to assert that p is true. But in exactly the same way, to hope that p is to hope that p is true; to imagine that p is to imagine that p is true; and so on. In none of these cases do I put p forward as true; indeed to be in such states typically precludes assent. So there is here no assertoric context. Yet the redundancy feature persists: "I hope that p" has the same sense as "I hope that p is true"; "I fear that p is true" says nothing more or less than "I fear that p." The same is true of non-assertoric contexts with which Frege explicitly concerns himself: to ask whether p is equivalent to asking whether p is true; to entertain the hypothesis that p is the same as entertaining the hypothesis that p is true. Since the truth predicate is redundant even where there is no assertion, we cannot adequately explain the redundancy feature by noting that it is already implied by assertion.

Some of Frege's own remarks seem to indicate a recognition of this point, and even those passages which may suggest the bookends explanation also include reflections which point us in other directions. Consider, for instance, a passage from the *Nachlass* which provides one of Frege's clearest statements of the redundancy point:

> If I attach [the word "true"] to the words "that sea-water is salty" as a predicate, I likewise form a sentence that expresses a thought. For the same reason as before I put this also in the dependent form "that it is true that sea-water is salty." The thought expressed in these words coincides with the sense of the sentence "that sea-water is salty." So the sense of the word "true" is such that it does not make any essential contribution to the thought.[43]

[42] Frege 1918–19: 356.
[43] Frege 1915: 251–52.

Frege goes on in this passage to discuss the redundancy of the truth predicate for assertion, but notice that the initial claim here is independent of and broader than the thesis about assertoric contexts. The redundancy is associated with the content, which Frege here marks with the artifact of the subordinate clause. This does not of itself yield an explanation of redundancy, but at least it locates it in the right place: *the redundancy of the truth-predicate for assertion is simply one instance of its ubiquity for content*. And this suggests an inversion of the bookends explanation: the truth-predicate adds nothing to an assertion *because* it is already implicitly a feature of the propositional content itself.

To see the redundancy of the truth predicate in these terms is to recognize a basic limitation on the expressive power of the judgment stroke. Here, it is helpful to consider the use we make of a signature on various legal documents: a witness signs his testimony; the prisoner signs a confession; a jury signs its verdict. As is often the case, these formalities of justice serve to render explicit significant features of the logic of judgment. Notice first that in these legal contexts the signature functions as something very much like a judgment stroke. The signed document graphically separates the judgeable contents (the text of the testimony, verdict, etc.) from the mark of judgment (the signature). But notice also how the legal formalities bring out the crucial point we have just noted. For in an important sense the document – even before the signature is appended – itself puts forward a set of truth-claims. The sentences of the testimony express various claims about events at a particular time and place; the text of the verdict makes a claim about the guilt of the accused. This feature of the content is itself sometimes formally inscribed in such documents ("The following is a true and faithful account of the events of . . . "). Such a preamble, of course, adds nothing to the substance of the testimony itself, but it provides a graphic formal enactment of the fact that here concerns us: in signing such a document, the witness signs on to (or as we say: "endorses") a claim to truth already expressed in the content of the unsigned document. The truth-claim is in this sense an implicit feature of the content affirmed as true.

It is just this feature of propositional contents, I submit, that is reflected in the celebrated redundancy of the truth predicate, and marks a principled limit on the disambiguating function of the judgment stroke. The claim to truth, as we might put the point, is the medium of complexity for judgeable contents. Just as space is the medium of complexity of a triangle and tonality the medium of complexity of a melody, so it is *as truth-claimants* that semantic elements together constitute complex judgeable contents. Frege's judgment stroke was intended to disambiguate both natural language and traditional logic by sharply separating the truth-asserting function of predication from its function as a mark of propositional form – *to dissociate assertoric force from the predicate*. But if the truth predicate is redundant for content, rather than simply for assertion, then this disambiguation cannot be fully carried out. The content itself – the predicative unity which a judgment acknowledges as true – is in some sense always already implicitly a truth-claimant. Indeed, it is precisely this truth-claiming function of the content which makes it, in Frege's phrase, "a possible object of judgment."

We must tread carefully here: this does not mean that every judgeable content must be endorsed as true; there are, of course, many propositions we expressly deny or from which we otherwise withhold our endorsement. What is more, we can and do adopt various conventions for demarking those contents we endorse from those we deny. But notice that even in these cases the redundancy feature persists: to deny that p is to deny that p is true; to consider whether p is to consider whether p is true. Accordingly, although we may indeed use a sign to acknowledge our assent, we should not suppose that we have thereby fully separated the mark of predicative unity from the sign of a claim to truth. For fully to drain a content of its truth-claim would be to leave oneself without an eligible content of judgment.

Nearly ten years after composing the ten-line fragment, Frege once again undertook a private accounting of his logical accomplishments. The opening line of "My Basic Logical Insights" connects judgment to truth, and then goes on to a statement of the redundancy thesis: "The word 'true' seems to make the impossible possible: it allows what corresponds to the assertoric force to assume the form of a contribution to the thought. And although this attempt miscarries, or rather through the very fact that it miscarries, it indicates what is characteristic of logic."[44]

What Frege here calls a miscarriage is, of course, exactly what befell him with his paraphrase of the judgment stroke in the *Begriffsschrift*. He tried to import the mark of assertion as a contribution to the content judged as true. The miscarriage exhibits the limits of Frege's logical representation of judgment: the expressive limit of the judgment stroke and the impossibility of fully excluding the truth-claim from the content available for judgment.

[44] Frege 1915: 252.

4 Frege, Heidegger, and the logical representation of judgment

In this final section I briefly consider the pertinence of the foregoing analysis for two claims in Heidegger's philosophical logic. The very suggestion that there is such pertinence may well be found surprising. Despite a modest recent revival of interest, Heidegger's writings in philosophical logic are still neither widely known nor well understood. Indeed, his reputation as a defiant critic of logic is still better known than his contributions in this area. Even among those who have concerned themselves with his logical writings, there is a fairly broad consensus that the significance of his work on logical topics is sharply constrained by an antiquated conception of logic. Regarding the particular case of Frege's logic, it is widely acknowledged that Heidegger simply missed the boat: his 1912 report on the "New Research in Logic" notoriously contains only the briefest mention of Frege (and then mainly in connection with his anti-psychologism), and he consistently expresses distrust for what he dismisses as the overly "logistical" approach of the mathematical logicians.[45] It is not my intention here to challenge this consensus directly, nor to argue that Heidegger had any more than a passing acquaintance with Frege's logical projects. Nonetheless, we are now in a position to see that there are significant points of contact here, and in particular that Heidegger's claims in philosophical logic bear quite directly on the issues we have been tracking in Frege's revolution. It is worth reminding ourselves in this connection that Heidegger's doctoral thesis was in philosophical logic, and indeed that it focused specifically on the issue of the logical representation of judgment.[46] Moreover, both Frege and Heidegger owe a common debt to Hermann Lotze, whose logical and metaphysical views can be traced in both thinkers. We should accordingly not be surprised that in this area there are points of contact between these otherwise disparate thinkers.

A full accounting of Heidegger's logical views would be a colossal undertaking, and certainly lies beyond the scope of these studies. In the next chapter I undertake a close examination of one source for Heidegger's logical views. Here, I focus my attention somewhat myopically on two Heideggerian claims that have direct bearing on the logical issues that have been my focus in the foregoing discussion. The first is found most strikingly in a passage from 1927, and echoed elsewhere in Heidegger's logical writings: "The copula is necessarily ambiguous; but

---

[45] Heidegger 1912: see in particular 20 and 43.
[46] Heidegger 1913.

this ambiguity is not a defect. It is the expression of the intrinsically manifold structure of the being of a being – and consequently of the overall understanding of being."[47]

Part of what makes this passage striking is its positive ontological thesis. Heidegger's central philosophical concerns lie with what he calls "the question of being," yet for the most part his ontological claims are framed negatively. This remark in his 1927 lectures thus stands out as an uncharacteristically direct positive ontological thesis. But what concerns us here is not the ontological thesis but the logical claim to which it stands in immediate proximity: *the copula is necessarily ambiguous, but this ambiguity is not a defect.* For Heidegger, the logical copula provides a fertile object of philosophical interest, mainly because in its canonical form it appears as a form of the verb "to be." It thus provides an exemplary case of the way in which the cognitive accomplishments we take for granted express an implicit understanding of being – an understanding which we nonetheless find difficult to make explicit. It is for this reason that we find Heidegger returning again and again to the logical problem of the copula, from the doctoral thesis of 1913 through many of the lecture courses of the Marburg period and beyond.

So what is Heidegger's logical claim here, and what bearing does it have on the issues we have been tracking in Frege's logical revolution? It will be useful to separate three distinct claims: the copula is ambiguous; the ambiguity is necessary; the ambiguity is not a defect. In each case, I suggest, we can illuminate the Heideggerian thesis by appeal to the fate of Frege's judgment stroke. I take each point in turn.

The copula is ambiguous. Heidegger himself distinguishes several dimensions of significance in the copula, but for our purposes the one that matters is the ambiguity between its truth-claiming function and its function as a mark of predicative unity. He traces the recognition of this ambiguity back as far as Aristotle's logic: "What Aristotle had already stressed recurs once again: on the one hand the 'is' signifies combination and on the other it means being true."[48]

The copula both marks a particular semantic complex as a proposition and at the same time serves to advance that proposition as true. This truth-claiming function is most evident, Heidegger suggests, in the patterns of emphasis we deploy in speech:

---

[47] Heidegger 1927b: 205. See also Heidegger 1929–30: 332.
[48] Heidegger 1927b: 200.

For example we say "The board *is* black." This stress expresses the way in which the speaker himself understands his assertion and intends for it to be understood. The stressed "is" permits him to be saying: the board is in fact black, is in truth black; the entity about which I am making the assertion is just *as* I assert it to be. The stressed "is" expresses the *being-true* of the assertion uttered.[49]

But he immediately goes on to insist that the emphasis marks a feature that is at work even where the emphasis is absent: "To speak more precisely, in this emphasis that sometimes occurs, we see simply that at bottom in every uttered assertion the being-true of the assertion is co-intended."[50] Understood as claims about the ambiguities of natural language, these remarks coincide closely with the point we encountered in our treatment of Frege. Indeed, as we have seen, Frege's introduction of the judgment stroke was designed to resolve just this lamentable ambiguity of natural language.

The ambiguity is necessary. Here we come to the first point of divergence from Frege. Where Frege saw a contingent feature of natural language, Heidegger alleges a necessity. This is a rather striking claim, and Heidegger says little explicitly to defend it. Notice, however, that if the ambiguity is indeed necessary, then it presumably cannot be avoided by the artifice of a disambiguating sign. And indeed this is just what we have seen in the fate of Frege's judgment stroke. The stroke cannot be inscribed without failing to fulfill its function; it cannot be paraphrased without self-defeating results. If we entirely drain predicative form of its truth-claiming function then we are left without a possible content of judgment. In short: the attempt at disambiguation fails. This does not of itself establish Heidegger's thesis as to the necessity of the ambiguity, but it provides some significant support for it: even a logical system which explicitly attempts to circumvent the ambiguity fails fully to do so.

The ambiguity is not a defect. As is well known, Frege harbored a deep distrust for the vagaries of natural language. Its vagueness and ambiguities make it quite unsuitable, as he sees it, for the tasks of rigorous proof. Heidegger, of course, has a rather different view of natural language, being more disposed to look for hidden insights behind its apparent failings. But the divergence here is not simply a matter of philosophical sensibilities but of philosophical logic. Frege sees the ambiguity of predicative form as flaw both in natural language and in

[49] Heidegger 1927b: 213.
[50] Heidegger 1927b: 213.

traditional logic, and accordingly as a defect to be overcome in a logically purified calculus. Heidegger takes exactly the opposite view: "By our critical discussion of the 'is' and its ambiguity, and above all in regard to its interconnection with being-true, we are driven back once more to the fundamental ontological question."[51]

For Heidegger, the ambiguity of the copula is not a defect to be avoided but a clue to be exploited. In particular, the truth-claiming function of predicative form can be used to unearth the ontological setting of logical discourse. From his earliest writings we find Heidegger seeking to exploit this clue – from his early endorsement of Lotze's claim that validity (*Geltung*) is the mode of being of judgments to his mature view of truth as unveiledness (*aletheia*). We have encountered at least one dimension of this insight in the issues surrounding Frege's treatment of the truth predicate: the redundancy of the truth predicate for propositional content reflects a fact about the medium of complexity of judgeable contents. A judgment, as Lotze had put it, has validity (*Geltung*) as its mode of being; in a proposition a predicate is united with a subject as something that holds (*gilt*) of it.[52] The ambiguity of the copula is not a defect insofar as it reflects these features of propositional complexity and thus serves to bring them to light.

Let me conclude this chapter by bringing out one further point of contact between Frege and Heidegger. The issue in this case concerns the expressive limits of logic.[53] Here, the mature Heideggerian claim is that logic must borrow its understanding of truth. Notoriously, Heidegger claims that logic presupposes an understanding of the truth of beings – an understanding which logic cannot itself articulate, which depends on the pre-logical availability of things, and which can only be properly investigated by an ontologically-oriented phenomenology. Once again I set aside Heidegger's ontological alternative in order to focus on his philosophical logic, in particular the claim that logic presupposes and cannot explicate a pre-logical understanding of truth.

Frege, in his mature writings, also came to recognize a principled limit on the expressive capacity of logic. This thought is perhaps most familiar

---

[51] Heidegger 1927b: 223.

[52] For Heidegger's most explicit endorsement of the Lotzean position see Heidegger FS 111–12. For a more critical accounting, see Heidegger 1927b: 218–19. Lotze's account of the distinction between existence (*Sein*) and validity (*Geltung*) is developed in Lotze 1874. See in particular Bk III, ch. ii.

[53] For a helpful recent discussion see Witherspoon 2002. Witherspoon's analysis focuses on the issue of the status of Fregean functions.

and explicit in Frege's writings as the doctrine of the indefinability of truth. Logic expresses the laws of truth, Frege holds, but it treats the notion of truth as primitive and indefinable.[54] Consider these remarks from the notes for Ludwig Darmstädter:

> What is distinctive about my conception of logic is that I begin by giving pride of place to the content of the word "true," and then immediately go on to introduce a thought as that to which the question "Is it true?" is in principle applicable. So I do not begin with concepts and put them together in order to form a thought or judgment; I come by the parts of a thought by analyzing the thought. This marks off my *Begriffsschrift* from the similar inventions of Leibniz and his successors, despite what the name suggests; perhaps it was not a very happy choice on my part.[55]

Notice that Frege's thesis about truth is here situated in the context of accounting for his logical revolution: *I do not begin with concepts and put them together in order to form a thought or judgment; I come by the parts of a thought by analyzing the thought.* Frege's target is clearly the subject-predicate account of judgment, which begins with parts (concepts) and combines them into judgments. But he casts his repudiation of the subject-predicate analysis in the context of a much broader logical revolution. Here, the revolving is quite literal: a reversal of the traditional direction of analysis in logic. The traditional logics typically begin with concepts or ideas – some kind of representational content which is taken as the primitive logical notion – with judgments and inferences then introduced as characteristic combinations of these primitives. This traditional progression amounts to a kind of *Aufbau*: inferences are "built up" out of judgments, which are themselves "built up" from concepts. As we see in the notes for Darmstädter, Frege's repudiation of subject-predicate logic is now cast as a repudiation of this whole approach to logical analysis. Indeed, he goes so far as to reconsider the very name he had given to his symbolism. *Begriffs-schrift* (literally: "concept-script") is a misleading title, insofar as it suggests the traditional approach which gives "pride of place" to concepts.

But if Frege now rejects the traditional *Aufbau*, then what is his alternative? In particular, what takes the place of concepts as the primitive logical notion? Commentators have sometimes presented Frege's

---

[54] There are many places where we find Frege developing this thesis, particularly in the late writings. See, e.g., the opening pages of Frege 1918–19 and the beginning of Frege 1879. I rely here mainly on Frege's notes for Ludwig Darmstädter, which is a particularly revealing source for Frege's mature reflections on this topic.

[55] Frege 1919: 253.

alternative as the doctrine of "the primacy of judgment." Judgments (or "thoughts"), on this reading, are logically and even ontologically basic for Frege, while concepts are generated by a kind of logical dissolution. What Frege insists here, however, is that the most basic logical notion is neither concept nor judgment but truth. In particular, what Frege now calls "thoughts" – propositional contents, the relata in inferences – are introduced by appeal to the notion of truth. The corollary of this approach, however, is that the notion of truth must itself be left as primitive. It is the first and last definiens, but never itself defined. Here, Frege effectively approaches the central claim of Heidegger's mature philosophical logic. The logician's account of judgment must *begin* with an understanding of truth. If I do not understand the notion of truth then I shall not understand "the question of truth," and I shall be quite at a loss to understand the logical definitions which depend on these notions.

This point of coincidence between Frege and Heidegger is noteworthy in its own right, but what I wish to emphasize here is its bearing on the paradoxes of the judgment stroke and the truth-predicate. As we have seen, the notions of truth and judgment are inexorably intertwined in Frege's logic. The initial introduction of the judgment stroke characterizes judgment as the acknowledgment of truth; the problems of the paraphrase exhibit its complex entanglement with the truth-predicate. In short: the recognition of truth is the character of judgment. As long as we already have an understanding of truth we shall be able to recognize predicative unities as the truth-claiming complexes that they are. In judgment we assent to some such complexes while withholding assent from others; and we communicate our assent to other judges who participate in this shared understanding. In this mundane sense something like the judgment stroke is unproblematically available to us. But such marks of assent cannot find a stable place in a logically purified language – in particular not in a language that sets out to express all and only that which is of inferential significance. For part of what is of significance for inferential is a pre-logical understanding of truth and judgment – an understanding that logic can neither express nor define.

4

HEIDEGGER AND THE PHENOMENO-LOGIC OF JUDGMENT: METHODS OF PHENOMENOLOGY IN THE DISSERTATION OF 1913

At the outset of these studies we distinguished three faces of judgment: psychology, logic, phenomenology. Our first three case studies have all concerned themselves in one way or another with issues at the meeting point of logic and psychology. In turning now to the work of Martin Heidegger we come at last to a figure explicitly associated with the so-called "phenomenological movement."[1] Even here, however, I propose to follow the strategy we have been using all along, and accordingly train our focus where phenomenology comes into closest proximity to the logical treatment of judgment. In this instance that means focusing on an almost entirely neglected source in Heidegger's corpus: his doctoral dissertation (1913), *Die Lehre vom Urteil im Psychologismus*.[2] Heidegger's thesis has not been widely studied, and there are a number of misconceptions about it, so I begin by dispelling a few myths. First, Heidegger's thesis was not supervised by Husserl. Although it is common and partly

---

I am grateful to Stephan Käufer, Joseph Schear, and Aaron Schiller for comments on an earlier draft of this chapter.

[1] On the treatment of phenomenology as a "movement," see Spiegelberg 1960.

[2] *The Doctrine of Judgment in Psychologism*. The thesis has been published at least three times, first in 1914 in a very limited edition (Leipzig: Johannes Barth Verlag), and then again in 1972 and 1978 (Frankfurt: Klostermann), but to my knowledge has never been translated. Citations to this work are preceded by FS, and refer to the pagination of Martin Heidegger, *Frühe Schriften* (Frankfurt: Klostermann, 1972). The 1972 pagination is provided in the margins of vol. 1 of the *Gesamtausgabe* (Frankfurt, Klostermann, 1978).

accurate to cast Husserl and Heidegger in the archetypal *Doktorvater* roles (pioneering professor, brilliant patricidal student), Heidegger's doctoral work was undertaken prior to his personal contact with Husserl. As we shall see, the only extended discussion of Husserl in the dissertation is sharply critical.[3] The thesis was in fact supervised by Arthur Schneider, who was mainly a medievalist, but also made a rather odd contribution to the history of psychology.[4] Second, Heidegger's thesis was not on Duns Scotus. It is true that Heidegger's *Habilitationsschrift* (the second thesis required in the German university system) dealt with the category theory of the medieval ontologist; or perhaps it would be more proper to say that Heidegger *intended* the Habilitation to deal with Duns Scotus. The text on which Heidegger focuses in the second thesis is now attributed rather to Thomas of Erfurt (a fateful omen for Heideggerian historiography, and an exercise for theorists of intentional reference). Heidegger's *doctoral* thesis was not in the history of philosophy at all; it was an attempt to review and assess a strictly contemporary debate *in logic*. In fact the topic of the thesis was more or less our topic in this book: the doctrine or theory of judgment – *Die Lehre vom Urteil*.

It is surprising, given the extraordinary scholarly attention that has been devoted to Heidegger's writings, that the doctoral thesis has received very little attention. This is very much as Heidegger thought it should be. Writing reflectively in 1972 he described the thesis as *hilflos* (helpless), and insists that at the time he knew nothing of the course his subsequent work would take.[5] Scholars, even those explicitly taking a biographical approach to Heidegger's thought, have implicitly shared this assessment and uniformly pass over the thesis with little or no comment. There are a few exceptions. Ott's biography does devote three pages to the thesis, but his discussion mainly focuses on Heidegger's decision to transfer out of the Catholic *Lehrstuhl* at Freiburg, and on his ambitions to succeed his supervisor when Schneider left for Straßburg in 1913. He says nothing of the content of the thesis itself.[6] It is perhaps more surprising to find the same silence in Kisiel's account of *The Genesis of Heidegger's Being and Time*.[7] Kisiel's exclusion of the thesis is accomplished in part by calendrical fiat (his focus is on the "years of silence"

---

[3] FS 55–56n. I discuss this note in detail in section 2 below.
[4] Ott 1988: 75. For Schneider's contribution in psychology see Schneider 1903–1906.
[5] FS ix.
[6] Ott 1988: 74–79.
[7] Kisiel 1993.

between the Scotus thesis and the publication of *Being and Time*). Nonetheless, in a book which so deliberately follows its title in purporting to provide "the Book of Genesis for a great classic,"[8] the silence over the dissertation carries an implicature. In recent years there has been a minor revival of work on Heidegger's logical writings.[9] But even among those who have explicitly concerned themselves with the early work in logic, the thesis has generally been dismissed as mere student work, "tedious and inconsequential in its details."[10]

All this neglect may well be justified; it is hard to tell in advance. Certainly it is the case that Heidegger's mature projects and commitments diverge radically from this work from his student days; indeed in no small part the thesis belongs to a vision for philosophical enquiry that Heidegger himself later came to scorn.[11] But we shall soon find, at the very least, that the dissertation does belong to the *Genesis* of Heidegger's mature thinking, if only perhaps as an Appendix A. I shall try to show more than that, however, and in what follows identify three central elements of mature Heideggerian positions that receive their first articulation in the thesis, albeit in an unfamiliar context and in one instance under insistent negation.

But these details about Heidegger's intellectual development are at most a subsidiary concern of the discussion that follows. My primary aim is to use Heidegger's dissertation as a resource in tackling the specifically phenomenological aspects of judgment: how does judgment figure in experience? how do judgments manifest themselves to us as what they

---

[8] Kisiel 1993: 2.

[9] See, e.g., Crowell 1981, 1992; Käufer 1998, 2001; Witherspoon 2002.

[10] Käufer 1998: 51. Although I shall dispute this assessment in what follows, I must add that I am enormously grateful for the guidance that Käufer's pioneering work has provided. A few other discussions of Heidegger's dissertation should also be mentioned here: Hobe 1971, Fay 1974, Crowell 1981, Mohanty 1988, Courtine 1997, Friedman 2000. For the most part these discussions of the dissertation pass almost entirely over its details. A detailed discussion of the administrative setting of the dissertation (including the CV Heidegger submitted with the dissertation and the text of the *Gutachten* by Heidegger's examiners) is provided in Sheehan 1988. The most comprehensive discussion of the dissertation of which I am aware is itself a doctoral thesis (Stewart 1977), portions of which were published as Stewart 1979. I am grateful to Käufer and to Steve Crowell for their help in this search of the literature. To provide some context and contrast, it is perhaps worth reporting that at the time of writing, a keyword search for "Heidegger" in *The Philosopher's Index* yields 5,985 hits.

[11] The best examples of Heidegger's scorn come from the Marburg lecture courses, where, among other things, he denounces speculation about some third realm of entities as "no less doubtful than medieval speculation about angels" (Heidegger 1927b: 306). As we shall see, there were very strong Platonistic elements in Heidegger's position in the thesis.

are? In particular, I focus in what follows on the lessons to be drawn from Heidegger's dissertation concerning the available *methods* for a phenomenological account of judgment. It is worth remembering that in the cases we have examined so far, attempts to tackle phenomenological questions about judgment have uniformly ended in failure. Hume sought to articulate the distinctive subjective manifestation of believing something to be true, but he first falsified the phenomenological facts with his claims about the force and vivacity of judgments, and in his second attempt was reduced to phenomenological silence – the two basic forms of phenomenological failure. In Libet's experiments we saw the failure to integrate the experience of judgment into a physiological timeline without distorting the temporality and logical dimensions of judgmental phenomena. And Kant based his account of the role of judgment in experience upon a logic of judgment that he himself helped to undermine. In light of these failures we face a real and substantive question about how and indeed whether a phenomenological account of judgment is possible at all.

In Heidegger's dissertation, I shall argue, we find significant resources for tackling this problem. Although the explicit topic of the thesis is the logic rather than the phenomenology of judgment, Heidegger's approach is informed by phenomenological analysis and in turn suggests a strategy for identifying and articulating the distinctive phenomenology of judgment. Indeed, I argue in what follows that the dissertation suggests two discrete and ultimately incompatible models for phenomenological reflection on judgment. The first is the explicit position of the thesis, which Heidegger himself describes as "logicism." The second emerges in Heidegger's critical exchange with the logical positions discussed in the thesis, and can perhaps best be described as a phenomenology of judgmental comportment.

The discussion proceeds as follows: in the first section I provide a preliminary orientation in Heidegger's thesis, reviewing in turn the context, targets, and methods of the dissertation, and specifying the character of Heidegger's logicism. In the following section I investigate the ontology of judgment as developed in the dissertation, comparing Heidegger's account both to Husserl's position in the *Logical Investigations* and also to Lotze's ontology of validity. The third section takes up some of the logical details of the thesis, particularly in connection with Heinrich Maier's account of negation and Theodor Lipps' account of the comportment of judgment. The final section draws out the significance of these results for the phenomenological investigation of judgment.

1 Heidegger's logicism and the content identity condition

Heidegger's doctoral dissertation is, somewhat surprisingly, a model of clarity, clear organization, and precision of expression. Indeed, one can in good conscience recommend it to any dissertator as a model to follow. It has a well-defined and clearly delimited aim, clear and substantive opponents, a systematic methodology, explicitly stated arguments, and definite conclusions. Its results are substantive and original, if also modest and in important respects derivative – particularly when compared to the astonishing originality of Heidegger's later writings.

In order to understand the argument of the dissertation it is perhaps best to begin with the last word in Heidegger's title: Psychologism. "Psychologism" seems always to have been a fighting word in philosophy, and the action of the dissertation is set against the backdrop of the Psychologism Wars which raged just as furiously at the beginning of the twentieth century as they did again at century's end.[12] I cannot here undertake a reconstruction of the whole heated debate, but offer at least this characterization of the contested issue. The central dispute concerned the question of whether logic is properly understood as the science of reasoning, and hence ought to be counted a branch of empirical psychology. As is often the case in heated academic battles, the debate was in part one about resources. It was mainly in the late nineteenth-century German-speaking universities that empirical psychology emerged as an experimental discipline and mathematical science. Within the universities, however, psychology continued to be treated as part of the philosophical curriculum. So the question, as ever, was in part about who would get the professorial chairs, and the money, to support their research. But at the same time, the psychologism disputes turned on much more narrowly defined and specifically philosophical questions. What, in particular, is the status of the laws of logic – the axioms and rules of inference one presupposes whenever an inference is made? How are they discovered or proven? What is the source and character of their normativity? The main proponents of the psychologistic program held that the laws of logic are ultimately the laws of thinking or

[12] For a detailed historical study of the nineteenth-century battle over psychologism, see Kusch 1995. As recently as 1989, Baker and Hacker described the debate over psychologism as of purely historical interest: "All these points are sound even if their restatement has little value in an era in which naturalist psychologism is not a serious disease among writers on philosophical logic" (Baker and Hacker 1989: 87). On the revival of psychologism at the end of the twentieth century, see Kitcher 1992, Maddy 2002.

reasoning well, that thinking is a psycho-biological operation of intelligent organisms, and hence that logic is properly a branch of psychology. This position often went along with a distinctively modernist stance toward the history and future of the discipline: if logic is to break out of its moribund state, it should be less deferential to traditional approaches and grounded instead in the latest psychological research.

The opponents of psychologism were the main founding figures of twentieth-century philosophy, both in its "analytic" and "phenomeno-logical" schools: Frege, Russell, Carnap on one side, Husserl and (as we shall see presently) the young Heidegger on the other. But the anti-psychologistic movement had deeper roots in nineteenth-century logic. Kant famously counted psychology as a source of impurity in general logic, and Lotze introduced the metaphysics of meaning that is now associated most closely with Frege's Third Realm.[13] The position of the anti-psychologistic camp was that logic could not be founded in psycho-logy on pain of circularity, relativism, and loss of strict generality. The classic statement of the anti-psychologistic position is the book-length Prolegomena to Husserl's *Logical Investigations* (1900), itself prompted in part by the charge of psychologism that Frege had levied against Husserl's own earlier work in the philosophy of mathematics. Among Husserl's many arguments against psychologism, three predominate. He argues first that logic cannot be treated as an empirical discipline since it is presupposed by all scientific inquiry: since any scientific reasoning must presuppose the law of non-contradiction (to take the most fundamental example) no scientific reasoning can establish it. Secondly, to treat logic as a science of thinking is to engage in what Husserl calls anthropologism – it is to make logical claims into claims about human thinking organisms (or whatever other organisms the logician happens to study). But this, Husserl argues, is fundamentally to mistake the scope and distinctive generality of logical laws, which apply not only to all judges but to all objects of judgment. The logical principle of identity does not apply simply to organisms like us; it is a constitutive law of thinking as such. The bottom of this slope is relativism, on Husserl's account. If logic is treated as laws of thought for creatures like us, our reasoning can have no legitimate claim upon anyone who happens to think differently than us – logical aliens, as Wittgenstein would call them. As is familiar from the more recent Psychologism

---

[13] For Kant's anti-psychologism see Ak. 9: 14. For an eloquent statement of the metaphysics of the Third Realm see Lotze's "The World of Ideas": Lotze 1874: II: 200–22.

Wars, the rhetoric in this debate was heated and revealing. Sigwart calls for logic to be founded "not upon an effete tradition, but on a new investigation of thought as it actually is in its psychological foundations"; Husserl expresses his fear that the naturalizing psychologizers are "a growing danger to our culture."[14]

In a debate in which the same grand charges and counter-charges are tossed back and forth, it is a great merit of Heidegger's dissertation that it focuses almost exclusively on matters of logical detail. Although Heidegger in places invokes the grand charges against psychologistic logic, he does not much rehearse them. Instead, he turns to examine in detail how psychologistic logicians handle a particular problem of logic: the problem of specifying the logical character and formal structure of judgment. Accordingly, the main work of the thesis is devoted to detailed exposition and assessment of four representative treatments of judgment in psychologistic logic. In each case Heidegger approaches the theory of judgment with a set of five questions: how is judgment in general defined? and how are four basic forms of judgment handled: negative, existential, hypothetical, impersonal? Each chapter is divided into two parts, the first summarizing the theory under scrutiny, the second critically assessing it. The thesis as a whole concludes with a chapter in which Heidegger answers the questions he had been posing of others.

In finding one's way in the dissertation it helps to have in hand characterizations in the theatrical sense. The argument of the thesis is carried out very systematically against four representative psychologistic theorists. Of the four, Wundt and Brentano are the figures now remembered. Wilhelm Wundt was a pioneer in the development of empirical psychology, and is often credited with having established the first ongoing research laboratory for psychological experimentation. But in the logic of judgment he is the most conservative of the four. His account of judgment closely follows Kant in its treatment of judgment as a feature of self-conscious mental activity, and it follows the Kantian definition in treating judgment as "a form of combination and division of concepts."[15] Brentano is another celebrated founding figure, in this case of the

---

[14] Sigwart 1873: I: x; Husserl 1911: 78. For a critical assessment of the anti-psychologistic arguments on which Heidegger relies, see Stewart 1979. For a broader reply to the stock arguments against psychologism, see Kitcher 1992.

[15] See FS 8–9. It is worth pointing out, though I will not take up this issue here, that Heidegger's Preface to the dissertation casts the project as an intervention in the appropriation of Kant's philosophical legacy. The struggle over that legacy continues to this day,

phenomenological movement. We have seen above the main elements of his approach to the logic of judgment, with his strenuous resistance to the synthetic model and his privileging of existential judgment. With the other two figures treated in the thesis we must turn to the dustier shelves in the history of psychology. Heinrich Maier's early work (to which Heidegger is responding in 1913) concerned the psychology of the emotions; one of his most insistently argued claims anticipates a thesis that has since become the received wisdom among psychologists: one cannot, Maier argues, sharply distinguish the emotional from the rational processes of the mind; the two are everywhere and inextricably intertwined.[16] Finally there is Theodor Lipps, an enormously prolific writer who made contributions in many areas of psychology – and also, according to Heidegger, shifted his basic views a lot. Lipps is treated last in the thesis, and the recounting of his various positions is undertaken in considerable detail. Where Heidegger's treatment of the other figures is harsh to the point of ridicule,[17] he treats Lipps as progressing away from early erroneous ("extreme psychologistic") positions toward a properly "pure" conception of the judgment of logic. As we shall see, Lipps is also responsible for introducing a central method of Heidegger's mature phenomenological approach – although in 1913 Heidegger still strenuously resists it.

In figuring Heidegger's place in the Psychologism Wars, we can begin with the term "logicism" – a slogan with which Heidegger more and more openly aligns himself as the thesis unfolds. In our own contemporary philosophical parlance, "logicism" has become the proper name of a proposition – the thesis, famously advanced by Frege and Russell, that the basic laws of arithmetic are wholly derivable from logic.[18] But although there are certain affinities between this familiar logicism and Heidegger's position (both are opponents of psychologism, in particular), the logicism of the dissertation bears only indirectly on issues in the philosophy of mathematics. Aside from one mathematical example, and

with many of the same lines of division that Heidegger marks out in the thesis. Some self-professed Kantians seek to take seriously Kant's psychological theories; others sharply reject the thesis that Kant's "faculties of cognition" are to be understood as psychological mechanisms. For a discussion of Heidegger's early projects in connection with the dominant neo-Kantian movement among his contemporaries, see Käufer 1998: ch. iv. For the two sides in the recent struggle over Kant's psychology see Allison 1983 and Kitcher 1990.

[16] For a recent treatment see Damasio 1994; the point is in fact as old as Aristotle.

[17] See, e.g., the critical assessment of Maier, whose theory Heidegger denounces as "*widersinnig*" (FS 52), and "noteworthy mainly for having hardly noticed the recent confrontation with logicism" (FS 56).

[18] For a dramatic instance of this usage see King 2003.

some remarks about the psychology of counting, Heidegger has virtually nothing to say about mathematical truth or knowledge. (Heidegger had originally announced that his *Habilitationschrift* was to concern the phenomenology of mathematics, but he later changed course toward historical topics.)[19] Accordingly our first task must be to determine the character of Heidegger's logicist commitments.

Although there are certain hints about this in the critical exchanges with the psychologistic logicians in the body of the dissertation, the clearest development of Heidegger's logicist commitments comes in the final, constructive, chapter of the thesis, where Heidegger sketches his own positions. Heidegger there begins by summarizing the critical points that had emerged in the particular studies, and concludes the first part of the chapter with an italicized paragraph of one sentence: *Die Problematik des Urteils liegt nicht im Psychischen* – "the problematic of judgment does not lie in the psychological domain."[20] In support of this he invokes the arguments, familiar from Frege and Husserl, that psychologism is essentially self-defeating: it aims to be science but ends up in relativism. But like Husserl, Heidegger is dissatisfied with this "merely negative" refutation: "Psychologism, it is often said, is ultimately refuted by its relativistic consequences, but a positive proof against it, that is, a proof that *alongside the psychological there is yet a domain of the logical*, can never be undertaken."[21]

A number of comments are in order concerning this formulation. Notice first Heidegger's appeal to "a domain of the logical [*ein Gebeit des Logische*]" which is in some sense "alongside [*neben*]" the psychological. Heidegger's early logicism is centered around this commitment to what he calls "logical objects [*logische Gegenstände*]," which he takes to be both the proper objects of investigation in logic and the ultimate truth-makers of logical principles. In some sense that we will need to specify, Heidegger's stance on psychologism thus turns on an ontological commitment – a claim about the metaphysical standing of the proper objects of logic. Some care must be taken here, however. In calling judgments objects, Heidegger does not mean to suggest that they are physically extended, spatio-temporal entities. Quite to the contrary: he sharply distinguishes logical objects from any physical or psychological object or process. An object (*Gegenstand*) in this context is anything about

[19] Sheehan 1988. For Heidegger's mature philosophy of mathematics see Heidegger 1952.
[20] FS 106.
[21] FS 107, emphasis added.

which there are objective truths. To mark this sense Heidegger sometimes uses the term "objectivities" (*Gegenständlichkeiten*) in connection
with logical objects. Irreal or abstract objects are explicitly included as
objectivities in this sense, since there are objective truths to be discovered
about them: "By the real [*das Wirkliche*] is to be understood anything that
becomes an object and stands in the possibility of objectivity, hence
also the Unreal."[22]

The objects to which the logicist is committed are thus objects only in
the minimal sense that there are objective truths concerning them. For
Heidegger, however, this is enough to distinguish the logicist position
sharply from its psychological rivals: a theory of judgment is *psychological*
if its truth or falsity turns on the acts or actions or processes of thinking
subjects. It is properly *logical* only if it wholly abstracts from such psychological facts and concerns itself exclusively with the "*Nebensbereich*" of
logical truth-makers. Heidegger is vigilant in denouncing as psychologistic any theory of judgment that strays from its focus on such logical
objects.[23]

But how are we to prove that there are such logical objects? This is the
crux of the question about a positive proof of logicism. It is one thing to
show that psychologism has seemingly absurd consequences, but this is
certainly not sufficient to show that there are logical objectivities as
Heidegger insists. Can there be a positive proof of logicism? Here we
arrive at the first recognizably phenomenological moment in the
dissertation. Heidegger insists, first of all, that the demand for a proof
makes little sense unless one already recognizes the difference between
psychological and logical processes. But he goes on to propose that what
is needed here is not a *proof* of logical objects, but rather an *exhibition* of
them: "It is important to note that the real as such cannot be proved, but
in any case only exhibited [nicht *be*wiesen sondern allenfalls nur *auf*-
gewiesen werden kann]."[24] And it is just such an exhibition that
Heidegger sets out to provide.

The exhibition comes by way of an extended phenomenological
description. Heidegger takes as his example his own judgment concerning the color of a certain book. He begins with a description of four cases
where he makes such a judgment:

---

[22] FS 107.
[23] Some examples: "A 'logic of judgment' is something nonsensical as long as judgment is
    considered as a psychological process" (FS 52). "As soon and as long as one considers the
    judgment of logic as a psychological reality, relativism is unavoidable" (FS 56).
[24] FS 107, original emphasis.

I look, for instance, at the book lying before me and I judge, without even being conscious of doing so: "The binding is yellow." The "judgment" arises suddenly in me, without my being aware of any intention to pass judgment concerning the binding of the book in question. In another case it occurs to me, as an arbitrary diversion of thought, to compare the books in front of me according to their color. I compare each book in the series to the one standing next to it. Arriving once again at the same volume as before I judge by distinguishing it from the grey one standing next to it: "The binding is yellow." Or I go out for my usual walk and see on the ground a yellow pen. I am reminded of the color of the binding and I judge again: "The binding is yellow." Or I am talking to someone about Natorp's book, *The Logical Foundations of the Exact Sciences*, and he asks the question at issue: How is the book bound? I answer and judge: "The binding is yellow."[25]

The first phenomenological point Heidegger makes about these cases is that the actual state of conscious awareness – what he calls the *Bewußtseinslage* – varies substantially from each case to the next. In one case I am explicitly asked about the binding, in others I come to judge quite without intention; in some cases the book is present to me, in others it is not, etc. Accordingly, the particular content of conscious experience at what Heidegger calls "the instant of passing judgment [*Augenblick der Urteilsfällung*]" varies dramatically. But the crucial point is that amidst all this thoroughgoing variation in psychological content we find a correlative constancy of judgmental content:

> It is clear that in all the different cases in which I judge concerning the binding, my state of conscious awareness [*Bewußtseinslage*] varies. The circumstances which occasion my judgment also vary. In answering a question, I may reflect carefully as to how I should answer, while in another case, prompted by the color of the pen, I am hardly aware of the judgment. Whether I arrive at the judgment through conscious deliberation or through an arbitrary association, whether the book in its specific format and size is explicitly present to me or not, with all these "modifications of consciousness" at the instant of passing judgment, with all the variation in the timing of judgment, I encounter in each act of judgment a *constant factor*, each time I say: "The binding is yellow."[26]

This "constant factor" becomes the phenomenological foundation for Heidegger's analysis: alongside variation of psychological (or what

---

[25] FS 109.
[26] FS 109, emphasis added.

Husserl would call *"reell"*) content, there is something that remains constant, something which retains its identity, something "perduring."[27] As Heidegger puts it: "We set out from an act of judgment – or more precisely from various discrete acts of judgment – but we have found something *non-psychological* [*ein Nichtpsychisches*]."[28]

It is worth emphasizing both the distinctively phenomenological approach that Heidegger takes here, and also the specific phenomeno-logical method on which he relies. The phenomenological aspects of the undertaking are most striking in the inclusion, in a work of logic, of this attention to and report on the author's own experience – the characteristic confessional idiom of first-personal phenomenology. But we should also recognize a distinctive method for phenomenology here, what we might well call the master method or master argument of the early phenomenological movement. One starts by noticing and emphasizing the dynamic flux characteristic of our conscious lives: the course of conscious experience, considered as occurrent content from moment to moment, is constantly changing. Heidegger invokes Bergson on this point, specifically his claim to have established that exactly the same conscious state can never occur twice.[29] Having noted such flux and variation, however, the phenomenological task is then to attend to and articulate what remains constant across it. This is the core of the method Husserl had proposed – the method of eidetic or imaginative variation.

In this case, what remains constant across these imaginative variations simply is the truth-evaluable judgment that the binding is yellow. Since it remains constant while psychological content varies, Heidegger claims title to conclude that the judgment is not itself to be identified as a psychological object: "The logical judgment, the judgment of logic, cannot be found in psychology, if logic and psychology concern them-selves with different kinds of objects and distinct realms of problems."[30]

---

[27] "Wir sind über die psychologischen Verschiedenheiten der gefällten Urteile hinweg auf etwas Beharrendes, Identisches gestoßen" (FS 109).

[28] FS 110–11, original emphasis. See also FS 110: "Und doch ist zuzugestehen, in den besagten Urteilen wurde 'das Gelbsein des Einbandes' in seiner unverrückbaren Derselbigkeit und Veränderungsfrendheit angetroffen. Also bleibt nur die eine Möglichkeit, es außerhalb des ständig fließenden psychischen Verlaufs zu stellen."

[29] Bergson 1889. Bergson argued that any purported second occurrence of an experience is inevitably colored by the fact that it has occurred before, by whatever has come in between, as well as by contextual variation between the two cases. In the unusual case of an experiential state that very exactly mimics an earlier experience, the second instance involves the further thought: *Déjà vu*, and thereby differs from the first.

[30] FS 107.

Notice that we here encounter once again a version of the content identity condition which has figured so persistently in the arguments of the preceding case studies. Whatever judgment is, it must be capable of retaining its identity through variation of psychological state or place in a proof. Heidegger here relies on the content identity condition to identify and distinguish the judgment of interest in logic from the psychological domain.[31]

Having "exhibited" the logical domain through phenomenological analysis, Heidegger proceeds to apply his discovery in support of a thesis that would be central to his mature position: once the distinctively logical domain has been recognized, we must also recognize the fundamental inadequacy of subject-object ontology for the task of phenomenological articulation. The argument on this point proceeds by way of a familiar dilemma. It has been customary, at least since Descartes, to divide the real between mind and world, or subject and object: a domain of extended physical objects on one side and a private internal space of subjective representational states (the stream of consciousness) on the other. If we follow the tradition and accept this disjunction, then we face the dilemma: are logical objects mind or world? Is the judgment about the color of the binding something subjective or objective? Psychical or physical? According to Heidegger, neither position will suffice. We have already seen that the judgment – the self-same "perduring" content common to discrete instances of judging – is not part of the fleeting psychological stream of representation. Should we say then that it is a physical object? This seems equally unacceptable. As Heidegger puts it: what the bookbinder binds is the book – not some judgment about it. The latter is not the kind of thing that we can encounter as a spatio-temporally extended particular, party to causal relations. So it seems that the judgment is not an object (*Objekt*) either:[32]

---

[31] Obviously much more would have to be said in order to defend or assess this argument. In particular, even if occurrent psychic content is constantly changing, one still might identify the judgment with some enduring or recurring *pattern* within that flux – much as certain kinds of clouds on mountain ridges maintain their form despite a constant exchange of water molecules in high velocity winds. This was in fact more-or-less Husserl's position in the *Logical Investigations*: the semantic content of an experience, he argues there, is a characteristic form or structure that is instantiated in our fluid experience. But the point is then that such forms or patterns cannot be identified with the fleeting conscious content itself. It retains its identity through variation, recurs in different individuals (whether at different times or simultaneously), and is the subject matter of various logical truths. For a discussion see Martin 1999.

[32] It is of course a *Gegenstand*, according to Heidegger – the subject matter of objective truths; but it is not a spatially extended *Objekt*.

> Does this puzzling identity [*rätselhaft Identische*] exist at all, if it can be counted neither in the psychic nor in the physical domain? Just as surely as either classification fails, just so certainly do we have something determinate before us [*ein bestimmtes Etwas vor uns*] – that is, it is some kind of object, something "standing over against," although of course not in the literal spatial sense. The mode of being and structure of this something is as yet of course still undetermined.[33]

If judgments are given to us in experience – and it should be evident that they are – then one cannot identify the content of our experience within the confines of a subject-object ontology. Whatever the metaphysical merits or demerits of Cartesian dualism, it simply fails as a framework for the phenomenological task of articulating the contents of experience.

I don't propose here to defend this argument from all objections – though I try to give it as forceful a statement as I can, since I confess to finding it compelling. At this point I content myself if I have established a first body of evidence in support of my two theses. First, against Kisiel and the elder Heidegger: however "*hilflos*" the dissertation may have been, it certainly does figure among the origins of *Being and Time*, if only because in it we find Heidegger's first invocation of a principle of ontological difference in support of the rejection of subject-object metaphysics as a framework for phenomenology. The more important result, however, is a first exhibit in support of my major thesis: that the doctoral dissertation proposes methodology for the phenomenology of judgment. So far we have seen one such method: in order to articulate the character of judgment as it figures in experience, focus on what remains constant across a range of cases of experienced judgment. What one finds holding constant is essentially a logical complex, distinct from both subjective psychological associations and spatio-temporal relations. The structure of this complex can be articulated in pure logic.

2 Ontological difference circa 1913

Before trying to identify a second phenomenological method in the dissertation, I pause in this section to address an objection – both because answering it is important to the defense of my thesis concerning the place of the dissertation in Heidegger's development, and because assessing it will illuminate the young Heidegger's distinctive concerns.

---

[33] FS 110. For a reiteration of this line of argument in the mature period see Heidegger 1927b: § 9b.

In particular, we must consider the objection that the phenomenology we have uncovered amidst the logic of the dissertation cannot properly be said to be *Heidegger's* phenomenology; that is, it does not really anticipate the phenomenological teachings of the mature Heidegger. As Kisiel provocatively puts it: Heidegger before 1919 was not *Heidegger*.[34] In particular, it seems, both the logical and the phenomenological doctrines of the dissertation are essentially Husserlian, indeed almost mimetically so.[35] If we have found Heidegger insisting on a kind of ontological difference in the logical theory of judgment, it is really the ontological difference of Husserl's *Logical Investigations*: the insistence on a difference of metaphysical kind between the fleeting contents of consciousness and the abstract objects which form the ideal intentional content of experience and are the proper objects of logical and phenomenological investigation. This would seem to be just the sort of appeal to a third realm of entities that Heidegger would ridicule in his mature writings as "no less doubtful than medieval speculation about angels."[36]

There is considerable truth in this objection, and it is indeed fair to say that the methodology we have discovered so far in the dissertation is in its fundamental orientation Husserlian. Note the central points of agreement: the intentional content of experience is said to be formal and abstract, distinct both from "psychic" content and from spatio-temporal objects in the world; it can be studied by systematically isolating what remains constant or retains its identity under imaginative or eidetic variation; the structure of this intentional content is articulated by logic.[37] Moreover, even the rhetorical structure of the dissertation is largely borrowed from Husserl: Heidegger relies on Husserlian arguments against psychologism; his dilemma is taken from Husserl's

---

[34] Kisiel 1993: 3.

[35] Heidegger himself emphasized the importance of Husserl's influence, most publically in his dedication and footnote in *Being and Time*, but also in the *Lebenslauf* (a narrative CV) that he submitted in 1915 with his application to teach at Freiburg: "Besides the *Small Summa* of Thomas Aquinas and individual works of Bonaventura, it was the *Logical Investigations* of Edmund Husserl that were decisive for the process of my scientific development." For a translation and analysis of the *Lebenslauf* see Sheehan 1988.

[36] Heidegger 1927b: 306: "The consequences of this impossible predicament of inquiry appear in the theory's being driven to every possible device – for instance, it sees that truth is not in objects, but also not in subjects, and so it comes up with a third realm of meaning, an invention no less doubtful than medieval speculation about angels." BP: s. 18a.

[37] Here is Heidegger, at what would seem to be his most Husserlian/Fregean: "Whenever I speak or write, I say *something*; I try to communicate *something*. In the case we have been discussing this is the being-yellow of the binding – that is, the static moment, the communicated content, the content or sense [*Sinn*] of the sentence." FS 112, original emphasis.

response to Brentano; and even his move from a negative to a positive critique of psychologism is borrowed from Husserl's phenomenological manifesto ("Philosophy as Rigorous Science"), published in the maiden volume of *Logos* just as Heidegger was writing up his dissertation.[38] Finally, there can be no denying that the mature Heidegger departs considerably from the position he had staked out in 1913. Nonetheless, it would be a mistake to read the thesis as simply parroting Husserlian doctrines. In fact, Heidegger explicitly considers the Husserlian position (in a long *Anmerkung* at the end of chapter 2) and explicitly rejects it. It will be worth considering this point in a bit more detail, if only to explode a third myth about Heidegger's development. It is often said (and sometimes heatedly so) that Heidegger turned against Husserl. But this is not so. Heidegger did not turn against Husserl; he was *always* against Husserl.

At the time that Heidegger was writing the dissertation, the main Husserlian texts to which he was responding were the *Logical Investigations* (first edition: 1900–1901; the much-revised second edition only began to appear in 1913) and "Philosophy as Rigorous Science" (1911). In the Prolegomena to the *Investigations* Husserl had developed his attack on psychologism, and as we have seen Heidegger echoes and endorses many of the Husserlian arguments. But for Husserl too, the attack on psychologism leaves open the question about its alternative. Like the young Heidegger, Husserl argues that the proper object of logical investigation is not to be seen as any kind of psychological or material reality. And like Heidegger, his alternative is to see the objects of logic as a kind of abstract entity. The position of the *Investigations* is that these objects are species (*Spezies*) – abstract universals that are instantiated in a subject who entertains a certain thought. Much as we find the species "horse" instantiated in individual horses, or "triangle" in particular triangular objects, so, Husserl maintains, a propositional content – say, the Pythagorean Theorem – is instantiated in a conscious subject each time someone thinks it. In numerically discrete and qualitatively different instances of thinking that thought, the stream of consciousness and subjective (*reell*) content may vary more-or-less dramatically, but each act of thinking nonetheless instantiates a common abstract form. According to Husserl, it is this abstract form that is party to inferential relations, but it is itself outside of time and space, and can be strictly identical across instances of thinking the same thought.[39]

---

[38] Husserl 1911.

[39] For an elegant treatment of Husserl's distinctive metaphysics of meaning, and its difference from Frege's account, see Willard 1972.

In a famous passage in the First Investigation Husserl clarifies this position with the example of the red slips of paper. The slips of paper are like our particular acts of judging: spatio-temporally located particulars. Yet all these tokens instantiate a common abstract essence or form, namely redness, which is itself an object (or objectivity) in the specific sense of being the topic of objective truths:

> The genuine identity that we here assert is none other than the *identity of the species*. As a species, and only as a species, can it embrace in unity ... and as an ideal unity, the dispersed manifold of individual particulars. ... The meaning is related to varied acts of meaning (the logical representation to representative acts, logical judgment to acts of judging, logical inference to acts of inferring) just as redness *in specie* is related to the slips of paper which lie here, and which all "have" the same redness. Each slip has, in addition to other constitutive aspects (extension, form, etc.), its own individual redness, i.e., its instance of this color-species, though this neither exists in the slip nor anywhere else in the whole world, and particularly not "in our thinking," insofar as this latter is part of the domain of real being, the sphere of temporality.[40]

Again here, we should emphasize that there are continuities and similarities between this position and Heidegger's in the dissertation: both reject the subject-object framework as inadequate for the specification of the meaning-content of consciousness; both locate the proper objects of logic as some kind of abstract, seemingly platonistic, objective reality. But Heidegger in 1913 already rejects the Husserlian position; his grounds for resisting it are instructive.

Two passages in the dissertation are particularly relevant to this point. We see a first important hint about it in the way Heidegger manages the dilemma discussed above. For where Husserl operates with a dilemma, Heidegger effectively substitutes a trilemma. As we have seen, Heidegger tries to show the inadequacy of subject-object metaphysics for phenomenology by showing that something we evidently encounter in experience – namely a judgment – cannot be accommodated as either a subjective psychological state or as an extended physical object in space and time. But after pressing this dilemma against the psychologistic position, Heidegger goes on to consider a third alternative. Should we perhaps conclude that judgments are neither subject nor object but rather some kind of metaphysical third thing?

---

[40] Husserl 1900–1901, First Investigation: § 31, original emphasis.

Heidegger's consideration of this alternative is one of the most striking passages in the dissertation. He starts by reemphasizing the basic
phenomenological observation and the negative conclusions to which he
claims title: "Something [*Ein Etwas*] stands before us in its identity; it is
there [*ist da*]. But we cannot yet illuminate this *existence* [*Dasein*] in its
essence. Negatively we know this much: the object in question is in no way
a physical, spatio-temporally determined thing, nor does it stand on the
side of the psychic occurrence."[41]

But he then goes on to consider (and reject) the appeal to some third
kind of entity, a "third thing," distinct from both subjective conscious
content and spatio-temporal object:

> There remains the possibility of assigning it some metaphysical standing.
> But this is also ruled out – not because there are no metaphysical beings, or
> because we could not know of their existence by way of some inference,
> but rather because such a metaphysical being is *never* known with *that*
> immediacy with which we become aware of the something in question.[42]

The appeal to a third realm, Heidegger insists, cannot account for the
presence to consciousness of a judgmental content. For if there are such
abstract metaphysical entities then they can only become manifest to our
experience through some mediating inferential path (*auf dem Wege der
Schlußfolgerung*) – perhaps in the way we become cognizant of irrational
numbers or black holes. But this clearly will not suffice. In the first
instance, we can only travel down such inferential paths if we are *already*
cognizant of judgments. And secondly, the mediation of such an inferential path is out of keeping with the distinctive immediacy with which
we find ourselves confronted with logical objects. Hence, the appeal to a
third realm of entities is idle.[43]

---

[41] FS 111. It is worth noting that Heidegger has not yet adopted his mature usage of "*Dasein*"
as a kind of successor term to "subject" or "human being" – a technical term for the kind of
being that we ourselves are. Here "*Dasein*" has its ordinary German sense of existence,
albeit with emphasis on the sense suggested by its etymology: something *is there* for us (*Es ist
da*); what we don't yet know is "the essence of this existence" (*dieses Dasein ... in seinem
Wesen*). In the continuation of the passage, as we shall see, Heidegger begins to draw a
distinction between *Dasein* and *Existenz*.

[42] FS 111, original emphasis.

[43] This argument is not conclusive, I think, since the Husserlian can always claim that the
universal *is* immediately given in experience, and that only a prejudice against *abstracta*
leads us to deny this. Encountering Mt. Humphries as I cross the Sierra Crest, I not only
experience a particular mountain as given; it is given in my experience *as a mountain*, and
in this sense a universal or species might be said to be immediately given in my experience.

On the basis of his trilemma, Heidegger claims title to rule out the possibility that judgments are any kind of thing or entity at all:

> Hence the last possible mode of existence is ruled out. The identical moment in the existing psychological process of judging therefore does *not itself exist, and yet it is there* [*existiert also nicht, und doch ist es da*] and imposes itself [*macht sich ... geltend*] with a force and irrefutability by contrast to which psychic reality can only be called fleeting and transient. There must accordingly be another mode of being-there [*Daseinsform*] alongside the possible modes of existence [*Existenzart*] of physical, psychical and metaphysical.[44]

Although Husserl is not named in this passage, we get a first sense of the line Heidegger takes against him, starting already here in the dissertation. Notice that Heidegger's difference with Husserl does not in the first instance have anything to do with the possibility or impossibility of the phenomenological reductions, nor with the difference between a transcendental and a hermeneutic phenomenology, nor in differences over the relation between theory and practice. It turns rather on the proper understanding of the ontological setting of judgment. If we reify judgments and other logical objects – whether psychologically or metaphysically – we effectively multiply the entities in our ontology. But the addition of logical entities fails to explain how such entities are intelligibly present to us in experience. What is needed, Heidegger concludes, is some account of how something can "be there" without existing – a "*Daseinsform*" as distinct from an "*Existenzart*." This is, I believe, Heidegger's first attempt at formulating a principle of ontological difference. Although he is not yet using the terminology which contrasts "being" (*Sein*) with "beings" or "entities" (*Seienden*), and while he has not yet settled into the mode of questioning he later describes in terms of "the question of being" (*die Seinsfrage*), he does here insist on an ontological difference which cannot be reduced to a difference between entities of different kinds (concrete v. abstract; material v. psychological; real v. *reell*) but must be cast rather as a contrast between existing things generally and some kind of reality that is not itself an existing entity.

(This is a position that I have heard defended most vigorously by students from what one might call the USC School of Phenomenology, in particular David Kasimir and Walter Hopp.) There is a danger here of a standoff over what is in fact given in experience – one of the characteristic dead-ends in which phenomenological inquiry can find itself caught.

[44] FS 111, emphasis added.

We get an important clarification of Heidegger's position on this point in a note that was very likely the last passage of the dissertation to be written. Heidegger's second chapter dealt with Heinrich Maier's account of judgment in *Psychologie des emotionalen Denkens* (1908). After Heidegger had defended his thesis (July 1913), but prior to its first publication (1914), a new essay by Maier appeared in a *Festschrift* for Alois Riehl.[45] In the published version of the dissertation Heidegger appended a long note to his second chapter, addressing this latest formulation of Maier's position. In its substance, Heidegger claims, nothing of significance has changed in Maier's psychologistic account. But the new essay undertook what Maier himself had called "a critique of absolutist logic," explicitly cast as a response to Husserl's attack on psychologism. Strikingly, Heidegger does not rise to Husserl's defense, but suggests rather that Maier has chosen an unduly weak version of the anti-psychologistic (or "absolutist") position:

> In his critique of "absolutist logic," Maier takes as his point of departure a distinction of Husserl's that I find to be not entirely satisfactory. The act of judgment is supposed to be a "particular" or "instantiation" of the valid sense of judgment [*geltendes Urteilssinnes*], which is itself taken to be a "universal" or "species." But sense and act belong in completely different realms of the real, realms which should not be assimilated to the relation between universal and particular – a relationship that itself applies within each of the two different worlds. The working out of the difference between the logical and psychological must emphasize other moments of which Husserl is at the very least unaware.[46]

Heidegger does not here explain how these "other moments" should be understood, but his rejection of the Husserlian position is unambiguous. Husserl is correct to distinguish logical objects from both subjects and objects, but he fundamentally mistakes their ontological character by treating them as abstract entities of a special sort – universals subsuming particular psychological events as their instances. What we see here, then, is that Heidegger does not follow Husserl's positive position. Indeed, he clearly signals that he views the ontological proposal of the *Investigations* as a mistake (*nicht glücklich*).[47] Moreover, as we have seen, in his resistance

---

[45] Maier 1914; for biographical details concerning the submission and examination of the dissertation, see Sheehan 1988.

[46] FS 56.

[47] FS 56. Husserl himself seems to have been sensitive to the concern that his species-instance model failed to capture the distinctive relation between the content and act of a thought or experience. In *Ideen* he famously introduces the notion of a noema in order to describe the

to the Husserlian position we find posed the problem of ontological difference that would be the overarching concern of the mature Heidegger.[48]

Finally, Heidegger's resistance to the Husserlian proposal also helps makes sense of the allegiance to the figure to whom he most consistently defers in the thesis: Hermann Lotze. Although Lotze was no longer living when the battle over psychologistic logic reached its peak around the turn of the century, his *Logic* (first edition, 1874) was an important source for the anti-psychologistic movement. Like Husserl and Frege, Lotze denied that logical objects can be treated as either subjective mental contents or as spatio-temporally determined objects. But whereas Husserl and Frege sought to accommodate logical objects as part of some third realm of entities, Lotze argues that they cannot properly be viewed as entities or "things" at all. His alternative is cast in the language of *"Geltung"* or validity, and in the dissertation, Heidegger very explicitly follows his lead and invokes his authority. A judgment, Heidegger writes, is properly not a thing at all, not something that exists. Rather, its mode of being is validity: *"The form of reality of this identical factor, uncovered in the process of judging, can only be validity. Being-yellow may be valid of the binding; but it never exists."*[49]

This is certainly not an easy thought to appropriate, but the central idea seems to be this. Judgments have a characteristic complexity – they have parts that contribute to the distinctive character of the whole – but the mode of their complexity is not the same as that of entities. Their parts are not spatially related to one another, nor are they causally or associatively related. It is helpful here to think of the analogous case of a geometrical shape or numerical series, which are likewise abstract truth-makers exhibiting a characteristic complexity. One might well say of geometrical shapes or number sequences that they are neither subjective states nor physical objects; on this point Frege, Husserl, Lotze, and the young Heidegger are all in agreement. But in order to

distinctive abstract entity at work in intentional experience and thought. But it should be clear from the dissertation that this position would not satisfy Heidegger either, turning as it does on appeal to yet another entity or "mode of existence" (*Existenzart*) rather than attempting to fathom the thought of some "realm of the real" (*Wirklichkeitsbereich*) that is not itself an entity at all. For various interpretations of the Husserlian noema, see the essays collected in Dreyfus and Hall 1982.

[48] For an overview of Heidegger's lifelong concern with the question of being see Olafson 1993.

[49] FS 111–12, original emphasis: "Die Wirklichkeitsform des im Urteilsvorgang aufgedeckten identischen Faktors kann nur das Gelten sein. Das Gelbsein des Einbandes gilt allenfalls, existiert aber nie."

understand what kind of *abstracta* are in question one needs to go further. Certainly in the mathematical case we have objects (*Gegenstände*) in the very broad sense of that term that Heidegger and Husserl rely on: there are objective truths about them. But in order to specify these correlates of objective truths – these objectivities – one must specify the medium of their complexity. In the geometrical case that medium is geometrical space: a triangle is a certain abstract objectivity whose parts relate to one another in space. In the case of judgments or propositions, by contrast, the medium of relation is validity. The judgment that Socrates is wise, for instance, relates wisdom to Socrates as something that is true or is valid or "holds" (*gilt*) of him. Lotze maintains that this form of *Geltung* is *sui generis* – a distinctive mode of complexity characteristic of logical objects, and not to be confused with or reduced to either spatial, physical, or psychological relations.[50] In the dissertation Heidegger follows Lotze's lead in insisting that the logical objectivities with which the pure logical theory of judgment is concerned are no kind of thing – neither mental nor physical nor somehow metaphysical. They *are* not; rather they *are valid*.

Heidegger himself would not long be satisfied by the Lotzean solution to the problems of the ontology of logic. By the time of the Marburg lecture courses on logic he was submitting the Lotzean position itself to ruthless critique. Nonetheless, his adherence to the position in the dissertation is of considerable importance. First, it illuminates his resistance to the Husserlian position: Husserl is right in distinguishing logical objects both from mental representations and from physical objects, but he mistakes their true ontological character in treating them as species or universals. This in turn helps us to recognize a logical impetus for the ontological project of Heidegger's mature philosophy. As we have seen, Heidegger explicitly rejects attempts to accommodate judgments as either subjective episodes or configurations of physical objects. He argues emphatically the judgments can retain their identity through both subjective and objective variation. But he also rejects the available proposals to assimilate judgments to some other metaphysical type. This leaves him with the problem of articulating an ontological difference which does not reduce to a difference in kind of entity.

---

[50] "As little as we can explain how it happens that anything at all *is* or *occurs*, so little can we explain how it comes about that a truth has validity; the latter conception has to be regarded as much as the former as ultimate and underivable, a conception of which everyone may know what he means by it, but which cannot be constructed out of any constituent elements which do not already contain it": Lotze 1874: II: 209–10.

In his later writings he would mercilessly criticize the leading anti-psychologizers for their failure to tackle this ontological problem.

In sum, then, we can see here another and deeper sense in which Heidegger's mature projects emerged from his early work on the judgment problem. The question of being (the *Seinsfrage*) is the uniting principle that brings together all of Heidegger's writings, early and late.[51] What we have seen here is that this question has its origins and finds its first expression in Heidegger's attempt to come to terms with the distinctive ontology of judgment.

3 World and comportment in the psychologistic logics of Maier and Lipps

So far we have concerned ourselves mainly with Heidegger's account of the ontological setting of judgment. But in fact the bulk of the dissertation is taken up not with this positive, metalogical proposal, but rather in the critical engagement with the logical specifics of the four psychologistic accounts of judgment. I turn in this section to consider two of these more narrowly logical engagements of the dissertation.

A Heinrich Maier on the logic of negation

Heinrich Maier was a follower of Christoph Sigwart, himself one of the leading figures of the psychologistic movement, and one of Husserl's principal targets in the *Investigations*. Maier's monumental work of 1908 undertook a *Psychology of Emotional Thought*, setting out to show the ways in which our broadly cognitive capacities depend on and are intertwined with emotional states and moods. One major portion of the work – the third of five major divisions – dealt with judgment, combining a psycho-genetic account of judgment with a reconstruction of the major forms traditionally treated in the logic textbooks. Although traces of Maier's approach to the emotions can be found in Heidegger's mature thought, in the thesis itself Heidegger sets aside Maier's broader thesis in order to focus on the logical theory of judgment to which Maier commits himself on psychological grounds. Even here, as we shall see, Heidegger's approach is highly selective: he sifts out most of Maier's psychological claims in order to focus on Maier's positions on the questions Heidegger

---

[51] Olafson 1993.

poses of each of the psychologistic logicians: how is judgment defined; what are its essential elements; and how are the logical forms of negative, existential, impersonal, and conditional judgments handled?

The point of departure in Maier's analysis is his critique of two strongly entrenched assumptions in epistemology and logic: first, that all knowing or cognizing (*Erkennen*) must be "dressed as judgments," and secondly that the elementary form of truth-evaluable representation requires subject-predicate synthesis. Maier rejects both claims. Against the former he argues that various emotional responses provide us with knowledge without themselves taking the form of judgments. (In feeling afraid I cognize my environment as dangerous without actually judging it to be so.) Against the latter he argues that some unsynthesized representations can – and indeed must – be counted as primitive, truth-evaluable judgments.

In making this case, Maier takes as his example the simple judgment that the sun is shining. If we trace such a judgment back to its psychological roots, he argues, we will find a form of judgment that does not conform to the traditional preconceptions. At the very least, he claims, we must distinguish the fully articulated and verbalized judgment from the perception on which it rests:

> If we want to confirm that what is thought in this judgment conforms to reality then obviously we consult perception. The perception of the shining sun is thus also the ground on which our perceptual judgment rests. So we are led back from the judgment "the sun is shining" to a corresponding perception.[52]

But now is this perception itself judgmental in character? Maier argues that it must be:

> But if the latter [the perception] is indeed to serve as the foundation of this judgment, then the perception itself must somehow carry in itself a subjective guarantee [*eine subjective Gewähr*], in virtue of which it is capable of underwriting the judgment. This guarantee, however, lies once again in a consciousness of validity [*Geltungsbewußtsein*], in the consciousness that in perception I represent something real. Indeed it requires considerable sophistical artifice if one tries to consider the perception in abstraction from this consciousness. But if one acknowledges it then one is forced to the assumption that in perception itself there is already a judgment taking place – a judgment in comparison

[52] Maier 1908: 146–47.

to which the judgment to be tested [the fully articulated judgment that the sun is shining] is obviously of a secondary nature.[53]

Since the perception of the shining sun involves a "consciousness of validity" – the recognition of something real – Maier argues that it must be counted as a variety of judgment.

Having distinguished the articulated judgment from the primary judgment "in perception itself," Maier then sets out to identify what this judgment in perception amounts to. The usual views, he argues, have made the mistake of reading the grammatical structure of declarative sentences back into this more primordial experience of validity, and accordingly treat even these inarticulate judgments of experience as involving some kind of subject-predicate synthesis. But Maier challenges this assumption, arguing that even the perceptual judgment that the sun is shining itself presupposes a yet more primitive judgment – viz., that *something* is shining, or better: *there is shine*:

> Just how little judgments of this kind – i.e., judgments of the kind expressed in grammatically completed assertions – can serve as the elementary confirmation for the judgment-function can be seen from the fact that we can always immediately contrast them to an undoubtedly more original judgment: the proposition, "it shines" [*der Satz: "es leuchtet"*]. Moreover, the judgment "the sun is shining" obviously presupposes yet another as already carried out. For even the subject term – namely, "the sun" – is only given through the perception; I carry out the judgment in the face of the shining sun. ... Indeed I represent the sun as a real thing, standing in the heavens, streaming heat, etc. All this rests on the basis of a perception that, although it is not the object of my representation, serves nonetheless as its foundation. To this as a completed, presupposed perception I add once again the consciousness of validity, which gives me the certainty that the perception corresponds to reality.[54]

On Maier's account, then, the conscious presence of an object (the sun), or indeed the presence of some as yet unattributed perceptual feature (shininess?), must itself involve primitive, inarticulate judgments. In these "wordless" judgments, I register some feature in my conscious content, which I experience with a kind of force of validity in virtue of which I interpret it as something corresponding to a real

---

[53] Maier 1908: 147.
[54] Maier 1908: 147.

feature in my environment.[55] Such primitive judgments cannot themselves be of the traditional subject-predicate form, Maier reasons, if they are providing the basic materials from which such synthetic judgments are composed.

> In short: the subject-representation, "the sun" is obviously itself already the result of a judgment, a perceptual judgment of a much more elementary nature than the judgment "the sun shines." Hence we trace the latter from two sides back to a simpler form of judgment – to judgments that are themselves included in perception itself.[56]

In a striking reversal of the standard logics, Maier proposes that the basic form of judgment is accordingly not the subject-predicate synthesis but rather the so-called "impersonal judgment" – as for instance "it is raining," "it is foggy," or "there's the tram." As we saw in Chapter 2, these grammatical forms of natural language had been a thorn in the side of the orthodox logics, since they had to be accommodated somehow to the requisite subject-predicate form. Maier, by contrast, argues that they are neither aberrations nor anomalies but rather the closest linguistic manifestation of the most fundamental form of judgment, in which a feature of one's experience is acknowledged as having validity, specifically as presenting something objective in the environment. Ultimately, however, even the impersonal grammatical form tends to misrepresent these psychologically primitive judgments, suggesting that there must be some subject-term, "*es*," of which the feature is predicated. In order to avoid this suggestion Maier introduces an orthographical device designed to resist any such assumption: "If I seek a linguistic garment in which to dress the judgment in which I perceive a tree then I don't say 'this is a tree,' but rather '– a tree.'"[57] The blank in such "sentences" is meant to indicate that we have here a judgment for which no subject is specifiable.

The remainder of Maier's account of judgment then takes its orientation from these psychologically primitive judgments. Maier's strategy is to identify what he calls the "constituent acts" (*Teilakte*) of judgment. Since our primitive judgments are not yet synthetic in the traditional sense (they do not involve the combination of a pair of simpler representations), we must look elsewhere to specify their constitutive structure. For while

---

[55] The similarities of this account to Hume's are striking, as Maier himself acknowledges (Maier 1908: 148). Heidegger's mention of this similarity (FS 36) is one of the very few explicit mentions of Hume in his entire corpus.

[56] Maier 1908: 147.

[57] Maier 1908: 148.

these primitive, inarticulate acts of judgment may be lacking in the traditional forms of complexity, they are by no means simple or unstructured.

Maier holds that the unfolding of these simple judgments reflects a structure that is in fact common to all judgments. He describes it as involving two interpretative acts performed upon a conscious content: an act of comparison (*Gleichsetzung*) and an act of objectification (*Objektivierung*). In the most primitive case, I compare some occurrent representation to some recalled content, and on the basis of this comparison I then interpret my subjective representation as applying to some independent object – to something alien outside me (*Etwas Fremdes außer mir*), as Maier puts it. Accordingly, the basic structure of judgments, from the most simple and silent to the most complex and articulate, involves at minimum three steps. Using another of Maier's examples we can divide them as follows:

a I register some conscious representational content, e.g., the characteristic rumbling caused by an approaching tram.
b I compare this occurrent content, either to some familiar remembered content or in some unfolding sequence of representations, e.g., I compare this registration of the rumbling to past similar experiences, or I notice a progression in the intensity of the rumbling as I see a particular shape looming larger in my visual field.
c On the basis of these comparisons I form the judgment, attributing the subjectively registered feature to an object posited as existing independently of me. In the preferred script for basic judgments: "– the tram."

In some cases, but by no means in all, this silent operation of the mind both occasions and warrants my fully articulated judgment: "The tram is coming." In this complex psychological unfolding, according to Maier, we find both the genesis of judgment and its fundamental character.

A crucial detail must concern us at this point, for it will be of considerable importance in what follows. In particular, we need to specify more closely the exact role of the comparison (*Gleichsetzung*) in the psychological process Maier describes. In the example we have just considered, the comparison of a present and a past conscious content forms the basis or ground for the perceptual judgment. But we must now ask more carefully about this "grounding." First, there is the question as to whether the comparison serves as a *cause* of the perceptual judgment or as its *warrant*. That is, is Maier's claim that my act of comparison simply *brings about* my act of judging that the tram is coming, or does it figure as the *justification* of that judgment? On this point Maier's position is not entirely explicit, but his answer seems to be *both*. While his aim is to identify the psychological unfolding of these basic judgments, he also holds that this largely involuntary causal process provides the evidence which warrants or justifies the judgment. As we shall see, this position is held by Heidegger to exemplify Maier's too-ready mixing of psychological and logical claims. But it also brings into focus a separate and important detail of Maier's position. For one might expect, given this claim about the role of comparison, that Maier would hold that the act of comparison is itself distinct from the judgment it purportedly both causes and warrants. But this is not Maier's view. The act of comparison, he claims, is not separate from and prior to the act of judgment, but is rather one of its component parts (*Teilakte*):

> The elementary act of judgment has two sides. On the one hand it carries out a comparison between the content which is grasped and the content of a reproduced representation; on the other hand it objectifies the representational content that it interprets in this way [*den so interpretierten Vorstellungsinhalt*]. A comparison of two representational contents occurs in every judgment, even the most primitive. The interpretation [*Auffassung*] of a representation arising in the soul is only possible insofar as its content is attached to the content of a familiar representation occurring in consciousness.[58]

Maier never squarely confronts the tension in this position. (Can a part be the cause of the whole of which it is a constituent? Can it serve to justify or warrant that whole?) But this claim about the role of comparison has important ramifications in his approach to the more complex forms of judgment. For on the basis of this account of the psychological role of comparison, Maier claims that all judgments, even the most simple, exhibit an inner complexity, and implicitly express a comparison or relation of some sort. This complexity is evident in some cases ("A man is on a horse," "The inn stands next to the church"),[59] but it is also at work in the simplest cases. When I judge that the tram is coming, I effectively compare or relate my subjective state to an object which I posit as its cause. In order to bring out the underlying psychological structure of different judgment forms, then, the psychologically informed logician must identify the comparisons at work in each of the traditional forms.

[58] Maier 1908: 149.
[59] Maier 1908: 218.

So how does Heidegger assess Maier's approach? No small part of his "critical evaluation" is devoted to documenting Maier's psychologism and anthropologism. He does not challenge Maier's psychological construction but vigorously disputes his equation of psychologically primitive acts of judging and logically elementary judgment-forms. Here is an exemplary passage, with emphasis and outraged punctuation taken from the original:

> At this point the *decisive* question arises: *Is there really a coincidence between the elementary judgment of logic and the primitive judgment that Maier identifies in his analysis?* ... From the outset of his investigation Maier moves in the domain of psychic *processes*, psychological activities, the course of representing. He investigates the *activity* of judgment, the *process* of judgment; he speaks of a "logical *doing*" (!); the *act* of judgment is put together out of logical component *acts*; the essence of judgment is an *activity* of objectification, at its most basic level indeed an *"involuntary process."* In short, the object of investigation is *judging* – something that, as a psychological activity, *necessarily belongs to the problems of psychology.*[60]

According to Heidegger, all this is of necessity a fundamental mistake – an error about the proper objects of investigation in logic, and a fallacy in moving from psychological premises to logical conclusions. If logical objects belong to a timeless, abstract reality, wholly distinct from any passing processes, acts, or activities, then Maier's investigations can make no legitimate claim to have touched the genuinely logical issues about judgment. Considered as logic, Heidegger concludes, Maier's theory is *"völlig wertlos."*[61]

This is, of course, a wholly external criticism of Maier's project; indeed in retrospect it is somewhat comic to find Heidegger going to such lengths and expressing such shock in showing that Maier is doing exactly what he said he would do, starting from the very first page of his book. Nonetheless, it is worth taking note of the strict standard Heidegger seeks to enforce here: *any mention* of acts, processes, activities, doings, etc. is enough to tarnish a theory of judgment with the taint of psychologism. A strictly logical account of judgment, it seems, must assiduously avoid any such appeal. But in addition to these merely external criticisms, Heidegger also takes up a more internal line of critical engagement, specifically in connection with Maier's strategy for applying his approach

---

[60] FS 47.
[61] FS 54.

to one of the basic forms of judgment: negation. It will be worth considering this part of Maier's approach in some detail.

As we have seen, Maier's account requires that every judgment involve the psychological registration of some subjective content (whether immediately given or recalled) which is then submitted to an interpreting comparison, typically to some remembered content and thence to a posited object. But now how is this sort of account to be extended to negative judgments? When I judge that my dog stinks then I may indeed compare my subjective psychological state to the objective state of my dog, perhaps by way of a comparison of a sequence of my own sensory states as I approach and back away from it. But what of the case where I judge that my dog does *not* stink? If " – the tram" is a primitive judgment in experience, should we also say that " – no tram" is such a primitive? If so, what kind of "comparison and objectification" are involved? If not, how do we arrive at the negative judgment on the basis of the psychologically primitive ones?

Maier addresses these questions in a brief chapter devoted to the issue of negative judgment, one of the longstanding puzzles in the history of logic. The discussion occupies only ten pages out of more than 200 that Maier devotes to the psychology of judging, but in this case import is not proportional to extent. Maier's basic strategy is to treat a negative judgment as a negative answer to a question: "The process of negation, which leads to the negative judgment, 'it is not burning,' corresponds exactly to the following course of representation: 'Is it burning? – No.' More precisely: the negative judgment is a complex judgment, in which *the underlying representation is the representation of a question*."[62]

This is, in its way, an ingenious solution, one that Frege would exploit in his own way in his famous treatment of this topic a decade later. It allows us clearly to distinguish the two basic forms of negation, since my denial that my dog stinks and my denial that I have a dog are now treated simply as negative answers to two different questions. But it still leaves Maier with the burden of showing how this account of negation fits with his general characterization of judgments as comparisons or relations. What, in short, are the relata in a negative judgment?

Maier recognizes this burden and proposes to discharge it as follows. Consider first the case where I deny that a particular object has a certain feature. In these cases, Maier claims:

[62] Maier 1908: 277, original emphasis.

a certain kind of comparison does take place: a comparison between the substrate-object ... and the available perceptual data [*den vorhandenen Auffassungsdaten*]. In this case I undertake the comparison not merely to that data which may have occasioned the act of judgment, but rather to the whole which is supplied by "the given thing" that has come under consideration [*sondern den sämtlichen, die das in Betracht kommende "Gegebene" überhaupt liefert*].[63]

Whereas in a positive judgment my comparison may involve a more-or-less discrete sensory datum (e.g., the rumbling of the tram, the distinctive smell of a wet dog), a negative judgment cannot proceed piecemeal in this way. Rather, the relata in my comparison must include a certain kind of totality – the whole set of perceptual states occasioned by the object in question.

This appeal to a totality is significant. In the simplest cases, the totality in question is the totality of given sensory data associated with a particular, actually existing object. But it is easy to see that the totality must quickly scale up, in particular when we move from a negation concerning a property or feature to a negative existential judgment. If I deny that I *have* a dog, I must compare my representation of a dog to my representation of the totality of my possessions. And what if I deny that there *are* any dogs? In that case, Maier claims, the comparison is between an objective representation and "reality" (*Wirklichkeit*): "[H]ence one can say: we measure the objective representation to be examined against reality, against that portion of the real in which the object, if it were real, would have to occur."[64]

In some cases, this "portion of the real" may be delimited. If you ask whether I have a certain book on my desk, I need only compare the thought of that book to the collection of entities on my desk. But it should be clear that in an unrestricted negative existential, no such limitation can apply. If I say that there are no angels or no unicorns or no elements of atomic weight 200, then the "reality" to which I undertake a comparison must be the totality of existent things.

In Maier's detailed table of contents, this account of negative existential judgment is included under the heading "various nuances of the act of negation."[65] But its significance outstrips this designation. First of all, it is hard to avoid the sense that the subject has here subtly been changed.

[63] Maier 1908: 277–78.
[64] Maier 1908: 278.
[65] Maier 1908: xi.

Can this comparison of a representation to a totality properly be construed as a description of an unfolding psychological process at work in every act of negative judgment? When I judge that I have a cat but no dog, do I undertake a systematic survey of the total collection of my possessions? Certainly not if that means that I undertake such a comparison piecemeal. It is true, of course, that the judgment that some x does not exist *entails* that nothing existent is x. But it seems odd to say that a survey of all existent things was part of the unfolding psychological process of judgment. Or if it was, then this survey must somehow have been undertaken wholesale – by comparing my representation of x to some overarching representation I have of the totality of things. Otherwise it would seem impossible ever to complete a negative existential judgment.[66] Further, such an overarching representation of the totality could not simply be a list, unless the list is somehow represented *as a totality*, for instance, as the *exhaustive* list of my possessions. But in that case we once again presuppose some prior representation of totality. So if Maier is right about the psychology of negation then I must *begin* every act of negation with some kind of representation of the whole of things – whether the totality of features of an object, the totality of psychological states occasioned by an object, or in the limiting case the totality of the real. This marks a significant break from the Aristotelian and Kantian tradition, which treated the relata of "Socrates is *not* wise" as identical to those in "Socrates *is* wise" – namely, Socrates and wisdom.

It is worth bringing out a connection between this issue in Maier's account of negative judgment and one strand in our earlier discussion of *positive* existential judgment. Recall in particular that Kant had explored four possible solutions to the problem of accommodating his own synthetic account of judgment to his thesis that being is not a predicate.[67] As we have seen, much of the nineteenth-century aftermath of Kantian logic involved the attempt to accommodate one-place thetic judgments in the broader context of the treatment of judgment as synthesis. But recall that Kant's own earliest strategy in dealing with this problem – the position of the 1763 essay on the ontological proof – was to propose that in existential judgment, being or existence is not a predicate but a subject. Under this proposal, the theist's defining commitment is to be rendered in these terms: "Something existent is God."

---

[66] It is important to appreciate that the issue here concerns the *formulation* of a negative existential judgment, not the *proof* of one.

[67] See Chapter 2, section 3.

Suppose we are walking across campus with a prospective graduate student and you say: "There is an interdisciplinary program in cognitive science at UCSD." According to Kant it would be a mistake to suppose that in such a judgment I am attaching a predicate (existence) to the subject concept (UCSD Cognitive Science Program). But then the question naturally arises: how is it that you have just managed to convey useful information to our visitor? According to Kant's 1763 position, the answer is not that I have conveyed information *about a particular program* (namely, that it exists) but rather that I have conveyed information *about UCSD* (namely, that a particular program is included among its formal offerings). It is easy to see that this strategy very naturally scales up to totality. For how do I now say that UCSD exists? Certainly not by predicating existence of it, but rather by saying of the University of California system, for instance, that it includes a campus in San Diego. And how do I then say that the UC system exists? Before long I arrive at a point of maximal totality: the totality of existent things includes that UCSD interdisciplinary program in cognitive science. In the nineteenth century it was once again Lotze who most explicitly embraced this solution to the vexed problem of existential judgment. In the "little logic" of 1883, he offers the following account of the much-discussed and contested judgment "*es blitzt*": "Instead of saying '*es blitzt*' one could therefore say '*das Sein ist (jetzt) blitzend.*'"[68] That is, the whole totality of things that exist includes an instance (now) of lightning. And in the major logic he says of the "*es*" in such statements that it refers to "the all-embracing thought of reality, which takes now one shape, now another."[69]

Maier's account of negation essentially applies the same approach to the case of negation. In negative judgments I effectively relate some particular representation to a totality – in the simplest case to a totality of features of a particular object which I posit as existing, but in the limiting case to the totality of objects with their totality of determinations amid the whole of all things that exist. But notice the corollary of this strategy: in order to make any existential claim (on Kant's 1763 position) or any negative judgment (on Maier's 1908 position) I must somehow have at my disposal some representation of the corresponding totality. Once such a position has been adopted one must eventually face the question: how are such totalities given to us? How do we come by our prior

---

[68] Lotze 1883: § 24.
[69] Lotze 1874: vol 1, § 49.

understanding of the whole of things or the totality of properties, given
that it cannot be by simply accumulating particulars into a long list?

B Theodor Lipps on judgmental comportment

Although now largely forgotten, Theodor Lipps was an influential and
prolific contributor to the foment of psychological research around the
beginning of the twentieth century. He was the author of over a dozen
books and many articles, on themes ranging, quite literally, from tragedy
to comedy, and all manner of topics in between, including hypnosis,
spatial illusions, and musical consonance.[70] He made contributions to
aesthetic theory and in the theory of intentionality; he translated Hume's
Treatise into German; and he was the founder of an influential book-
series in aesthetics and the philosophy of art. Although he published a
logic textbook that went through several editions between 1891 and
1923, his most important contributions in this area came in his *Leitfaden
der Psychologie* (first edition 1903), and in a pair of long essays published in
1905, one on the relation between consciousness and its objects, the other
on the distinction between the content and object of thought.[71]

Lipps is the last theorist treated in Heidegger's dissertation, and his
views are handled quite differently than those of the other theorists
Heidegger discusses. The chapter on Lipps is the longest in the thesis,
and rather than providing the usual synopsis followed by his "critical
assessment," Heidegger undertakes a careful reconstruction of the
development of Lipps' views. He divides this development into three
stages, which he characterizes as exhibiting a movement from a strictly
psychologistic position, through a middle period in which Lipps recognizes the distinction among the act, content, and object of judgment, and
culminating in his most fully developed views in the essays from 1905
and the textbook most closely associated with them. Although it seems
clear that Lipps himself retains his psychologistic commitments (all three
editions of his logic textbook begin with the claim that "Logic is a
psychological discipline"),[72] Heidegger detects a progression in his

---

[70] See Knight Dunlap's overview of Lipps' major publications in the editor's preface to the
one work that has appeared in English translation: the second edition of *Psychologische
Studien* (1905; English edition 1926). For his treatment of tragedy see Lipps 1891; the
psychology of laughter is examined in *Komik und Humor* (1898).

[71] Lipps 1905a, 1905b.

[72] Lipps 1893, 1912², 1923³: 1: "Die Logik ist eine psychologische Disziplin, so gewiß das
Erkennen nur in der Psyche vorkommt und das Denken, das in ihm sich vollendet, ein

development from an "extreme psychologistic formulation"[73] at the earliest stages to a position which approaches (but never quite attains) the viewpoint of "a pure logic of judgment."[74] In what follows I shall not attempt to revisit the details of Heidegger's biographical reconstruction, but concentrate on the two ideas in Lipps' mature position which Heidegger considers most original and important.

With each of the four psychologistic theories broached in the dissertation, Heidegger proposes a brief, one-sentence slogan. These slogans do not always manage to capture what is in fact most central or original in the theories under question, but they do serve as an important indicator of what Heidegger himself seeks to emphasize. In the case of Lipps' theory of judgment, Heidegger's slogan reads as follows: "The essence of judgment lies in the comportment of the psychological subject as demanded by the object."[75] Two notions must occupy our attention in understanding this claim. The first is the notion of a demand (*Forderung*); the second is the idea of judgmental comportment (*Verhalten*). I consider each in turn.

At the heart of Lipps' account of judgment, early and late, is the idea that judgment involves the awareness of some kind of demand or felt necessity. In his *Logic*, Lipps' chapter on judgment opens with an invocation of this necessity: "The judgment is the individual act of real or purported knowledge; accordingly, any consciousness of an object, regardless of whether it is sound or unsound, or any consciousness of being necessitated [*genötigt*] in representation by the represented object, is a judgment."[76] When he comes to provide his formal definition of judgment, once again an appeal to conscious necessitation figures centrally: "[Judgment is] the consciousness of the objective necessity of a belonging together or ordering ... of the objects of consciousness."[77]

Notice the double-occurrence of "consciousness" in Lipps' definition. In many (or perhaps all) forms of consciousness I am aware of some object. But in the case of judgment, Lipps claims, there is in addition a second-order consciousness: I am conscious not only of the objects

psychisches Geschehen ist." Husserl's critique of Lipps' *Logik* is developed in ch. III of the *Prolegomena*.

[73] FS 76.

[74] See, *inter alia*, FS 96, 101, 105–6.

[75] FS 67: "Das Wesen des Urteils liegt in dem vom Gegenstand geforderten Verhalten des psychischen Subjekts."

[76] Lipps 1893: 16.

[77] Lipps 1893: 17.

themselves but also of a certain necessity in the way they are ordered or combined. The clearest exemplars of this felt necessity come in perception. Taking in a certain visual array I am aware not only of a particular book and a particular color, but of the necessity of representing the book *as being of that color*. According to Lipps, an analogous necessity is also at work in non-perceptual judgment, for instance in counting or in considering the ordering relations of the days of the week. Here again, I feel the necessity of ordering the objects of my conscious attention in one particular way rather than any other. This "felt necessity," Lipps claims, is the psychological hallmark of judgment.

But just what kind of necessity could be involved here? This is a problem with which Lipps continuously struggles. In saying that I feel the necessity of representing the book as yellow, I certainly do not mean to say that it is *necessarily* yellow – as if it could not have been a different color if the printers had decided differently. The necessity, it seems, must attach to my act of representing, rather than to the relations that I represent. But in what sense should we say that my act of representing is necessary? In his earliest formulations Lipps characterizes this felt necessity as a kind of felt compulsion or strain.[78] In hearing one tone followed by another I simply cannot hear them in any other serial ordering.[79] But as a general characterization of judgment this does not seem quite right either. There may be some cases where I find it impossible to see the book as having any other color than yellow. In such cases the perceptual situation might indeed be said to compel me to judge as I do. But this hardly seems to be a general feature of judgment. In many celebrated cases (e.g., cases of hard choices) I have trouble making up my mind precisely because the evidence fails to push me decisively into one judgment or another. So if indeed there is some felt necessity characteristic of judgment, it seems to lie neither in the represented state of affairs nor in any kind of subjective compulsion.

In Lipps' later formulations of this approach to the psychology of judgment he introduces two important distinctions. The first is the distinction between a felt *necessity* (*Nötigung*) and a felt *demand* (*Forderung*). Lipps still insists that there are indeed cases where I feel necessitated to represent in some particular way – where a judgment simply overwhelms me. (One important example is found in the phenomenon of moral revulsion, where I simply find myself unable to

---

[78] *Zwangsgefuhl; Anerstrenung;* see FS 73.
[79] Lipps 1883: 397.

withhold a judgment of moral condemnation of some scene with which I am confronted.) But Lipps now claims that the hallmark of judgment is not this feeling of being bowled over by a compulsion but rather the acknowledgement of the authority of a demand.

> The object [*Gegenstand*] is something that stands over against me; it is as it is not because of my will, but simply, factually, in or of itself – in short, "objectively" [*objective*]. And of this object I am conscious; I have an objective consciousness. The object confronts me with a "demand," [*Forderung*] a requirement of justice [*Recht*] or validity [*Geltung*], as something that demands acknowledgment [*Anerkennung*].[80]

On this view, the necessity at work in judgment is a matter of authority rather than a matter of force. In judging, I am sensitive to a demand made upon me in my act of representing. In short: I feel myself subject to the demand to represent an object or state of affairs *as it actually is*. In some cases I may not succeed in satisfying this demand; in other cases I may indeed find myself compelled into conformity with it. But the crucial feature of judgment is my awareness of the authority of this demand over my conscious representation.

The second distinction in Lipps' refined theory concerns the locus or source of this demand. Normally when we think of being placed under some demand we think of that demand as originating from some person or agent who places the demand upon us. An officer of the law demands to see my identification; the landlord demands the rent; my neighbor demands that I turn down the music. Lipps calls these "demands of the will" (*Willensforderungen*), since the demand can be traced to the will of another. In such cases it is always at least in principle possible to remove the demand by petitioning the originating agent to reconsider or retract the demand that has been made. The demand that lies at the essence of judgment, according to Lipps, is quite different. In perceiving the book as yellow, on his analysis, I experience *the book itself* as the locus or source of the demand that I represent it as such. Against this kind of demand there can be no intelligible appeal. Lipps calls these demands "objective," "logical," or "absolute":

> What I am speaking of here are not the demands of a will. Rather, the demands that I mean are logical demands. This means nothing more than that they are "objective" demands, or demands of the object. ...

---

[80] Lipps 1903: 58.

> One can make no appeal against the demands of an object. They are the
> absolute, the final authority.[81]

According to this refined account, then, it is part of the experience of
judgment to be sensitive to the absolute authority of a demand placed
upon us by an object or objective state of affairs.

An example may help bring these claims into sharper focus. Suppose
we are climbing together and after a long, difficult day we finally reach
the top of the pass. Elated that the hard work of the day is finally done,
we start to hunt around for the way down the other side. It soon becomes
apparent that the way down may be just as difficult and dangerous as the
way up. Anxious to be on our way, we pick a likely route and start to pick
our way down. At first our choice looks promising, but before long it
becomes clear that the would-be route leads to an avalanche chute, or
a sheer cliff, or a near-vertical debris flow. Initial optimism turns to
despair and we grudgingly recognize the route for what it is: a death-
trap rather than the way home. In such a case I exercise my judgment,
and in doing so I am sensitive to a demand. In part the demand is that of
my own life-force, struggling mightily to keep me alive in my foolish
endeavors. But there is also a felt demand that might indeed be experienced as emanating from the object itself: its demand to be recognized
for what it is. The demand is salient in this case because it so evidently
runs counter to my wishful thinking. But according to Lipps it is a
demand that is at work in every case of judgment, subtly or dramatically
guiding and constraining my representation of the object. Notice that
while there are many intermediary steps between the mountain pass and
my judgment (the light reflected from stone and snow, the images on my
retina, the electrical impulses cascading through my visual system – to
say nothing of the tense deliberation among the members of the party),
the *object* of judgment is that entity or state of affairs which I experience
as the locus of this demand.

Already with this example we have come to the second key notion in
Lipps' position: the idea of a comportment (*Verhalten*) characteristic of
judgment. *Verhalten* is of course a central term of art in Heidegger's own
mature philosophy. In section 12 of *Being and Time* he characterizes
Dasein as "an entity which, in its very Being, comports itself understand-
ingly toward that Being."[82] And in the Marburg lecture courses of the

---

[81] Lipps 1903: 58–59.
[82] Heidegger 1927a: 52–53: "Dasein ist Seiendes, das sich in seinem Sein verstehend zu
diesem Sein verhält."

1920s, *Verhalten* and *Verhaltungen* have become Heidegger's central terms for characterizing the phenomenon of intentionality.[83] In the dissertation of 1913, Heidegger seems to have introduced the term for the purposes of summarizing Lipps' views; Lipps himself tends to speak rather of acts (*Akte*), actions (*Handlungen*), or sometimes apperception (*Apperzipieren*). Whatever term is chosen, what is central here is the thought of a certain kind of behavior of the judge, undertaken in response to a demand experienced as originating from the object of judgment. This idea of judgmental comportment is in fact the strict correlate of the idea of a felt demand. If in a certain process I feel the force of certain demands, then I also pro tanto experience myself as a locus of agency. This is clearest in the case of demands of the will. To be oriented by the felt demands of a parent, foreman, conductor, or instructor is to experience myself as an agent, called to determine my own behavior in conformity to such demands. Something analogous is at work, according to Lipps, in the case of the "logical demands" that are experienced as originating from objects. The object of a judgment is that which guides and constrains my conscious representation. As Heidegger puts the point, summing up Lipps' views: "I hear the call of the demand, and what follows from that hearing is ... my consent, my affirmation." "My reaction ... is the acknowledgement of the demand, or the act of judgment."[84] Lipps himself, in a poetic moment, describes this comportment toward the object as a game of question and answer:

> In apperceiving the object, I make it such that the object is an object for me, and accordingly that its demands are demands upon me. The apperception is my question as to what the object demands. The demand is the answer. My relation to the object lies in this game of question and answer [*dies Frage- und Antwortspiel*].[85]

For Lipps, then, judgment is ultimately to be understood as a characteristic way in which I consciously behave or orient myself toward objects. It is to engage in conscious representation in ways that are sensitive to and guided by a demand for recognition that I experience as emanating from objects themselves.

---

[83] See, e.g., Heidegger 1927b: 16: "Dergleichen wie Sein gibt sich uns im Seinsverständnis, im Verstehen von Sein, das jedem Verhalten zu Seiendem zu grunde liegt." For a discussion see Dreyfus 1991: 57–58 et passim.

[84] FS 87; the language of "call and answer" (*Ruf und Antwort*) is taken from ch. 6 of Lipps 1905a.

[85] Lipps 1903: 60.

How does Heidegger view Lipps' proposal? His "critical assessment" is in fact considerably more moderate than those he offers of the other theories treated in the dissertation. In Lipps' movement away from a model of psychological compulsion, and in his distinction between psychological necessity and logical demands, Heidegger finds "undeniable progress."[86] Moreover, in the idea that judgment is somehow situated in the face of an unconditional demand for acknowledgement, Heidegger sees in Lipps an incipient awareness of the logical objects which, on his own position, must be the focus of a strictly logical theory of judgment. And in his recognition that this demand is strictly neither a determination of the judging subject nor of the object of judgment, Lipps comes to the edge of recognizing the inadequacy of the subject-object model.

But none of this suffices to save Lipps from Heidegger's antipsychologistic knife. Indeed, in the very proposals which bear the closest affinities to Heidegger's own mature positions, he finds the most damning evidence of Lipps' psychologistic errors. In the idea of a judgmental action or comportment, Heidegger claims, Lipps has clearly failed to transcend the domain of the psychological; in the idea that the demand for judgment could be cashed out as some kind of "logical feeling," Heidegger descries a contradiction no less blatant than an appeal to wooden iron.[87] He thus concludes: "The decisive step out of psychology and into the sphere of pure logic has thus not yet been taken. ... [T]he idea that the essence of logical judgment lies in the *act* of recognition remains psychologism."[88]

In short, since Lipps' account of judgment steers logic into the domain of actions, feelings, and comportments, it ends in the same absurdities that beset the whole psychologistic tradition.[89]

4 Methods of phenomenology in the dissertation of 1913

It is time to return to the two theses broached at the outset of this chapter. As regards Heidegger's development, we are now in a position to see that important elements of Heidegger's mature position are indeed

[86] FS 93.
[87] FS 97.
[88] FS 101.
[89] Heidegger's rejection of Lipps' position rather sharply raises the question of whether the mature Heideggerian philosophy of logic amounts to psychologism, as measured by Heidegger's own youthful standards. This question points beyond the limits of the present study.

found articulated in the doctoral dissertation of 1913. In particular we have found that versions of the principle of ontological difference, the criticism of subject-object metaphysics, and model of intentional comportment toward objects, all receive a first articulation in Heidegger's student work in logic. Here we must take care not to overstate the case. By no means do I mean to suggest that Heidegger's mature positions were already worked out in 1913. There are many central Heideggerian doctrines that find no trace in this early work, and even in these cases where important early formulations are to be found, the early and the mature positions differ in important respects.[90] This is most obviously and dramatically the case with the notion of comportment, where a notion that becomes central for the mature Heidegger is dismissed in the dissertation as both psychological and psychologistic. Having registered these qualifications, however, it should I hope be clear that the Heidegger of 1913 was indeed *Heidegger*, and that important elements of his mature philosophy were worked out in his attempt to think through the state of the art in turn-of-the-century psychologistic logic.

My second thesis was not historical but more squarely philosophical, and concerned the available methods for pursuing a phenomenological articulation of judgment. How might we go about giving voice to the experienced character of judgment? Is there some way of developing a theory or at least a systematic description of judgment as a phenomenon? Here I believe that Heidegger's dissertation yields two rich leads. We have already seen one in the explicit positive proposal in the constructive chapter of the dissertation. Close attention to and systematic variation of the circumstances of judgment allow us to isolate a moment in our experience of judgment that remains constant through the perpetual flux of human experience. This constant element proves to be an abstract logical complex in the medium of validity and party to

[90] There is virtually no end to the list of examples one might cite in support of this claim. The thesis has no discussion of anxiety or death, for example, nor of the phenomenological structure of the workshop; there is no distinction between *Zuhandensein* and *Vorhandensein*, no mention of *das Man* or authenticity or resoluteness; Heidegger has not yet adopted his distinctive usage of the term *Dasein*. One particularly important difference between the Heidegger of 1913 and the Heidegger of *Being and Time* is that in the dissertation Heidegger is happy to write of the "instant" (*Augenblick*) of judgment, without any indication that the structure of this instant might itself exhibit considerable complexity. This idea that judgment might take place (or be experienced to take place) in a simple instant or "now" stands in tension with the mature Heidegger's view about the structure of temporality as a complex knitting together of past, present, and future.

inferential relations. In this way the explication of the structure of the experience of judgment can be carried out in what Heidegger calls a pure logical theory. When the logician provides a systematic account of the parts of an inference and the rules governing their valid composition, she is in effect also providing an account of the structure of a certain feature of the experience of rational agents like ourselves.

But we are also now in a position to see a second method of phenomenology articulated in Heidegger's dissertation. In 1913 Heidegger does not endorse this second method; indeed, in important respects he resists it as unacceptably psychologistic. Nonetheless, in his critical engagement with the psychologistic logics of his day we can recognize the outlines of a method that would become central to the mature Heidegger. This second approach to the phenomenology of judgment brings together two doctrines explored in the dissertation. The first emerges in Heidegger's engagement with Maier's theory of the constituent acts of judgment, in particular in connection with his account of the act of negation. As we have seen, Maier's theory of the psychological process of judgment leads him to recognize, in negative judgment, a certain essential prerequisite. In order to carry out a negative judgment, according to Maier, a judge must have at his disposal some representation of totalities of various kinds – a totality of perceptual data, a totality of features of an object, a totality of existent things. In individual acts of judgment (especially but perhaps not exclusively negative judgments), we come to some conclusion about a particular only against the background of a prior representation of these wholes. The second doctrine comes with the idea of demand-sensitive comportment toward things, as that idea was developed in Lipps' later account of the necessitation at work in the act of judgment. As we have seen, Lipps comes to treat judgment as a distinctive way in which judges orient themselves toward entities, adjusting their behavior in responses sensitive to demands experienced as emanating from the objects themselves.

Both of these ideas originated in psychological investigations of judgment, and specifically in an attempt to place the logic of judgment on the purportedly secure foundation of empirical psychology. But when placed together they suggest a method for undertaking a specifically phenomenological investigation of judgment. If we wish to understand and articulate the place of judgment in experience, we should not make the mistake of reflectively looking inward in search of the distinctive subjective quality of judgment. Nor should we confine our attention to the inferential structures of logical objects as abstract contents. In place of these strategies we can instead take our lead from two results from century-old psychologistic logic. In judgment we situate ourselves in the context of a whole we already understand (Maier); in judgment we comport ourselves toward entities in response to experienced demands they place upon us (Lipps). I shall not attempt here to show that these two ideas were indeed central to Heidegger's mature method, particularly during the "phenomenological period" associated with *Being and Time*. But in the chapter which follows I try to put the method to work to illuminate the phenomenological structure of a celebrated act of judgment.

5

ELEMENTS OF A PHENOMENOLOGY OF JUDGMENT: JUDGMENTAL COMPORTMENT IN CRANACH'S *JUDGMENT OF PARIS*

The case studies we have undertaken to this point have examined episodes from the history of the theory of judgment – theories spanning a range of scientific and philosophical disciplines. In this final chapter I turn to theories of quite a different sort, drawn not from science or philosophy but rather from the history of painting. The English word, "theory" derives from the Greek, $\theta\varepsilon\tilde{\alpha}\sigma\theta\alpha\iota$, to look at or contemplate, and the "theories of judgment" I consider here are theories in just this sense: attempts by painters to present or represent the act of judgment to our contemplating vision. My aim is to follow the lead that emerged from Heidegger's doctoral dissertation: the strategy of seeking a phenomenological articulation of judgment by focusing on the characteristic comportments or intentional orientations of the judge. Painting is a medium well-suited to the representation of comportments, and in the painterly representation of judgment we find significant resources for exploring its phenomenological structure. This will be surprising only if one continues to labor under the idea that phenomenology must report on some secretive, entirely inner experience. But to follow Lipps and Heidegger is to reject that particular straightjacket in favor of an approach which finds the phenomenological structure of judgment in the ways judges comport themselves toward the entities in their surrounding world.

I am grateful to Laurie Bussis and Dana Nelkin for comments on earlier drafts of this chapter and to Leslie Tait, who first drew my attention to Cranach's treatment of judgment.

The account that I propose here can at best be described as a phenomenological sketch; it is anything but the last word. But with that qualification firmly registered, let me anticipate the position I seek to defend. I shall argue that judgment involves intentional comportment in four "directions" or toward four different targets: the objects of judgment, the authority of evidence, Others (i.e., other judges), and oneself. In each case the characteristic comportment is thoroughly normative, and I propose four corresponding ideals at work in this distinctive comportmental space: a judge ought to be objective; a judge ought to be reasonable; a judge ought to be articulate; a judge ought to be free.

1 Cranach's *Paris-Urteilen*

In the painterly tradition, one finds the setting of judgment represented most frequently under three different scenarios. One is the religious theme of final judgment. With its all-encompassing scope and recounting of ultimate justice, the final judgment has tempted many painters to works on a very grand scale, most famously in Michelangelo's rendering at one end of the Sistine Chapel. A second scene of judgment explored by painters is also biblical: the judgment of King Solomon concerning the disputed maternity of an infant. In this case it is the intense pathos of the scene which becomes the focus – sword drawn over an unknowing child, mother writhing in anguish at the sight. But neither of these biblical scenes provide much insight into the phenomenology of judgment itself. In the one case the judge is divine and often absent from the representation; in the other a royal judge provides little more than the occasion for portraying the anguish of the witnesses. If our interest is in the phenomenology of judgment then we will do well to concentrate on a third case: the tale from classical mythology concerning the judgment of Paris.

Recall the main elements of the myth: the young Paris, said to be the fairest of mortal men, is called upon by Zeus to settle a dispute that has broken out among three goddesses. The three – Hera, Athene, and Aphrodite (Juno, Minerva, Venus) – are brought to Paris by Hermes (Mercury), who also brings a golden apple to be awarded to the one deemed most beautiful. Paris is faced with an impossible choice, made considerably worse as each of the three divinities tries to bribe the judge: Hera offers power, Athene victory in war, and Aphrodite the love of the most beautiful woman. Paris chooses Aphrodite, and the result (after a few mediating steps) is the Trojan War. Here is the opening speech from Lucian's treatment in *The Judgment of the Goddesses* (second century A.D.):

> *Zeus*: Hermes, take this apple; go to Phygria, to Priam's son, the herds-man – he is grazing his flock in the foothills of Ida, on Gargaron – and say to him: "Paris, as you are handsome yourself, and also well schooled in all that concerns love, Zeus bids you judge for the goddesses, to decide which of them is the most beautiful. As a prize for the contest, let the victor take the apple." (*To the goddesses*) You yourselves must now go and appear before your judge. I refuse to be umpire because I love you all alike and if it were possible, should be glad to see you all victorious. Moreover, it is sure that if I gave the guerdon of beauty to one, I should inevitably get into the bad graces of the majority. For those reasons I am not a proper judge for you, but the young Phygrian to whom you are going is of royal blood and near of kin to our Ganymede; besides, he is ingenuous and unsophisticated, and one cannot consider him unworthy of a spectacle such as this.[1]

The scene of Paris's judgment holds obvious attractions for the painter: dramatic tension, a familiar narrative, an exotic setting. (The judgment takes place deep in the woods of Mt. Ida, where Zeus sends the goddesses after they have disrupted an Olympic wedding with their squabbling; it also happens to be the place where Paris had been abandoned as an infant after a seer foretold his role in the destruction of Troy.)[2] And, of course, the theme presents an occasion for painting three beautiful goddesses (three nudes, in most renderings) alongside the most beautiful (and usually fully clothed) mortal man. Examples of the theme in painting go back almost as far as the surviving history of painting itself. We find instances from unknown Greek vase painters (as early as 500 B.C.), in medieval and Renaissance paintings (Penni in 1395; Benvenuto, c. 1500; Rubens, 1636); in eighteenth-century French painting (Watteau, David), and repeatedly among nineteenth and twentieth-century painters (Blake, Sargeant, George Frederick Watts, Renoir, . . .). Indeed the theme has been so systematically revisited through the history of painting that it provides something of a survey of Western conceptions of feminine beauty, at least as viewed and valued by male painters and their clients. By the time of Dali's rendering the goddesses have become supermodels sketched in the

---

[1] Lucian, *The Judgment of the Goddesses* [ΘΕΩΝ ΚΡΙΣΙΣ]; LL Lucian III 1921: 385.
[2] Ehrhart 1987.

style of a fashion designer (or Barbie dolls, in another twentieth-century treatment).[3]

In what follows I focus mainly on the work of the German Renaissance painter, Lucas Cranach the Elder (1472–1553). The *Paris-Urteil* was one of Cranach's favorite themes. Over a dozen variations survive: at least eleven paintings composed over more than a quarter century, at least one early woodcut, as well as a rare pen-and-ink drawing. Cranach's compositions follow a retelling of the ancient tale from a popular thirteenth-century romance: Guido della Colonne's *Historia Destructionis Troiae*.[4] In this version of the story, Paris has been out hunting and has stopped with his horse to rest in the woods. Hermes (or rather Mercury in this Latin version) and the goddesses find him sleeping and he either dreams or is awakened to find that he is face-to-face with an extraordinary scene. Told by Mercury of his assigned task, Paris's first reaction is to take the most advantage of the situation: "I replied to him that I would not give the truth in this judgment unless they all presented themselves naked to my sight, so that by my observation I might be able to consider the individual qualities of their bodies for a true judgment."[5] At Mercury's command the goddesses comply.

Cranach's various renderings of the scene provide a series of close variations on this unfolding male fantasy. In all the paintings the three goddesses stand nude before Paris, trailing wispy veils which float about their bodies but hide nothing.[6] Mercury is portrayed as an old bearded man in a variety of extravagant hats. He holds the prize, which is not an apple but a large orb – usually crystalline and highly reflective, in some cases wrapped in a band of gold.[7] The scene has been transposed from an ancient to a medieval setting: a medieval castle in the background represents Olympus, and Paris himself is shown in medieval attire, usually partially prone and sleepy in a full suit of armor. Paris' horse looks on, tied to the thick trunk of a tree which typically divides the panel. Paris is presented on the left side of the panel, resting on a quiver filled with arrows. The three female figures

---

[3] For extensive analysis of the history of Paris paintings, and reproductions of many of the paintings mentioned in this brief survey, see Damisch 1992.

[4] Colonne 1287; Cranach's source was first identified in Förster 1898.

[5] Colonne 1287: VI: 234–39.

[6] An exception is Cranach's *Paris-Urteil* in the Metropolitan Museum, to which a strategic degree of opacity has been added to the veil of the one frontal nude, presumably by some well-intentioned but prudish owner of the work. See Nickel 1981: 120 n. 7.

[7] On the use of reflective spheres in painting see Martin 2005.

are arrayed on the right of the painting. One is portrayed frontally, one from the rear but looking back over her shoulder; the third typically stands in three-quarter profile. The three female figures are not identical to one another, but there are no obvious signs to distinguish which is which, nor any obvious way in which the beauty of one is made to outshine that of the others.

So much as to what Cranach's paintings have in common; what then of their differences? There are various divergences in the attire of the male principals (in particular among Mercury's variously spectacular hats and Paris' elaborate armor), in the position of the horse, in the inclusion or absence or a winged cherub overhead, in the postures of the nudes, and in the architecture and landscape in the distance. (It is characteristic of Cranach's compositions to combine long landscape views with tight portraits, put together in paintings with impossibly extended depth of field.) But the most important differences concern the precise instant of the narrative captured by the image. For while each of the paintings represents the scene of Paris' judgment, the different paintings capture different stages in an unfolding encounter. The 1517 panel (Seattle Art Museum) and another from the 1530s (Graz), show Paris sound asleep, with Mercury reaching down to wake him. The 1527 rendering (Copenhagen) shows Paris awake, but still listening to Mercury, to whom his attention is entirely directed while the goddesses look on. In the New York Metropolitan version (undated) Paris is finally looking toward the goddesses, to whom Mercury seems to be directing some remark. In the 1528 painting (Basel) and again in the very last of the series to be painted (Gotha, after 1537), one of the goddesses (presumably Aphrodite/Venus) seems to be communicating with Paris directly, who in turn seems to be listening attentively, even though the goddess's lips show no sign of movement. In the Basel painting, a sword or arrow is shown rising between Paris' armored legs. In a lost 1535 rendering (stolen from Harz in 1945), all four Olympians look on impatiently as Paris looks dejectedly away, apparently lost in thought; one of the goddesses gives him a kick to rouse him from his indecision. Finally, two of the paintings (including the earliest extant, c. 1513, now in Cologne, and one of the latest, 1537, now in St. Louis) seem to represent the moment of choice. In one Aphrodite reaches down to Paris (who is always represented below the immortals, at the lower left of the panels); in the other she already has her hand on the prize, while Paris looks anxiously (toward Mercury?) to see how his decision has been received. Taken together the paintings represent the whole course of the visible action, in a scene which manages somehow to be both comic and erotic.[8]

Can we learn something about the phenomenology of judgment by looking to Cranach's paintings? Let me here be careful about what I claim. I do not intend to make any particular claim about the meaning of Cranach's Paris paintings, if that means advancing some thesis about Cranach's intentions or the significance of the works in their original context.[9] Nor do I mean to suggest that the highly unusual circumstances of the Parisian judgment should be taken as common to or exemplary of judgment in general. Nonetheless, I shall argue that Cranach's paintings do capture something of the phenomenological structure of judgment; or to put the point even more modestly: that we can use the paintings to reveal and articulate some of the fundamental structure of the experience of judgment.

As an initial point, consider the way Cranach conveys Paris' dawning realization of both the freedom and the necessity of his judgment. In many versions of the Paris story, we hear Paris expressing both reluctance and fear in the face of his assigned task, as he quickly comes to the realization that whatever decision he makes will earn him the enmity of two powerful deities. In Lucian's influential rendering this is the first thought we hear from Paris, as he tries to excuse himself from his assigned task. "How could I, a mere mortal and a countryman, be

---

[8] I have relied on Friedländer and Rosenberg 1978 for this survey of Cranach's various renderings, but even this collection is incomplete, omitting at least one late version of the theme from the British Royal Collection, recently reported as having been moved from Hampton Court to the State Apartments at Windsor Castle. Royal Collections Trust 2004: 16.

[9] It may well have been that their significance for Cranach himself was in large part alchemical. The artist seems to have had a serious interest in alchemy, and is reported as having owned an apothecary's shop. The judgment of Paris was commonly used in alchemy textbooks as a symbol for the crucial step in transforming base matter into gold. Nickel 1981 proposes an interpretation of the Metropolitan's *Paris-Urteil* as an elaborate alchemical recipe, with the bearded god representing white mercury, Venus as a symbol for copper, even the horse and species of tree an indication of the fuels to be used in the combustion. There is somewhat more direct evidence that the significance of the Paris theme for Cranach's original audience was in part genealogical. At the beginning of the sixteenth century, there was fashion among a number of prominent royal households to trace the family lineage back to the Trojan diaspora. The Hapsburgs, Kaiser Maximilian of Bavaria, Frederick the Wise of Saxony, and one of Cranach's own patrons (Johann, brother of Frederick of Saxony) were all claimed as descendants of Trojan princes. If nothing else this must have had an effect on the market for representations of Trojan history. Significantly, Cranach's woodcut of 1508 incorporates two coats-of-arms, hanging from a branch above Paris' encounter with the goddesses. One of the two has been identified as belonging to the House of Saxony. See Koepplin 2003: 153.

judge of an extraordinary spectacle, too sublime for a herdsman? To decide such matters better befits dainty, city-bred folk."[10] Failing to escape the task, Paris goes on to plead with Hermes (fruitlessly, as it happens) to convince the goddesses that the two who lose should not be slighted by his decision. "Do me this one favor, Hermes: persuade them not to be angry with me, the two that are defeated, but to think that only my sight is at fault."[11] But it is clear that for Paris there is no escaping the judgment, a point that Cranach makes in several of the works by showing Mercury towering menacingly above him, in two cases threatening him with a short staff held against his breastplate.

But if Paris is shown to be forced to his judgment, there is also a clear sense in which he also finds himself free to decide. Although each of the goddesses do their best to influence his decision with their promises, they either cannot or will not force his choice. After all, in decreeing that Paris decide, Zeus has effectively made him the agent of judgment. The powers and promises of the goddesses figure here not as mechanical determinants of choice but rather as information (and incentives) to be weighed. This connection between judgment and freedom is reflected in the language of judgment, in particular in the Latin term "*deliberare*": to deliberate. The root here is not in fact *liber* (free) but rather *libra* (the scales), but the terms are clearly related, both etymologically and in substance. Deliberation involves a kind of weighing, hence *de-libra*: from the scales. But in order to function properly, scales must be allowed to swing free; scales held in place are not properly scales at all. In Cranach's painting this judgmental or deliberative freedom is vividly conveyed in the extraordinary scene of four Olympians, forced to stand by, waiting upon the decision of a rather pathetic mortal.

To sum up this first point, then, the Paris of Cranach's paintings is a judge struggling through the dawning realization: "*I must decide.*" *I* am the agent of this decision; *I* am the one who will be praised (by one) and blamed (by the others); I am the one who will reap both the rewards and the wrath. But this awareness of freedom is balanced by the palpable sense of necessity, here brought to a focus in Mercury's threatening staff and combining with the heavy weight of his absurd armor to render Paris incapable of even standing to face his task. In portraying this combination of the sense of agency ("I") and the sense of necessity

---

[10] LL Lucian III 1921: 395.
[11] LL Lucian III 1921: 395.

("must") Cranach exhibits something of the phenomenological structure of the Parisian judgment.

So far all this might well be taken to be a special feature of the highly unusual circumstances of Paris' judgment. After all, it is certainly not the case that human judgment is typically carried out under a divine command, which is here what provides the distinctive constraint of the judgmental task. But in another sense, I think, Cranach's representation of judgment does indeed convey features common to judgment in general. As we saw emphasized in Theodor Lipps' account, to judge is in some sense to find oneself bound or constrained in representation. In particular, the judge is bound by the evidence – not mechanically or otherwise deterministically, but in something like the form of a command from an authority. To return to Lipps' formula: in judgment I am conscious of a felt necessity or demand upon my representation of objects. To recognize clear evidence in support of p is, pro tanto, to find oneself under an obligation to judge that p.[12] Even when the evidence is mixed or unclear, to be a judge is to be sensitive to and oriented by its authority. In this sense, finding oneself subject to determination is a constitutive feature of judgment itself; to experience oneself as a judge is to be alive to the authority of evidence, even if one does not always obey it.

At the same time, as Kant famously insists in his moral philosophy, to deliberate is to discover oneself under a certain idea of freedom. Deliberation is only intelligible for the judge under the assumption that the outcome can in some sense be the result of the deliberator's decision. This presupposition of deliberation is most salient where the condition is not met. There can be no intelligible sense in *deliberation* about some matter I take to be settled quite independently of my act of judgment – e.g., about where I should be born or how the planets should be ordered. I may engage in various idle speculations about such matters; I might even tot up the pros and cons of various options. But going through the motions of deliberation in this way does not amount to deliberating over these matters any more than running the bases at the stadium makes me a major leaguer. If this is right, if freedom and determination are indeed both constituent moments of judgment, then Cranach's painting can be said to articulate (in its own distinctive medium) an insight into the phenomenology of judgment as such.

---

[12] That obligation may be defeasible in various ways, for instance if I am under some independent obligation to suspend judgment about the matter at hand.

Here we need to defend and clarify two key elements of this claim. First, even if we grant that freedom and determination are constitutive features of judgment as such, is it really fair to describe these as *phenomenological* features? Do we experience our freedom and determination, and if so in what sense? Secondly, we have here moved very quickly between claims about deliberation and claims about judgment, although the relation between the two is far from clear. Some clarification and qualification is required on both points.

Start with the latter. If Kant was right, then deliberation requires that we act under the idea of freedom. We cannot deliberate about some matter if we take the relevant facts to be settled quite independently of our deliberation. But the act of deliberation is not the same as the act of judgment; the former involves some kind of conscious weighing of options, whereas the latter is the opting for one choice or another. Opting may be the outcome of the weighing, but it certainly need not be. Deliberation may be cut short without issuing in judgment, and in the case of snap judgments I seem to do the opting without any conscious weighing. So the conclusion about deliberation does not immediately carry over to a conclusion about judging.

Two points are in order here. First, although it is true that deliberation is not essential to a particular act of judgment, the *capacity* for deliberation is essential to the capacity for judgment. Someone who is incapable of deliberation may indeed opt for one choice or another when presented with options – in something like the way that a simple organism propels itself in one direction or another through a salinity or nutrient gradient. But where the capacity for deliberation is absent, such opting may be a more-or-less suitable reaction but it does not properly amount to judgment. This is related to the second point: for while prior conscious deliberation may not be required for every instance of judgment, it is a paradigmatic instance of something that is essential: the capacity to weigh conflicting evidence. In this sense, the ability to "hang free" as scales do, and to consider one's weighing as at least potentially playing a role in the outcome, can indeed be said to be at work in judgment as such.

What about the second worry? Even if we grant that freedom and determination are in some sense constitutive elements of judgment, is it fair to describe them as phenomenological features? Do we (ever? always?) *experience* ourselves as simultaneously free and determined in judgment, or are these attributions rather those of the theorist – claims about conditions upon judgment that are themselves rarely (if ever) salient features of the judge's experience itself? If these were the only choices then we should surely opt for the latter rather than the former position. Although the sense of one's one own freedom and determination may be intensely felt in particularly wrenching judgments (e.g., that of a jurist in a capital case), it would be a colossal mistake to read that experience back into mundane judgment. In sorting the laundry I may be conscious of the laundry or the ballgame on the radio or the looming election or perhaps of nothing at all, but it would be an absurd imposition on the phenomenological facts to say that I am conscious of my own freedom to sort, or of my being determined by the available evidence as to which socks should go together.

But these are not the only options. One of the main aims of this study has been to bring into view both the difficulty of phenomenological investigation of judgment and certain methods and strategies for meeting those challenges. In particular, we have seen that phenomenological investigation of judgment falls quickly into intractable difficulties if it sets out to identify some distinctive occurrent contents or conscious features which are characteristic of all and only judgments. There simply is no such common conscious denominator of judgment. But we have also found a proposal for a radically different approach to the phenomenology of judgment. Rather than casting phenomenology as a search through the private files of our subjective conscious lives, phenomenology can be cast instead as a study of our comportment (*Verhalten*) toward things in response to the demands they place upon us. We can seek a phenomenology of judgment by teasing out the distinctive orientation toward things that is at work in the experience of judgment. To follow this path is accordingly not to look for a conscious content associated with judgment but to ask instead how, in judgment, the judge orients himself toward various entities and authorities in play in his world. It is in this sense, I submit, that the experience of freedom and determination are ever and always part of the experienced structure of judgment. Let me try to develop this a bit more systematically, adverting once again to Cranach's paintings in order to distinguish four directions or targets of the characteristic comportments of a judge.

2 Four comportments of judgment

By way of conclusion I hazard a mapping of sorts: a mapping of the constituent intentional comportments of judgment. This is meant as a sketch; I do not mean to suggest that the four comportments I identify exhaust the phenomenological structure of judgment, and in each instance I identify various problems and issues without proposing definitive solutions. Taken together, however, these four directions of judgmental comportment provide an indication and an articulation of the experienced space in which judgments unfold and manifest themselves as such in our experience.

A In judgment I comport myself toward an object

This is the point that requires the least elaboration. Paris' judgment is *about* the goddesses, and it is surely true of all judgments that they are, in Brentano's sense, intentional: they are of or about some object or state of affairs. Certainly the most salient comportment of judgment is toward its object. Even here, this need not mean that my conscious attention is actively directed to or focused on the object of judgment – at least not if that is taken to mean that the object of judgment is a focal object of conscious attention. This is a point that has now often been emphasized in connection with the judgments passed in the course of skillful activity.[13] Merging onto the freeway or finding a seat on a crowded bus, my focal attention may be primarily taken up in the conversation I am having with my friend or the lyrics of the music on the headphones or in trying to remember the ten-digit phone number on a help-wanted sign. At the same time, however, I exercise judgment in choosing how fast to accelerate, whether to sit up front or in the back row, and which among the various commuters I am to join in an overheated rush hour.

Although this intentional direction toward the objects of judgment need not be a matter of focal attention, in some sense it must be a matter of awareness. I can hardly pass judgment about nothing, nor about something which in no way figures in my experience. The sense of object-directedness can be captured, I submit, in terms of the notions of comportment and orientation we encountered above. For better or for worse, drivers merging onto the freeway are often not focally attentive to the vehicles they are joining in the stream of traffic, but their activity is intelligently coordinated with them and sensitive to the subtle variations in their demands. If for some reason the occasion demands it, they are capable of bringing those objects of judgment into focal attention. It is in this sense that judgment can be said to be oriented toward an object: it is coordinated with the demands of the object in the context of an

---

[13] A classic study is Dreyfus and Dreyfus 1980.

unfolding situation; and the object of judgment is at least "within reach" of conscious deliberative attention, should such attention be required.

One famous problem about this object-direction arises with the much-discussed problems of hallucination and failed reference. What am I oriented toward if someone tricks me into guessing at the name of the present King of France? It seems clear that I might hazard a judgment about such a matter (perhaps I know the statistical frequency of "Louis" as the name of French monarchs, though not that France is now a Republic), but there is also an obvious sense in which there is no object to orient or comport myself toward in such cases. Is this then a counter-example to the thesis that judgment always involves comportment toward an object? The issue is a fraught one, and I have no ambition to settle it here. Suffice to remind ourselves that it is all too easy to be oriented by things which turn out not to exist. The history of both religion and science is replete with examples.

B In judgment I comport myself toward evidence

The second judgmental comportment requires more extensive comment. A judge's comportment toward evidence is closely connected with his comportment toward the object of judgment, and in certain cases the two may very nearly coincide. Nonetheless they are not to be confused with one another. If I am called upon to judge whether the accused is guilty, then the defendant (a person) is the object of my judgment. But in so judging I must also comport myself toward and be guided by the available evidence: the tape-recordings, the bank records, the testimony of whistle-blowers, etc. If the orientation toward the object is the most salient orientation of judgment, this orientation toward evidence is perhaps the most fundamental. As is emphasized at the outset of every trial, a competent juror (that is, a competent judge) must be capable of rendering judgment in response to and on the basis of the evidence presented at court. In this case the comportment very explicitly takes the form of guidance. If I am incapable of being guided by the evidence – whether in general because of some cognitive incapacity or in the specific case at hand because of some prejudice – then I have a fundamental responsibility to recuse myself from the deliberations in question.

This responsive comportment toward evidence is constitutive of judgment in two different senses. First, at the level of general capacities, the ability to be guided by evidence is an essential prerequisite for the capacity of judgment. But it also plays a constitutive role in a narrower but crucial sense, in determining the content of the judgment that is passed. This point is not at all obvious, but we can clarify it by considering a question that we have thus far avoided: *What exactly did Paris decide?*

So far we have been speaking quite freely about *the* judgment of Paris. But what was that judgment? In one sense, of course, the answer is clear from his actions: Paris awarded the apple to Aphrodite. But in knowing this much we do not yet know what judgment led to this action. What, in short, was the *content* of his judgment? Or to put the point another way: what was the question to which Paris finally arrived at an answer? Recall that Paris in effect faced two questions. One concerned the relative beauty of three goddesses; the second concerned the relative value (to him) of three bribes. Did Paris award the apple as he did because he judged: "Aphrodite is more beautiful than either Hera or Athene"? Or did he rather act as he did because he judged: "the love of Helen is more desirable than either political power or victory in battle"? Or did he perhaps draw both these conclusions?

Modern retellings of classical mythology sometimes treat this question as settled, but the ancient sources are far more nuanced. The Homeric treatment of the judgment (in the *Cypria*) has not survived, but ancient reports on it leave the issue studiously unsettled. A summary from the Library of Apollodorus summarizes the Homeric treatment in these terms (note that Alexander was the name Paris was given by the shepherds who raised him before his royal lineage was discovered):

> Strife threw an apple as a prize of beauty to be contended for by Hera, Athene, and Aphrodite; and Zeus commanded Hermes to lead them to Alexander on Ida in order to be judged by him. And they promised to give Alexander gifts. Hera said that if she were preferred to all women, she would give him the kingdom over all men; and Athene promised victory in war, and Aphrodite the hand of Helen. And he decided in favor of Aphrodite.[14]

In this summary the word "and" hides the issue that here concerns us: did Paris award the apple *because* of the rewards that were promised him, or simply *after* they were offered? Apollodorus does not tell us. Other ancient summaries are more definite, as for instance in this report from *Chrestomathy*: "Alexandrus, lured by his promised marriage with Helen,

---

[14] LL Apollodorus II 1921: 173.

decided in favor of Aphrodite."[15] When we move to later traditions, we get all manner of different answers. Ovid has Paris profess insistently that he was already moved by the beauty of Aphrodite before any mention of the gifts,[16] while in the *Fabulae* (an important source for the transmission of the text into medieval times), Hyginus very explicitly makes the decision turn on consideration of the rewards: "Paris placed the last gift first and judged Venus to be the most beautiful, whereupon Juno and Minerva were angry with the Trojans."[17] Isocrates' *Encomium on Helen* has Paris so overwhelmed that he cannot even face the goddesses, but he seems to be moved by yet another motive: his ambition to secure an Olympian lineage for his progeny.[18]

It is worth considering how this disputed matter can be settled – not, of course, as a matter of the historical facts, but rather as a matter of what I shall call *representational determinacy*. How, that is, does an author represent Paris as having decided one question rather than the other? How might a painter address this issue? And finally, how might Paris himself have made the basis or content of his judgment determinate?

Once again here, the answers vary dramatically with the medium. In most of the ancient sources we are told of the events on Mt. Ida only through the medium of monologues after the fact – most importantly through Paris' speech before Priam at court, through his subsequent communications with Helen, or even more indirectly through reports of others who were not witness to the event at all. This is also the case with the medieval source on which Cranach relied. In Colonne's recounting, Paris is emphatic in maintaining that his choice was guided by his aesthetic judgment concerning the goddesses themselves:

> When the aforesaid three goddesses had put aside their clothes, and when each of them in turn had presented herself naked to my sight, it seemed to me, by following the judgment of truth [*prosequendo iudicium veritatis*], that Venus in her beauty excelled those other two, and accordingly I decided that she was mistress of the apple.[19]

This is quite unambiguous as a report, but it nonetheless leaves the crucial question unanswered. For we must remember that Paris is here

---

[15] Proclus, *Chrestomathy*, LL Hesiod 1936: 491.

[16] Ovid, *Heroides* 16; LL Ovid I 1977: 201–3.

[17] Hyginus, *Fabulae*, Fable #92.

[18] Isocrates, *Encomium on Helen*; LL Isocrates III 1966: 60–97. See Ehrhart 1987, ch. 1 for a more systematic survey of the ancient sources of the Paris myth.

[19] Colonne 1287: VI: 240–44.

speaking to his father, Priam, the King of Troy, seeking to persuade him to grant use of the Trojan fleet for the unlikely purpose of marrying a woman whom Paris has never met, and who happens to be married to a powerful Greek prince. Priam is rightfully skeptical (whether or not he recalls the prophecy of the seer), and Paris is desperate to convince him. Paris, in other words, has every reason to cast his judgment in the most favorable possible light, even if this means lying to his father about the judgment he had actually formed. In short: *if* the proper content of the judgment is a private matter, known only to Paris himself, then he has every opportunity to misrepresent it without fear of contradiction. Note that a similarly rhetorical context (seduction) prevails in the other case where we hear Paris reporting on his judgment: in the love letters to Helen which serve as the medium of narrative in Ovid's *Heroides*. Once again Paris assures us that his judgment was based on the beauty of the goddesses, but we have no particular reason to trust his report.

So far we have been assuming that Paris himself knows the content of his own judgment – that there is some private but determinate truth, known only to the agent of judgment, about which Paris himself may publically speak either truth or falsity. But this is an assumption that must be challenged. In the pressure of the moment there may indeed have been many private thoughts that raced through poor Paris' mind, and about these he may indeed speak either truthfully or untruthfully. But it is important to see that this does not of itself determine the content of his judgment. Presumably in the crucial moments preceding judgment, Paris considered *both* the beauty of the goddesses *and* the distinctive advantages of the three rewards. (Wouldn't you?) And after some period of such thinking and fretting he acted, giving the apple to Aphrodite. But nothing in that sequence of events, private and public, as yet determines the content of the judgment that was passed. Even if his inner voice pronounced explicitly "Aphrodite is the most beautiful," we cannot rule out that this was itself a case of motivated self-deception or rationalization, occasioned to justify the choice that would bring him Helen, whose seduction Aphrodite had already quite vividly described.[20] Once this possibility is allowed we might wonder whether anything could render of the content of Paris' judgment determinate. In a narrative medium one might, of course, interpose the voice of some omniscient narrator, which would at least yield determinacy to the

[20] See, e.g., LL Lucian III 1921: 405–7.

representation, but this is simply to push back the question of the basis of *that* knowledge.

Here, it proves both interesting and instructive to return to the painterly tradition. This may be surprising. If the content of judgment were indeed some private, potentially embarrassing fact which Paris himself is reluctant to reveal, or about which he may even be uncertain, then how could a painterly representation of the scene possibly settle the question, or even show us a determinate answer? Before considering how Cranach manages this detail, it is worth considering the provocative rococo rendering of the judgment by Jean Antoine Watteau. Watteau's *Judgment of Paris* (1720) is remarkable for a number of reasons, most dramatically because in it Paris' view of the goddesses is sharply restricted. Watteau's Paris is once again a rather pathetic, almost childlike figure, nearly falling over backwards as he rather impishly extends his arm upwards to bestow the apple. One recent scholar describes him as follows:

> Watteau's Paris is relegated to the lower left, diagonally opposite the withdrawing Hera, and strikes a note very different from that of the attentive judge to whom Mercury concedes in most earlier depictions: seated, inclined slightly backwards, eyes uplifted to look at the looming Venus, who exhibits herself in a way that clearly conveys her domination of him, he surrenders the apple to her like one conquered, while Mercury looks over his shoulder.[21]

But what is most distinctive about Watteau's Paris is that he is shown making his choice on the basis of a very narrow consideration of the evidence. Hera is shown behind him and to the right, out of the line of sight altogether; Athene is mostly obstructed from view (both his and ours) by her helmet and shield. Aphrodite is here made the central focus of the work, and indeed her figure, shown to the viewer from behind, dominates the canvas. In a departure from the tradition, she squarely faces Paris, who is accordingly presented with (and apparently is quite overwhelmed by) the sight of her frontal exposure. But even this exposure is incomplete in Paris' line of sight, as an intervening cherub arranges the obligatory veil in such a way as to obscure Paris' view of the goddess from the waist up. In short, the whole arrangement of the scene is carefully contrived so that Paris has a wholly unobstructed view of the divine genitals, and very little else. As Watteau has it, this seems to

---

[21] Damisch 1992: 297. My discussion here follows Damisch's insightful analysis on several details.

have been quite enough to settle the contest, and the apple is awarded accordingly.

There is, I think, a question in Watteau's rendering about whether Paris is properly deemed a judge at all. As I have argued above, the freedom to arrive at one's own decision is a constitutive condition on judgment, and in Watteau's rendering Aphrodite seems to have placed her weight pretty firmly on the scales. (Both of the other goddesses are quite evidently disgusted at the way the contest has been decided.) But what is important for our argument here is the distinctive way in which Watteau manages to provide a determinate representation of the basis and content of Paris' decision. What makes the representation determinate are not words that Paris utters, nor some private internal dialogue shown to be coursing through his head. Rather, his judgment (if indeed it is that) is determinately represented by exhibiting his orientation toward the evidence by which he is guided. Watteau's Paris decides neither which goddess is fairest (he doesn't bother to look at them) nor which reward is most valuable, but only that he is ready to go along with the promptings of the figure standing before him. What we see, then, is that the evidence toward which one is oriented, and one's comportment toward it, can serve to fix the representational content of a judgment. Notice that this may or may not be a matter about which a judge has self-knowledge.

We find the same route to representational determinacy exploited in Lucian's theatrical treatment of this issue. As a play, Lucian's treatment once again provides the viewer with access only to the public events of the judgment scene; there are no voice-overs, no "thought-bubbles," not even a monologue or stage directions. If the determinate content of the judgment were indeed some private matter, then one might suppose that this would leave the true content of judgment once again hidden. But the closing exchange of the play shows clearly how Paris has settled the matter. Having privately heard Aphrodite's offer, and her description of the devices she plans to use in the seduction, Paris replies:

Paris: I am afraid you may dismiss me from your mind after the decision.

Aphrodite: Do you want me to take an oath?

Paris: Not at all; but promise once again.

Aphrodite: I do promise that I will give you Helen to wife, and that she shall follow you and come to your people in Troy; and I myself will be there and help in arranging it all.

Paris: And shall you bring Love and Desire and the Graces?

Aphrodite: Have no fear; I shall take with me Longing and Wedlock as well.[22]

Lucian shows us the basis of Paris' judgment here, not simply through the use of words (words by themselves may deceive or dissemble) but by showing us how Paris comports himself toward the evidence. The final exchange with Aphrodite shows him very clearly concerned with the evidence at hand, but the evidence he is oriented by is that concerning the promise rather than the beauty of the goddess. Having shown us this comportment, Lucian's final line in the play is strictly redundant, for it tells us only what we have already been shown:

Paris: Then on these conditions I award you the apple; take it on these conditions.

Are Cranach's portrayals of the judgment representationally determinate on this question? The answer is not entirely clear. It is striking, however, that in the earliest surviving work, the prize held by Mercury bears a partially legible inscription. Although Cranach's literary source had explicitly identified the inscription as "written in Greek letters," Cranach's inscription is clearly Latin. And while Colonne had followed the rest of the tradition in describing the inscription as "for the fairest," the visible portion of Cranach's inscription reads: "AMORTX.N".[23] The significance of this departure is unclear (perhaps it figures in one of Cranach's alchemical recipes),[24] but it is noteworthy that the seven visible letters include both the Latin root for love (*amor*) and the Latin root for death (*mort*). This has clear bearing on Paris' choice. With the exception of a rather agitated horse, Paris is the one mortal at the scene, so it seems clear that the word "death" could only apply to him (rather than to Aphrodite, for instance, who wins the inscribed prize, or to Eris, who manufactured it). And, of course, the two words might well be taken as a concise summary of his fate: he chooses love and in doing so prepares the way to a great many deaths, including his own. Read in this way we might well see the deviant inscription as Cranach's way of lending representational determinacy to the Parisian judgment. It is worth noticing that the words are not here presented as issuing from

---

[22] LL Lucian III 1921: 409.

[23] Koepplin and Falk 1976, vol. 2: 629.

[24] See Nickel 1981.

Paris at all. If they nonetheless represent his judgment it is because he decides, in effect, to sign on to their truth-claim concerning his fate.[25]

C *In judgment I comport myself toward Others*

A third comportment of judgment is toward Others, that is, toward other judges. Typically that means orientation toward human beings other than the judging agent, although in Paris' exceptional circumstances it includes divine Others, and as we shall see there are cases and senses in which the pertinent Other may be the judge himself. The role and structure of the experience of the Other is an enormously complex question, and one of the richest in the phenomenological tradition. Properly it is the topic for another book, but I allow myself here a few comments, drawing once again on the *Paris-Urteil*.

Cranach is quite explicit in exhibiting the ways in which Paris' decision is carried out before Others. As we have noted, the four Olympians all look on as witnesses to the judgment, and Paris himself is intensely aware that he will have to answer for the decision he reaches. In the one painting where the judgment has most clearly been reached (the work of 1537, showing Aphrodite taking possession of the prize), we see Paris apparently looking to Mercury, as if to gauge the reaction to his decision. Real and projected Others figure in our judgments in many different ways, whether as authorities to whom we may be called for an accounting, peers to whom we may go for counsel, or those who are victims or beneficiaries of our judgments and may "answer back," questioning or protesting our judgments in a variety of different ways. This Other-directedness of judgment is in fact closely related to the sense of agency at work in judgment, as discussed above. To be the agent of judgment is also to be the one *responsible* for judgment; that is, it is to be the one who is called to *respond* to those who may question it. Although in Colonne's representation, Paris may indeed carry out his judgment in the privacy of his own dream, he ultimately finds himself accountable for it to a whole horde of Greeks and Trojans adversely affected by his decision. Indeed, the most immediate consequence of the judgment, as we have noted, is that he finds himself having to explain it to his own father at court.

Here, it may be protested, however, that this comportment toward Others is not itself essential, but figures only in certain cases, and perhaps

---

[25] On the idea that judgmental contents themselves incorporate a truth-claim, see Chapter 3.

not even the majority. Is it not possible to pass judgment as a wholly private affair, without any registration of an orientation toward Others? If this means that judgments may be kept secret then there is certainly no denying the point. But it is worth remembering that the keeping of secrets is itself a very distinctive comportment toward Others. To hide my judgment and keep it private I must be careful what I say, I must think before I answer even seemingly innocent questions, I must be sure that I cover any traces of that which I seek to hide. So the undeniable possibility of hiding judgments does not show that comportment toward Others is inessential to judgment; it much rather exemplifies the principle.

Still, it will be asked, by those who want to press the case, isn't it nonetheless possible for a solitary individual to pass judgment? Couldn't some extreme variant of Robinson Crusoe decide this way or that about a particular matter? This question raises substantive issues that must be postponed for another occasion – questions about the role of Others in the aspiration to objectivity, and about the role of the ideal of objectivity in the passing of judgment. But at the very least we should recognize a sense in which even a solitary Robinson Crusoe may be called to provide an answer to a questioning Other: the Other that is his own future self. If he is faced with the question of which rock is most beautiful, choosing which of three to haul back to his hut, he is minimally responsible to the Robinson Crusoe he will become once he gets back to the hut, wondering whether his earlier self made the right choice. "What was I thinking?," we ask in such contexts. In so asking, I become my own Other.

But for phenomenological analysis the more significant questions concern not the possibility or impossibility of radically solipsistic judgment, but rather the problem of understanding the mode or texture of the judgmental comportment toward Others. In the case of the judge's comportment toward evidence, by comparison, the character of the relevant comportment is relatively straightforward. The judge should be *guided* by the evidence: gathering it, weighing it, and following its authority. To be guided by it is to follow its inferential (i.e., logical) significance. Even here there are difficulties, to be sure. One notorious problem is that of knowing when to cut off the evidence-gathering stage, and of *responsibly* doing so without initiating a regress. But the general form of the comportment toward evidence (guidance by an authority) is at least in this case clear. In the comportment of a judge toward other judges, the situation is far more complex.

One principled solution to this problem will no doubt seem unduly extreme. The stance of the judge toward other judges, one might propose, is effectively the demand for assent. In judging, as we might put it, I take a stand and I make a demand. I take a stand as to how things are with the object of my judgment, and I demand of Others that they share my assessment. This sounds massively imperialistic, but there is nonetheless a simple line of argument which seems to require it. First, as we have seen, to judge concerning some matter is always to judge concerning *the truth* of that matter; to judge *that p* is to judge *that p is true*. But in judging before Others I judge before those whom I judge to be judges themselves. And to treat an Other as a judge is to treat them as someone who ought to be guided by the ideal of judging truthfully. Here we can see the imperialistic consequence looming. If I take it to be true that p, and if I take you to be a judge and hence answerable to the truth, then it seems that in judging p to be true I treat you as someone who ought to recognize p's truth too. If this is right then one can only be speaking in bad faith if one says (as is often said): "I am only expressing my opinion; I am not telling you what to think."

Now clearly something has gone wrong in this line of reasoning. If nothing else we must obviously allow that the scope of this demand is limited to those who have access to the relevant evidence. It would be absurd to suppose that in judging that the cat is on the mat, I demand assent of someone who has neither seen nor heard testimony concerning the cat. So at a minimum we must retreat to a demand *of those who are properly situated* – in particular those who share access to the relevant evidence and have the requisite cognitive capacities and background to see what the evidence shows me. They are the ones of whom I demand assent. We should also be clear that such a demand must be sharply distinguished from an expectation. Paris has no reason to expect that the losing goddesses will share his judgment; indeed, he has every reason to suppose that they will not. The claim here is not that suitably situated Others *will* share my judgment, but only that in judging I effectively claim that they *ought* to. Even this will likely seem too much, especially in a cultural situation where the demand for assent is often viewed as (and sometimes *is*) a form of clumsy bad taste. But this should not prevent us from recognizing something quite special in an encounter where we find an Other who has reviewed the same evidence, who shares the same cognitive resources, who seems not to be blinded by any obvious prejudice, and yet nonetheless withholds their assent from the content I endorse. Such an Other is both a distinctive cognitive threat and a distinctive cognitive opportunity. If the disputed matter is of any serious import then I ought to be shaken by the encounter.

It is just here, however, that the imperialism at work in judgment may take different forms. Simply to shrug off such an encounter, as if such a difference were nothing to me ...; that really is a form of bad faith. Certainly there can be all manner of good reasons for letting the matter drop without pressing the demand incipient in every judgment. But the alternative is not flatly to demand the assent of this Other but rather to engage them. "Where do we differ in this matter? On what points do we agree? How do you reconcile q, r, and s, with your seemingly firm conviction that not-p?" Such conversations are anything but imperialistic, and yet they obtain their distinctive seriousness and significance from a comportment that is in its way demanding: the demand either to agree or to participate in a collaborative exploration of disagreement, guided in either case by a common commitment to truthfulness.

It is worth reiterating in this context a point that has now been emphasized several times in the foregoing: in order for the assent of an Other to be of any significance for the judge, that assent must be freely undertaken. It is part of the complexity of judgmental comportment that the demand I make of Others is a demand that they exercise their own freedom.[26] Notice also that in order to engage in such conversations, a judge must be *articulate*. Not only must he have the general capacity for speech; he also requires the capacity to express the reasons which sway him. Thus, while many particular instances of judgment may well be silent, the idea of a wholly silent judge (a judge incapable of articulating his reasons) is ultimately unintelligible.[27] Notice that in order to engage in such conversations, a judge must be articulate, both in the sense of being capable of linguistic expression, but also in the more rigorous sense of being capable of articulating the evidence that sways him.[28]

---

[26] This complex "calling out" (*Aufforderung*) of the freedom of the Other is the fundamental notion in Fichte's liberal political philosophy. See Fichte 1796.

[27] I do not mean here to rule out the possibility that a deaf-mute, for instance, might be capable of judgment. The articulacy to which I here appeal need not take the form of utterances created with the vocal cords; what is required is the ability to articulate one's reasons for judgment in exchange with Others. The vocal cords are the paradigmatic organ for such an undertaking, but they need not be the exclusive one.

[28] This is, of course, a theme that has been central to the work of Robert Brandom. See Brandom 1994, 2000.

D In judgment I comport myself toward myself

Here we come to the most complex issue. Is there some sense in which judgmental comportment is self-directed or self-oriented? What can it even mean to speak of comportment toward oneself? Start once again with some negative claims. It is certainly not the case that in judgment the judge typically or even commonly thematizes himself or his own act of judgment. There may indeed be circumstances where this is the case, but these are exceptional. In the ordinary cases, the attention of a judge is and ought to be taken up with the other three targets of judgmental comportment – with the object of judgment, with the pertinent evidence, and with the viewpoints of those who may be expected to question or challenge the judgment that is made. Judgment is thematically self-directed only in the special cases where the judge happens also to be the object of judgment (e.g., "Should I keep working or try to get a few hours of sleep?").

Nonetheless, if properly functioning judgment is typically directed *from* the judge rather than *toward* it, there is nonetheless a complex of ways in which judgmental comportment is and must be self-related. Perhaps the best way to tease this out is to start from the realization that judgment is a form of self-determination. At various junctures in the foregoing discussion we have touched on the point that judgment has certain prerequisites, that various capacities are required of any would-be judge: the capacity to be sensitive to the inferential structure and authority of evidence and to be guided by it, the capacity to "hang free" of mechanical determination by some force or power, the capacity to suspend judgment until evidence has been presented, etc. It is part of the art of jury selection to be cognizant of these prerequisites, and to find ways of sorting the pool into those who satisfy them and those who do not. Among all these prerequisite capacities, however, one predominates. A judge must be capable of self-determination; or more precisely: he must be capable of determining, in response to the evidence, his own representation of the objects or states-of-affairs he is judging.

It was precisely because he thought they lacked this capacity that Aristotle insisted that women should be excluded from positions requiring judgment, and in particular, from politics:

> Hence there are by nature various classes of rulers and ruled. For the free rules the slave, the male the female, and the man the child in a different way. And all possess the various parts of the soul, but possess

them in different ways; for the slave has not got the deliberative part [βουλευτικόν] at all, and the female has it, but without full authority, while the child has it, but in an undeveloped form.[29]

Aristotle was badly wrong about women and slaves, but he was right about the prerequisites of judgment, political and otherwise. To appreciate this it is useful to introduce the notion of a *representational wanton*. The more familiar form of wanton is the character who simply cannot resist indulging whatever pleasures are presented to him. In effect, the wanton lacks effective control over his desires and simply follows their lead toward whatever delight presents itself most saliently. The cognitive wanton lacks the analogous control over his own representational capacities, particularly the capacity for belief and judgment. The idea of a total wanton may not be fully intelligible in either the cognitive or the conative case, but to tend toward cognitive wantonness is in effect to be gullible, following the appearances wherever they initially lead. Young children are cognitive wantons in this sense, and so, according to Aristotle, are women. Women and children, as Aristotle understands them, lack the ability to discipline their judgment, and hence while they may indeed deliberate about various matters, their deliberation is not reliably effective in guiding and determining their exercise of judgment.

It should be obvious that cognitive wantons do not make effective judges. Indeed, whether we would be ready to call them judges at all is open to question. (They might indeed *function* as judges in some particular administrative setting, but this is not quite the same as *being* judges.) What interests me here, however, is not the demarcational question, but rather the issue of what cognitive wantons lack. That lack, I submit, is a certain kind of self-relation, most centrally the capacity to step back from initial appearances in order to inquire as to how things objectively stand. This capacity, as we might put it, of navigating the boundary between appearance and reality, between seeming and being, is *not* a form of self-consciousness or self-thematization. The judge who effectively navigates the boundary will usually find his (or her!) attention fully taken up with the object, the evidence, and the Others of judgment. But it *is* a kind of self-relation: the ability to discipline one's own representation of the facts in light of a sustained consideration of evidence – a capacity to discipline one's gullibility, in order to see things as they are, and not simply as they initially appear to be.

[29] Aristotle, *Politics* 1260a.

This form of cognitive self-discipline must itself be understood as a distinctive, self-directed comportment of judgment, but in its execution it brings us back to the other three comportments we have considered. For the self-discipline that is involved requires adversion to the other three targets we have here identified. I discipline my representation of the object by seeking objective representation. My capacity for representational objectivity in turn depends on my capacity to be guided by the inferential structure of the evidence, rather than by the first blush of appearances. And all this comes out in the comportment I take toward Others, most importantly in my comportment toward those who dissent from the judgments I advance.

Cranach's Paris shows us very little of the self-determining self-discipline that Aristotle requires of judges. Barely awake, freighted by his heavy armor, and overwhelmed by the scene unfolding before him, the Paris that Cranach displays is shown near the brink of judgmental incapacity. As we have seen in Watteau's rendering, a further step along this path may indeed leave Paris no longer recognizable as a judge, insofar as he is no longer recognizably in control of his representational faculties: a cognitive and conative wanton. The crucial difference between Watteau's Paris and Cranach's lies in the ways that the Others on the scene press his judgmental task upon him: Mercury with his insistent, even threatening demand for an answer, and the goddesses in waiting upon the decision of their unworthy judge. In this way the self-comportment of judgment and the Other-directedness of judgment prove to be intricately intertwined: we make Others into judges by allowing, expecting, and demanding that they exercise the autonomous self-discipline that lies at the heart of judgmental comportment.

3 Conclusion: the fourth face of judgment

At the outset of these studies we distinguished three areas of investigation where judgment becomes a central topic of concern. Judgment figures in the explanation of behavior, in inference, and in experience; hence the theory of judgment has a place in psychology, in logic, and in phenomenology. The integrity of our notion of judgment depends on the possibility of integrating these three faces of judgment without distorting the facts in any one of the three domains. The episodes we have investigated from the history of the judgment problem have shown that this task of integration is by no means simple. In the psychological studies, Hume's psychological and logical commitments drove him to distort the phenomenological facts, while Libet found himself forced to efface the logical character of judgment in order to render it tractable in his experimental protocol. Like Hume, Kant used logic to guide his investigation of the structure of judgment in experience, but his account betrayed fundamental tensions between his general logical characterization of judgment and his account of the distinctive cognitive act at work in singular existential judgment. Frege undertook to insulate logic from any invocation of claims about human cognition, but this enterprise encountered a limit precisely where it attempted to represent judgment in symbolic form.

With the phenomenological map just sketched we begin to see that the tensions in our understanding of judgment do not originate in these theoretical investigations; they are part of the experience of judgment itself. As a phenomenon – that is, as a structure of experience – judgment is fraught with underlying structural tension. To experience oneself as a judge is to find oneself both free to judge and yet determined by evidence. To treat an Other as a judge is both to demand their free assent and to be open to their reasoned dissent. To occupy the place of judge requires that one be guided by the appearances and yet disciplined in one's gullibility. And in all this we must somehow make sense of ourselves both in causal interchange with objects and Others, while also autonomously guided by inferential relations among the abstract contents of judgment.

The difficulties we have encountered in understanding judgment are thus not simply difficulties in theory; they manifest themselves as challenges in cultivating and sustaining a coherent practice of judgment. The fragility of those practices is most visible where they are first emerging or are in danger of being lost. In the relations between children and the adults who care for them we find one example of the emergence of judgment in a context notorious for its tensions as well as its delights. Among the many skills the child comes to acquire is that of judgment: weighing evidence, sorting appearance from reality, reaching a decision, and facing responsibility for the outcome. In cultivating young judges, parents, guardians, teachers, and various Others must learn to leave room for the (sometimes painful) exercise of judgmental authority. In the case of the emerging young judge, however, it may be hard to appreciate the fragility of these judgmental practices. Though the child's relation to those around him may at times be fraught with tension, the inexorable force of psychological maturation makes the emergence of a fully-formed judge all-but-inevitable.

What then of the case where the practices of judgment threaten to disintegrate? Imagine if you can the perfect Faustian campaign consultant, a maximally extreme version of the much-maligned characters that have played such an important role in democracies from ancient to modern times. Highly paid and highly accomplished, the Faustian consultant is the master of his game. What is that game? The consultant is not himself a candidate but rather advises candidates and designs campaigns. The Faustian consultant has no particular political convictions; he simply works behind the scenes for the highest bidder or the most interesting challenge. His expertise rests on his knowledge of the electoral process, his keen instinct for the political life of the nation, and his sense for the grooves in which voters' deliberations are likely to run. He shows the candidate's team how to produce just the right sequence of programming – free media, paid political advertising, political speeches, the control of images, the campaign event, the "hot-button" issues, etc. – that will have the intended (that is to say: the paid-for) election result.

The Faustian consultant is the product of a form of human interaction that has judgment as its focus. To vote, after all, is to judge. But if the Faustian consultant finds his distinctive place in this context of formalized judgment, he also acts in ways that undermine the very possibility of judgment. To see this, ask about the comportment of this character toward members of the electorate, in particular toward me as a voter. How does he view me? How does he treat me? How does he orient himself toward me? Although he treats me as a choice-point, he does not, I submit, engage me as a judge. This is most obvious where campaigns are run as a barrage of images and rhetorically loaded but indeterminate slogans, all set to a background of an emotional soundtrack. If there are reasons and arguments mixed in with the brass band and the cheering crowd, these have become, for the consultant, simply so much more in the multimedia extravaganza: causes of an intended effect rather than premises in support of a conclusion. But where this logical dimension is effaced, judgment itself disintegrates and is ultimately no longer distinguishable from the thoroughly a-rational exercise of power. Taken to its extreme, the campaign consultant becomes interchangeable with the callous advertising executive. He treats voters as intricate but manipulable bio-psychological mechanisms, for whom various sorts of political programming comprise input, and behavior at the polling station is output. His distinctive talent lies in choosing the right inputs to yield the preferred outputs. What is lacking in this is the comportment toward Others that is partly constitutive of judgment.

The Faustian consultant does not treat me as a free and self-disciplining representational system, guided by evidence and responsible for my choice. His stance toward me is utterly unlike that of the respectful but partisan peer who presents me with information and expects me to make up my own mind. In short: he bypasses any engagement with my character as a judge.

With this we arrive at the fourth face of judgment. Judgment is not only logical, psychological, and phenomenological; it is political. That is, it takes place in and presupposes certain forms of social interaction. This political context of judgment applies not only in the specialized cases of elections we have just considered, nor is it confined to the political framework of democracy. The Faustian campaign consultant is a limiting case of a degenerate stance that we sometimes take toward each other in many different contexts, and in its very degeneracy it helps us recognize the political and phenomenological structure in which judgment must take place. To be a judge is not simply to be a representational mechanism, nor is it to treat Others as reducible to such mechanisms. It is to adopt a stance toward oneself and Others as autonomously and responsibly representing the objects with which one is concerned.

BIBLIOGRAPHY

Allison, Henry. 1983: *Kant's Transcendental Idealism: An Interpretation and Defense* (New Haven, Conn.: Yale University Press)

Aristotle, *Politics*; citations refer to translation by H. Rackham (Cambridge, Mass.: Loeb Classical Library, 1932)

Baker, Gordon and Hacker, Peter. 1984: *Frege: Logical Excavations* (Oxford: Oxford University Press)

    1989: "Frege's Anti-Psychologism" in M. Notturno (ed.) *Perspectives on Psychologism* (Leiden: Brill), 75–127

Beaney, Michael. 1997: *The Frege Reader* (Oxford: Basil Blackwell)

Bergson, Henri. 1889: *Essai sur les données immédiates de la conscience* (Paris: Alcan); translated by F. L. Pogson as *Time and Free Will: An Essay on the Immediate Data of Consciousness* (London: Allen and Unwin, 1971)

Biedermann, Gottfried. 1981: "Die Paris-Urteile Lukas Cranach d.Ä" *Pantheon* 39: 310–13

Brandom, Robert. 1994. *Making it Explicit* (Cambridge, Mass.: Harvard University Press)

    2000. *Articulating Reasons* (Cambridge, Mass.: Harvard University Press)

Brandt, Reinhard. 1989: *Die Urteilstafel, Kritik der reinen Vernunft A67–76; B92–101* (Hamburg: Felix Meiner Verlag); English translation by Eric Watkins (Atascadero, Calif.: Ridgeview Publishing, 1995)

Brentano, Franz. 1870–77: *Die Lehre vom Richtigen Urteil*, published posthumously in an edition edited by Franziska Mayer-Hillebrand (Bern: Francke, 1956)

    1874: *Psychologie vom empirischen Standpunkt* (Leipzig: Dunker und Humblot); citations refer to the pagination of the English translation by L. McAlister *et al.* (London: Routledge and Kegan Paul, 1973)

Carman, Taylor. 2003: *Heidegger's Analytic: Interpretation, Discourse, and Authenticity in Being and Time* (Cambridge: Cambridge University Press)

Carnap, Rudolph. 1930: "The Old and the New Logic" *Erkenntnis* 1; citations refer to reprint in A. J. Ayer (ed.), *Logical Positivism* (Glencoe, Ill.: Free Press, 1959), 133–46

Castañeda, Hector-Neri. 1969: "On the Phenomeno-Logic of the I" in *Proceedings of the 14th Annual Congress of Philosophy* (Vienna: University of Vienna), 260–66; reprint in Q. Cassam (ed.), *Self-Knowledge* (Oxford: Oxford University Press, 1994), 160–66

Cerbone, David. 2003: "Phenomenology: Straight and Hetero" in C. G. Prado (ed.), *A House Divided: Comparing Analytic and Continental Philosophy* (Amherst, NY: Humanity Books)

Chisholm, Roderick. 1976: "Brentano's Non-Propositional Theory of Judgment" *Midwest Studies in Philosophy* 1: 91–95

    1982: "Brentano's Theory of Judgment" in *Brentano and Meinong Studies* (Atlantic Highlands, NJ: Humanities Press), 17–36; first published in R. Haller (ed.), *Studien zur Österreichischen Philosophie* vol. III (Amsterdam: Rodopi, 1982)

Colonne, Guido della. 1287: *Historia Destructionis Troiae*; translated from Latin by Mary Elizabeth Meek (Indianapolis: Indiana University Press, 1974)

Courtine, Jean-François. 1997: "Martin Heidegger's Logical Investigations: From the Theory of Judgment to the Truth of Being" *Graduate Faculty Philosophy Journal* 19/20: 103–27

Crowell, Steven Galt. 1981: *Truth and Reflection: The Development of Transcendental Logic in Lask, Husserl, and Heidegger* (University Microfilms International, Yale University Ph.D Dissertation)

    1992: "Lask, Heidegger and the Homelessness of Logic" *Journal of the British Society for Phenomenology* 23: 222–39

    2001: *Husserl, Heidegger, and the Space of Meaning* (Evanston, Ill.: Northwestern University Press)

Damasio, Antonio R. 1994: *Descartes' Error: Emotion, Reason, and the Human Brain* (New York: Putnam)

Damisch, Hubert. 1992: *Le Jugement de Pâris: Iconologie analytique* (Paris: Flammarion); citations refer to the translation by John Goodman, *The Judgment of Paris* (Chicago, Ill.: University of Chicago Press, 1996)

Dreyfus, Hubert. 1991: *Being-in-the-World: A Commentary on Heidegger's Being and Time, Division I* (Cambridge, Mass.: MIT Press)

Dreyfus, Hubert and Dreyfus, Stuart. 1980: "A Five-Stage Model of the Mental Activities Involved in Directed Skill Acquisition", *Operations Research Center Report* 80:2 (Berkeley, Calif.: University of California)

Dreyfus, Hubert and Hall, Harrison. 1982: *Husserl, Intentionality and Cognitive Science* (Cambridge, Mass.: MIT Press)

Drobisch, Moritz Wilhelm. 1836 (1st edn), 1851 (2nd edn), 1863 (3rd edn): *Neue Darstellung der Logik nach ihren einfachsten Verhältnissen, mit Rücksicht auf Mathematik und Naturwissenschaft* (Leipzig: Voss)

    1876: *Ueber die Fortbildung der Philosophie durch Herbart: Akademische Vorlesung zur Mitfeier seines hundertjährigen Geburtstags gehalten zu Leipzig am 4. Mai 1876* (Leipzig: Voss)

Dummett, Michael. 1993: *Origins of Analytical Philosophy* (London: Duckworth)

Ehrhart, Margaret J. 1987: *The Judgment of the Trojan Prince Paris in Medieval Literature* (Philadelphia, Pa.: University of Pennsylvania Press)

Fay, Thomas. 1974: "Heidegger on Logic: A Genetic Study of His Thought on Logic" *Journal of the History of Philosophy* 12: 77–94

　　1977: *Heidegger: The Critique of Logic* (The Hague: Martinus Nijhoff)

Fichte, Johann Gottlieb. 1796: *Grundlage des Naturrechts* (Jena: Gabler); translated by Michael Bauer as *Foundations of Natural Right* (Cambridge: Cambridge University Press, 2000)

　　1812: *Ueber das Verhältniß der Logik zur Philosophie oder Transscendentale Logik*; citations refer to the pagination of vol. I of I. H. Fichte (ed.), *Johann Gottlieb Fichtes Nachgelassene Werke* (Bonn: Adolph-Marcus, 1834–35); photo-mechanically reprinted as vol. IX of *Fichtes Werke* (Berlin: de Gruyter, 1971)

Fischer, Kurt and Miller, Leon. 1976: "Notes on Terrell's 'Brentano's Logical Innovations'" *Midwest Studies in Philosophy* 1: 95–97

Förster, Richard. 1898: "Neue Cranachs in Schlesien" *Schlesiens Vorzeit in Bild und Schrift* 7: 265–69

Freeman, Anthony. 1999: "Fear of Mechanism: A Compatibilist Critique of the Volitional Brain" *Journal of Consciousness Studies* 6: 279–93

Frege, Gottlob. 1879: *Begriffsschrift: A Formula Language of Pure Thought Modelled upon the Formula Language of Arithmetic* (Halle: Nebert Verlag); citations refer to the section number and to the pagination of the translation by Terrell Ward Bynum in *Gottlob Frege: Conceptual Notation and Related Articles* (Oxford: Clarendon, 1972)

　　1880–81: "Boole's Logical Calculus and the *Begriffsschrift*" in Frege 1969; translation by Peter Long and Roger White in Frege 1979: 9–52

　　1891: "Comments on Sense and Reference" in Frege 1969: 128–36; citations refer to the pagination of the translation by Peter Long and Roger White in Frege 1979: 118–25

　　1897a: "Logic" in Frege 1969: 137–63; citations refer to the pagination of the translation by Peter Long and Roger White in Frege 1979: 126–49

　　1897b: "On Mr. Peano's Conceptual Notation and My Own" *Verhandlungen der Königlich Sächsischen Gesellschaft der Wissenschaften zu Leipzig* 48: 362–68; citations refer to the pagination of the translation by Victor Dudman in Frege 1984: 234–48

　　1906: "What May I Regard as the Result of my Work?" in Frege 1969: 200; citations refer to the pagination of the translation by Peter Long and Roger White in Frege 1979: 184

　　1915: "My Basic Logical Insights" in Frege 1969: 271–72; citations refer to the pagination of the translation by Peter Long and Roger White in Frege 1979: 251–52

　　1918–19: "The Thought" *Beiträge zur Philosophie des deutschen Idealismus* 1: 58–77; citations refer to the pagination of the translation by Peter Geach and R. H. Stoothoff in Frege 1984: 351–72

　　1919: "Notes for Ludwig Darmstädter" in Frege 1969: 273–77; citations refer to the pagination of the translation by Peter Long and Roger White in Frege 1979: 251–53

　　1969: *Nachgelassene Schriften*, edited by Hans Hermes, Friedrich Kambartel, and Friedrich Kaulbach (Hamburg: Felix Meiner, 1969)

1979: *Posthumous Writings* (Oxford: Basil Blackwell, 1979)

1984: *Collected Papers*, edited by Brian McGuinness (Oxford: Basil Blackwell)

Friedländer, Max and Rosenberg, Jakob. 1978: *The Paintings of Lucas Cranach* (Ithaca, NY: Cornell University Press); revised and translated edition of *Die Gemälde von Lucas Cranach* (Berlin: Deutsche Verein für Kunstwissenschaft, 1932)

Friedman, Michael. 2000: *A Parting of the Ways: Carnap, Cassirer, and Heidegger* (Chicago, Ill.: Open Court)

Geach, Peter. 1965: "Assertion" *The Philosophical Review* 74: 449–65

Gilden, L., Vaughan, H. G., and Costa, L. D. 1966: "Summated Human EEG Potentials with Voluntary Movements" *Electroencephalography and Clinical Neurophysiology* 20: 433–38

Greimann, Dirk. 2000: "The Judgement-Stroke as Truth Operator: A New Interpretation of the Logical Form of Sentences in Frege's Scientific Language" *Erkenntnis* 52: 213–38

Gumppenberg, Rudolph. 1974: "Die tranzendentalphilosophische Urteils- und Bedeutungsproblematik in M. Heideggers 'Fruhe Schriften'" in *Akten des 4. Internationalen Kant-Kongresses*, Teil II.2: 751–61

Heidegger, Martin. 1912: "Neuere Forschungen über Logik" in *Literarische Rundschau für das Katolische Deutschland* vol. 38; citations refer to the reprint in Martin Heidegger, *Gesamtausgabe* vol. 1 (Frankfurt: Klostermann, 1978), 17–43

1913: *Die Lehre vom Urteil im Psychologismus: Ein kritisch-positiver Beitrag zur Logik*; citations refer to the pagination of *Martin Heidegger: Frühe Schriften* (Frankfurt: Klostermann, 1972), 1–129

1927a: *Sein und Zeit* translated by J. Macquarrie and E. Robinson as *Being and Time* (New York: Harper and Row, 1962)

1927b: *The Basic Problems of Phenomenology*; German text first published in Martin Heidegger, *Gesamtausgabe* vol. 24 (Frankfurt: Klostermann, 1975); citations refer to the pagination of the translation by Albert Hofstadter (Indianapolis: Indiana University Press, 1982)

1929–30: *The Fundamental Concepts of Metaphysics: World, Finitude, Solitude*; German text first published in Martin Heidegger, *Gesamtausgabe* vol. 29/30 (Frankfurt: Klostermann, 1975); citations refer to the pagination of the translation by William McNeill and Nicholas Walker (Indianapolis, Ind.: Indiana University Press, 1995)

1952: "Die Zeit des Weltbildes" in *Holzwege* (Frankfurt: Klostermann); translated by William Lovitt as "The Age of the World Picture" in *The Question Concerning Technology and Other Essays* (New York: Harper, 1977)

Herbart, Johann Friedrich. 1813: *Lehrbuch zur Einleitung in die Philosophie* (Königsberg: Unzer)

Hillebrand, Franz. 1891: *Die neuen Theorien der kategorischen Schlüsse* (Vienna: Holber)

Hobe, Konrad. 1971: "Zwischen Rickert und Heidegger: Versuch über eine Perspektive des Denkens von Emil Lask" *Philosophisches-Jahrbuch* 78: 360–76

Hume, David. 1739: *A Treatise of Human Nature* (London: John Noon); citations refer to the pagination of *Hume's Treatise of Human Nature*, edited and with an Analytical Index by L. A. Selby-Bigge, second edition revised by P. H. Nidditch (Oxford: Clarendon Press, 1978)

1748: *An Inquiry Concerning Human Understanding* (London: Millar); citations refer to the pagination of *An Inquiry Concerning Human Understanding*, edited and with an introduction by Charles Hendel (Indianapolis, Ind.: Bobbs-Merrill, 1955)

Husserl, Edmund. 1900–1901: *Logische Untersuchungen*; citations refer to translation by J. N. Findlay, *Logical Investigations* (London: Routledge and Kegan Paul, 1970)

1911: "Philosophie als strenge Wissenschaft" *Logos* 1: 289–341; citations refer to the pagination of the translation by S. J. Quentin Lauer in *Phenomenology and the Crisis of Philosophy* (New York: Harper, 1965)

1913: *Ideen zu einer reinen Phänomenologie und phänomenologischen Philosophie*; citations refer to translation by R. Boyce-Gibson, *Ideas: General Introduction to Pure Phenomenology* (London: George Allen and Unwin, 1931)

Kant, Immanuel. 1902ff: *Kants Gesammelte Schriften* (Berlin: Königlich Preußischen Akademie der Wissenschften); citations preceded by the abbreviation "Ak." refer to volume and page of this edition

Käufer, Stephan. 1998: *Heidegger's Philosophy of Logic* (University Microfilms International, Stanford University Ph.D Dissertation)

2001: "On Heidegger on Logic" *Continental Philosophy Review* 34: 455–76

Kenny, Anthony. 1995: *Frege* (London: Penguin Books)

King, Jeffrey. 2003: "Complex Demonstratives, a Quantificational Account" *Mind* 112: 734–40

Kisiel, Theodore. 1993: *The Genesis of Heidegger's Being and Time* (Berkeley Calif.: University of California Press)

Kitcher, Patricia. 1990: *Kant's Transcendental Psychology* (Oxford: Oxford Univesity Press)

Kitcher, Philip. 1992: "The Naturalists Return" *Philosophical Review* 101: 53–114

Kneale, William and Kneale, Martha. 1962: *The Development of Logic* (Oxford: Clarendon Press)

Koepplin, Dieter. 2003: "Ein Cranach-Prinzip" in W. Schade (ed.), *Lucas Cranach: Glaube, Mythologie und Moderne* (Ostfildern: Hatje Cantz), 144–65

Koepplin, Dieter and Falk, Tilman. 1976: *Lukas Cranach: Gemälde, Zeichnungen, Druckgraphik: Zur Ausstellung im Kunstmuseum, Basel, 15. Jun ibis 8. September 1974* (Basel and Stuttgart: Birkhäuser), two vols

Kornhuber, Hans and Deecke, Lüder 1965: "Hirnpotentialänderungen bei Willkürbewegungen und passiven Bewegungen des Menschen: Bereitschaftspotential und reafferente Potentiale" *Pflügers Archiv für Gesamte Physiologie* 284: 1–17

Kuhn, Thomas. 1962: *The Structure of Scientific Revolutions* (Chicago, Ill.: University of Chicago Press)

Kuroda, S. Y. 1972: "The Categorical and Thetic Judgment" *Foundations of Language* 9: 153–85

Kusch, Martin. 1995: *Psychologism: A Case Study in the Sociology of Philosophical Knowledge* (London: Routledge and Kegan Paul)

Ladusaw, William A. 1994: "Thetic and Categorical, Stage and Individual, Weak and Strong" in *Proceedings of the Conference on Semantics and Linguistic Theory* vol. 4 (Ithaca, NY: Cornell University Press), 220–29

Libet, Benjamin. 1965: "Cortical Activation in Conscious and Unconscious Experience" *Perspectives in Biology and Medicine* 9: 77–86

    1966: "Brain Stimulation and the Threshold of Conscious Experience" in J. C. Eccles (ed.), *Brain and Conscious Experience* (New York: Springer), 165–81

    1985: "Unconscious Cerebral Initiative and the Role of Conscious Will in Voluntary Action" *Behavioral and Brain Sciences* 8: 529–66

Libet, Benjamin *et al.* 1982: "Readiness-Potentials Preceding Unrestricted 'Spontaneous' vrs. Pre-planned Voluntary Acts" *Electroencephalography and Clinical Neurophysiology* 54: 322–35

    1983: "Time of Conscious Intention to Act in Relation to Onset of Cerebral Activities (Readiness-Potential): The Unconscious Initiation of a Freely Voluntary Act" *Brain* 106: 623–42

Libet, Benjamin, Freeman, Anthony, and Sunderland, Keith (eds.). 1999: *The Volitional Brain: Toward a Neuroscience of Free Will*; published as a double issue of *Journal of Consciousness Studies* 6

Lipps, Theodor. 1880: "Die Aufgabe der Erkenntnistheorie und die Wundtsche Logik" *Philosophische Monatshefte* 16: 28–58, 198–226, 427–45

    1883: *Grundtatsachen des Seelenlebens* (Bonn: Cohen)

    1891: *Die Streit über die Tragödie* (Hamburg: Voss)

    1893 (1st edn), 1912 (2nd edn), 1923 (3rd edn): *Grundzüge der Logik* (Hamburg and Leipzig: Voss)

    1894: "Subjektive Kategorien in objektiven Urteilen" *Philosophische Monatshefte* 30: 97–128

    1898: *Komik und Humor: Eine Psychologisch-Ästhetische Untersuchung* (Hamburg: Voss)

    1903, 1906^2, 1909^3: *Leitfaden der Psychologie* (Leipzig: Engelmann)

    1905a: "Bewuβtsein und Gegenstände" *Psychologische Untersuchungen* 1: 1–203

    1905b: "Inhalt und Gegensatand; Psychologie und Logik" in *Separat-Abdruck aus den Sitzungsberichten der Bayerische Akademie der Wissenschaften, Philosophisch-Historische Klasse* 4: 511–669

Longuenesse, Béatrice. 1993: *Kant et le pouvoir de juger: sensibilité et discursivité dans l'analytique transcendantale de la critique de la raison pure* (Paris: Presses Universitaires de France); translated from the French by Charles T. Wolfe as *Kant and the Capacity to Judge: Sensibility and Discursivity in the Transcendental Analytic of the Critique of Pure Reason* (Princeton, NJ: Princeton University Press, 1998)

Lotze, Hermann. 1874: *Logik; drei Bücher, vom Denken, vom Untersuchen und vom Erkennen* (Leipzig: Hirzel); citations refer to the reprint of the translation by Bernard Bosanquet (Oxford: Clarendon Press, 1888; reprinted New York: Garland, 1980)

    1883: *Grundzüge der Logik und Enzyklopädie der Philosophie* (Leipzig: Hirzel)

Maddy, Penelope. 2002: "A Naturalistic Look at Logic" in *Proceedings and Addresses of the American Philosophical Association* 76(2): 61–90

Maier, Heinrich. 1900: "Logik und Erkenntnistheorie" in Benno Erdmann *et al.* (eds.), *Philosophische Abhandlungen: Christoph Sigwart zu Seinem Siebzigsten Geburtstage 28. März 1900 Gewidmet* (Tübingen: Mohr)

1908: *Psychologie des emotionalen Denkens* (Tübingen: Mohr)

1914: "Logik und Psychologie" in *Festschrift für Alois Riehl* (Halle: Niemeyer), 311–78

Martin, Wayne. 1999: "Husserl's Relapse? Concerning a Fregean Challenge to Phenomenology" *Inquiry* 42: 3–4, 343–70

2005: "Bubbles and Skulls: The Phenomenology of Self-Consciousness in Dutch Still Life Painting" in Mark Wrathall (ed.), *The Blackwell Companion to Phenomenology and Existentialism* (Oxford: Blackwell)

Marty, Anton. 1908: *Untersuchungen zur Grundlegung der allgemeinen Grammatik und Sprachphilosophie* vol. 1 (Halle: Niemeyer)

McCrone, John. 1999: *Going Inside: A Tour Round a Single Moment of Consciousness* (London: Faber and Faber)

McNally, Louise. 1997: *A Semantics for the English Existential Construction* (New York: Garland)

1998: "Stativity and Theticity" in S. Rothstein (ed.), *Events and Grammar* (Kluwer: Dordrecht), 293–307

Mill, John Stuart. 1843: *A System of Logic, Ratiocinative and Inductive: Being a Connected View of the Principles of Evidence and the Methods of Scientific Investigation* (London: Parker)

Mohanty, J. N. 1988: "Heidegger on Logic" *Journal of the History of Philosophy* 26: 107–35

Nickel, Helmut. 1981: "The Judgment of Paris by Lucas Cranach the Elder: Nature, Allegory, and Alchemy" *Metropolitan Museum Journal* 16: 117–29

Olafson, Frederick. 1993: "The Unity of Heidegger's Thought" in C. Guignon (ed.), *The Cambridge Companion to Heidegger* (Cambridge, Cambridge University Press), 97–121

Ott, Hugo. 1988: *Martin Heidegger: Unterwegs zu seiner Biographie* (Frankfurt: Campus Verlag)

Owen, David. 2003: "Locke and Hume on Belief, Judgment and Assent" *Topoi* 22: 1

Peano, Giuseppe. 1895: "Review of Frege's *Grundgesetze*" *Revista di Matematica* 5: 122–28; citations refer to the pagination of the translation by Victor Dudman in *Southern Journal of Philosophy* 9: 25–37 (1971)

Pinder, Tillmann. 1998: *Immanuel Kant, Logik-Vorlesung: Unveröffentlichte Nachschriften* (Hamburg: Meiner)

Poli, Roberto. 1993: "Ontologia e logica in Franz Brentano: giudizi categorici e giudizi tetici" *Epistemologia* 16: 39–76

1998: "La teoria del giudizio di Franz Brentano e Anton Marty: giudizi tetici e giudizi doppi" *Epistemologia* 21: 41–59

Reich, Klaus. 1932: *Die Vollständigkeit der Kantischen Urteilstafel* (Berlin); English translation by J. Kneller and M. Losonsky as *The Completeness of Kant's Table of Judgments* (Stanford, Calif.: Stanford University Press, 1992)

Royal Collections Trust, Trustees of the. 2004: *Annual Report and Financial Statements for the Year Ended 31 March 2004* (London: Royal Collection)

Russell, Bertrand. 1903: *Principles of Mathematics* (New York: Norton)

1914: "Logic as the Essence of Philosophy" in *Our Knowledge of the External World* (London: George Allen and Unwin)

1945: *A History of Western Philosophy* (New York: Simon and Schuster)

Sasse, Hans Jürgen. 1987: "The Thetic/Categorical Distinction Revisited" *Linguistics* 25/3: 511–80

Schneider, Arthur. 1903–1906: *Die Psychologie Alberts des Grossen* (Münster: Aschendorff)

Schröder, Ernst. 1880: "Review of Frege's *Begriffsschrift*" *Zeitschrift für Mathematik und Physik* 25: 81–94; citations refer to the pagination of the translation by Victor Dudman in *Southern Journal of Philosophy* 7: 139–50 (1969)

Shadlen, Michael *et al.* 2001: "Neural Computations that Underlie Decisions about Sensory Stimuli" *Trends in Cognitive Science* 5/1: 10–16

Sheehan, Thomas. 1988: "Heidegger's Lehrjahr" in John Sallis *et al.* (eds.), *The Collegium Phaenomenologicum* (Dordrecht: Kluwer), 77–137

Sigwart, Christoph. 1873 (1st edn), 1895 (2nd edn): *Logik* (Freiburg: Mohr); citations refer to the pagination of Helen Dendy's translation of the second edition (New York: Macmillan, 1980)

Simons, Peter. 1984: "A Brentanian Basis for Lesniewskian Logic" *Logique et Analyse* 27: 297–308

　　1987: "Brentano's Reform of Logic" *Topoi* 6: 25–38

Sluga, Hans. 1980: *Frege* (London: Routledge and Kegan Paul)

Smith, Barry. 1994: *Austrian Philosophy: The Legacy of Franz Brentano* (Chicago, Ill.: Open Court)

Smith, Nicholas. 2000: "Frege's Judgment Stroke" *Australasian Journal of Philosophy* 78: 153–75

Spiegelberg, Herbert. 1960: *The Phenomenological Movement: A Historical Introduction* (The Hague: Nijhoff)

Stewart, Roderick M. 1977: *Psychologism, Sinn and Urteil in the Early Writings of Heidegger* (Syracuse University Doctoral Dissertation)

　　1979: "The Problem of Logical Psychologism for Husserl and the Early Heidegger" *Journal of the British Society for Phenomenology* 10: 184–93

Stroud, Barry. 1977: *Hume*. Arguments of the Philosophers Series (London: Routledge and Kegan Paul)

Terrell, Burnham. 1976: "Franz Brentano's Logical Innovations" *Midwest Studies in Philosophy* 1: 81–90

　　1978: "Quantification and Brentano's Logic" in R. Chisholm and R. Haller (eds.), *Die Philosophie Franz Brentano: Beiträge zur Brentano-Konferenz Graz, 4–8 September 1977* (Amsterdam: Rodopi), 45–65

Trendelenburg, Adolph. 1870: *Logische Untersuchungen* (Leipzig: Hirzel, third edition)

Willard, Dallas. 1972: "The Paradox of Logical Psychologism: Husserl's Way Out" *Philosophical Review* 9: 94–100

　　1984: *Logic and the Objectivity of Knowledge: A Study in Husserl's Early Philosophy* (Athens, Ohio: Ohio University Press)

Witherspoon, Edward. 2002: "Logic and the Inexpressible in Frege and Heidegger" *Journal of the History of Philosophy* 40: 89–113

Wittgenstein, Ludwig. 1921: *Tractatus Logico-Philosophicus*; first published in *Annalen der Naturphilosophie* 14

Young, J. Michael (ed.). 1992: *Immanuel Kant: Lectures on Logic* (Cambridge, Cambridge University Press)

INDEX